MJ

WITHDRAWN

THE THEORY AND WORKING OF STATE CORPORATIONS

THE THEORY AND WORKING
OF STATE CORPORATIONS

WITH SPECIAL REFERENCE TO INDIA

BY

OM PRAKASH

FREDERICK A. PRAEGER, *Publisher*

NEW YORK

BOOKS THAT MATTER

Published in the United States of America in 1963
by Frederick A. Praeger, Inc., Publisher
64 University Place, New York 3, N.Y.

© George Allen & Unwin Ltd., 1962

Library of Congress Catalog Card Number: 63-9173

PRINTED IN GREAT BRITAIN
in 10 point Times Roman type
BY SIMSON SHAND LTD
LONDON, HERTFORD AND HARLOW

TO MY MOTHER

PREFACE

My interest in the study of industrial organization first manifested itself in the publication of *Principles and Problems of Industrial Organization*, the first edition of which appeared in 1950. Since nationalization was a widely debated topic in India at that time, I examined the pros and cons of industrial planning in India. Public Corporations, however, formed only a small part of that discussion. The second edition of that volume, which appeared in 1953, contained a brief account of a number of State enterprises which had appeared in India by that time. It was followed by a six-year research on the theory and working of State Corporations with special reference to India, leading to the degree of Doctor of Letters approved by the University of Allahabad in the year 1961.

In this book, the term 'State Corporations' has been used as a generic connotation to cover Public Corporations as well as Government Companies in India. When applied to other countries, the description includes Crown Corporations, Statutory Corporations, Government-sponsored Corporations and Government Corporations. In India, only those Corporations have been taken into account which fall under the jurisdiction of the Central Government. Particular attention has been given to the Government Companies functioning under the aegis of the Ministry of Commerce and Industry. The Appendices include details about the working of two Public Corporations of India, the Damodar Valley Corporation and the Life Insurance Corporation of India, representing respectively initial and later stages of development. The other two Public Corporations, the National Coal Board and the Tennessee Valley Authority, indicate the growth of this institution in England and America respectively. Of the three Government Companies which find a place in the Appendices, Hindustan Steel Limited falls in the category of Industrial Companies, the State Trading Corporation of India Limited is a Commercial Company and the National Industrial Development Corporation Limited belongs to the family of Development Corporations, which have brought a new institutional pattern to the fore in the economies of underdeveloped countries.

State Corporations have been examined in their theoretical setting in the first two chapters and again in the sixth, seventh, eighth and ninth chapters. The genesis and the peculiarities of the corporate device, the transition from Privately-owned Corporations to State Corporations, and the distinctive characteristics of State Corporations constitute the first chapter. It also presents a definition of socialized industry. The second chapter indicates the importance of the public sector, the classification of Public Authorities, and the functional rôle of State Corporations. The other four chapters contain an examination of certain specific issues relating to the organization and working of State Corporations. The critical analysis is based on the structure of State enterprises in a large number of countries. Accordingly, the concluding chapter relates to State Corporations not only in India but also elsewhere.

I must express my gratitude to the various Public Corporations

Government Companies, Government Departments and other official and non-official organizations in India who were good enough to provide me with much of the information which has formed the basis of this volume. I am particularly grateful to the authorities of the Tennessee Valley Authority, the Canadian National Railways, the British Broadcasting Corporation, the Port of London Authority and the National Coal Board, for not only sending their printed literature but also for answering my queries. I am thankful to Sir Roy Harrod for permitting me to reproduce my paper on 'Industrial Development Corporations in India and Pakistan' which appeared in *The Economic Journal* of the Royal Economic Society, March 1957.

I cannot forbear to mention the names of certain individuals who evinced personal interest in my work and sought to resolve my difficulties from time to time. They are: Mr H. R. Balls, Comptroller of the Treasury, Canada; Dr P. S. Lokanathan, Director General, National Council of Applied Economic Research; Dr V. K. R. V. Rao, Director, Institute of Economic Growth (then Vice-chancellor, University of Delhi); Professor J. J. Anjaria, then Chief Economic Adviser, Ministry of Finance, Government of India; Mr P. C. Suri, Director, Public Management Studies, Planning Commission; Mr P. S. Rau, then Chairman of the Damodar Valley Corporation; Mr Y. R. Seth, of the Administrative Branch, Rourkela Steel Plant; Mr O. K. Ghosh, Accountant General, Posts and Telegraphs; Mr N. C. Chaudhri, Research Officer, Department of Company Law Administration; and Mr M. S. Ramayyar, Deputy Director, Indian Institute of Public Administration. I am much beholden to the late Professor M. K. Ghosh, who inspired me to undertake this ambitious research work, and to Dr A. N. Agarwala, whose untiring zeal enabled me to sustain my perseverence. I have benefited immensely from intellectual discourses afforded by Professor J. K. Mehta and all my colleagues in the Department of Economics and Commerce.

University of Allahabad
January 5, 1962   OM PRAKASH

CONTENTS

CHAPTER I

THE CORPORATE DEVICE AND STATE CORPORATIONS

According to the Encyclopaedia of the Social Sciences, 'A Corporation is a form of organization which enables a group of individuals to act under a common name in carrying on one or more related enterprises, holding and managing property and distributing the profits or beneficial interests in such enterprises or property among the associates. Its structure is defined and sanctioned by a statute, charter or certificate granted by the State; its shares are transferable; its life is independent of the lives of the individuals; and its debts do not usually create a liability for the latter.'

Thus the basic idea of establishing a corporation is to enable a number of individuals to unite together for the purpose of acting in concert. But this unifying desire, by itself, is not enough, for individuals might as well unite in partnership or other non-corporate associations. The additional factor, which is of cardinal importance, is that the life of a corporation is independent of the lives of the individuals who go to constitute it. Mathematically, therefore, when 'n' persons (number of human beings) unite together to form a corporation, there comes into existence a $(n+1)$th person (non-human legal person). Such an entity may be called a juristic person, a fictitious person, an artificial person or a moral person.

This $(n+1)$th person is a right-and-duty-bearing unit. The recognition of the principle of limited liability, which is a later development, has strengthened the doctrine of segregated personality. It is this individuality that makes a corporation something more than a mere collectivity. A one-man partnership is an impossibility but a one-man company, although sometimes subjected to judicial strictures, is a perfectly legal entity.[1] The plurality of corporators is indicated by the fact that there exists a contract between the corporation and each corporator. Besides this initial contract, every

[1] See the interesting decision of the House of Lords in *Salomon* Vs. *Salomon & Co.* (1897). This judgment may be considered to be the precursor of the spectacular progress made by corporate enterprise during the twentieth century. On the one hand, the decision granted far reaching protection to the members of a corporation (i.e., it did not allow the principle of limited liability to become farcical); on the other hand, it did not see anything wrong in the concentration of economic power and influence through the corporate device.

corporator is free to enter into any business contract with the corporation (except for the restrictions which may be imposed on such of the corporators who are Directors, Managing Agents, etc.). The corporators, i.e. the shareholders, are not the agents of the corporation unless specially appointed (as Directors, Managers, etc.). Again, although the corporators are very much interested in the prosperity of the corporation, they are not recognized as the owners of corporate property. The result of incorporation is that the creditors must look to corporate assets for the satisfaction of their claims and not to the property owned by individual corporators. Likewise, the alienation and mortgage of corporate property must be made in the name of the corporation. This makes for perpetual succession in the matter of property and continuation in the matter of business activities. Thus the death of any corporator does not affect the life of the corporation, though it may certainly undermine the efficient working thereof if that individual corporator happened to be the moving spirit behind the corporation.

The corporate device is an amalgam of four peculiarities. First, it provides the comenting force without which the *group-person* would be pulverized into *grouped persons*. This grouping is of special importance for modern social activities—particularly those which require massive capital investment and a long waiting period, or such activities which are not based on private profit. Secondly, incorporation means the birth of a new entity in the eyes of law. The existence of a corporation depends on registration and continuous recognition by the State. So to say, even a privately-owned corporation is created and maintained by the State. As such, the State is directly interested in all corporate activity. The relationship subsisting between one corporate entity and another and between the members of a corporation *inter se* is to a large extent determined by the State. Thirdly, the membership of a corporation, in principle, depends upon voluntary acceptance. The status of corporators can, therefore, be distinguished from that of the citizens of a State. That is, one can help being a corporator, but he is generally helpless in the matter of citizenship. However, in the context of Municipal and State Corporations, this distinction is not so important. It is true that one may not become a member of the Governing Board of a State Corporation (unless compelled to do so in an *ex-officio* position), but the very fact of citizenship carries with it the status of a corporator in all nationalized enterprises. Finally, all corporations, whether nationalized or privately owned, carry with them an element of autonomy. If a corporation is, by definition, autonomous, it could be argued that the term 'autonomous corporation' is unnecessary. However, there can be varying degrees of autonomy in the matter of corporate activities. As such, the term 'autonomous'

12

symbolizes the fact (or desire) that a particular corporation is (or should be) more autonomous than certain others. This autonomy may not only be self-regarding, it may also be extra-regarding. Thus a corporation may, as a self-sufficient unit, add to its membership and change its internal regulations (Articles of Association) without any specific authorization by law. It may forfeit the shares of the corporators under certain circumstances. Within the limits set by the law of the land, and its own constitution (Royal Charter, Incorporating Legislation or the Memorandum of Association), the power of the corporation is supreme. Like the fabulous island in Thomas More's *Utopia,* a corporation is a smaller world inside a bigger universe.

The concept of autonomy offers considerable difficulty in its application to State Corporations. We can even put the blunt question: Can a State Corporation be really autonomous? In a privately-owned corporation almost the sole interest of corporators is a high and stable rate of dividend. So long as this is assured, the corporators do not mind giving a long rope to the Directors and Managers. On the other hand, the performance of State Corporations is judged on the basis of a large number of criteria, many of them being not amenable to objective assessment. Hence the concepts of autonomy and accountability are often to be found in hostile camps.

FROM PRIVATELY-OWNED CORPORATIONS TO STATE CORPORATIONS

The increase in the number, size and influence of Privately-owned Corporations created an impression that the corporate device could be employed only in the private sector of industry and commerce. Berle and Means went to the extent of comparing the 'corporate system' to what was once the 'feudal system'. Taking account of the divorce between ownership and management, and the vast concentration of economic power, Berle and Means smelled in the modern Corporation a formidable rival to the modern State. They expressed their fears that the future might see the economic organism (now) typified by the Corporation, not only on an equal plane with the State, but possibly even superseding the dominant form of social organization.[2] However, Berle and Means had only the Privately-owned Corporations in mind. Little did they visualize that the rivalry between the State and the corporate device might be avoided by the former adopting the latter, i.e. through the growth of State

[2] Adolfe A. Berle, Jr., and Gardiner C. Means, *The Modern Corporation and Private Property,* Macmillan, New York, 17th printing 1950, p. 357. The study relates to 200 giant corporations in the USA for the year 1929.

Corporations as the dominant form of industrial and commercial organization.

In recent discussions, it has often been ignored that the long history of corporate evolution has much to do with the influence of the State. In fact, State Corporations (e.g. the State Officers' Associations in Roman times) can claim much greater antiquity than Privately-owned Corporations. Moreover, we cannot ignore the fact that the State infuses its life even into the Privately-owned Corporations by granting legal status to artificial persons. Again, it is interesting to observe that the phenomenal rise of Privately-owned Corporations,[3] in no small measure, paved the way for the growth of State Corporations of the present era. By blocking the path of individual entrepreneurs, giant corporations in the private sector have proved to be inconsistent with the very ideal of free enterprise which gave them strength. The entire chain of anti-trust and anti-monopoly laws is enough testimony of the grave social problems and contradictions caused by Privately-owned Corporations. The recent cry about 'People's Capitalism' is another phase of that contradiction.[4]

Monopolistic Corporations in the private sector have been the precursors of State Corporations in many cases. This has happened for several reasons. First, where monopoly is inevitable because of technical, physical or historical factors, the creation of State Corporations has been found to be an urgent social necessity. Secondly, the passage of nationalizing legislation has been quite convenient in

[3] An estimate (supposed to be very careful and unbiased) by Professor M. A. Adelman of the Massachusetts Institute of Technology reveals that 135 corporations own 45 per cent of the industrial assets of the United States, or about one-fourth of the manufacturing volume of the globe. (See Adolfe A. Berle, Jr.: *The Twentieth Century Capitalist Revolution*, 1955, pp. 15-16.) The share of fifty biggest companies (in the value added by manufacturing) in the USA rose from 17 per cent in 1947 to 23 per cent in 1954. Again, during 1952-57, firms with assets of over $100 million increased their net worth by 53 per cent (*Concentration in American Industry*, Report of the Sub-Committee on Anti-trust and Monopoly to the Senate Committee on Judiciary, July 12, 1957). The number of shareholders in the American Telephone and Telegraph Company rose from over half a million in 1929 to far in excess of a million in 1954. However, the total number of stockholders in the USA was only 8,630,000 (5.1 per cent of population) in 1956 as against an estimated 9-11 million in 1930 (7.3 to 8.9 per cent of population).

[4] The expression was developed by the Advertising Council which prepared a 'People's Capitalism' exhibit, shown internationally under the auspices of the United States Information Agency (*New York Times*, February 14 and September 3, 1956). Mr Victor Perlo concludes as follows: 'The basic claim of "People's Capitalism", that the rank and file of the population are becoming owners of the means of production in American industry, is without foundation in fact. The widespread diffusion of this theory signifies only the effectiveness of organized propaganda.' (*The American Economic Review*, June 1958, p. 347.)

14

such cases because the monopolistic Corporation can be taken over as a going concern. Thirdly, when regulatory measures fail to protect the public interest, the psychological atmosphere is most favourable for the birth of State Corporations. Fourthly, the reaction against Privately-owned Corporations is still greater when 'subsidiary' Corporations are under the thumb of 'holding' Corporations (the situation being further complicated in case of intermediate holding Corporations, i.e. when a Corporation is 'holding' and 'subsidiary' at the same time). Finally, whereas the corporate device has taken away much of the flexibility, initiative and sense of responsibility in the case of private enterprises, the institution of State Corporations has made public enterprises more acceptable.

CHARACTERISTICS OF STATE CORPORATIONS[5]

1. *Statutory Body.* A Public Corporation of the British pattern is established under an Act of Parliament (Legislature), i.e. it is a statutory body. In rare cases it may be established under a Royal Charter, e.g. the British Broadcasting Corporation. An ordinary Corporation or Joint Stock Company comes into existence automatically by fulfilling certain legal requirements as provided in Company Law. But the Public Corporation is an embodiment of an express wish on the part of the State to create a new agency. It is, however, possible that in course of time we may have a Law of Public Corporations, under which Public Corporations can be established as and when found convenient, obviating the necessity of obtaining a fresh mandate from Parliament on every occasion. Already, in case of Corporations established under the State Government, in India, there are several such Laws. Thus, under the Road Transport Corporations Act, 1950, States are free to establish State-owned Corporations. Similarly, we have the State Financial Corporations Act, 1951. State Warehousing Corporations can be established under the Agricultural Produce (Development and Warehousing) Act, 1956—the very Act under which two Public Corporations were established at the Central Government level.

2. *Insulated Personality.* As a corollary to the above point, we can say that a Public Corporation possesses a legal personality separate not only from the persons who conduct its affairs, but also separate from the State as such. *It is a child of the State which grows into maturity as soon as it is born.* But Professor Friedmann states that

---

[5] Here we have examined the characteristics of Public Corporations. However, except for the first (statutory body), eighth (no shares and shareholders), and in many cases the ninth (public monopoly), other characteristics are applicable to Government companies as well.

15

there can be exceptions to this general rule.[6] He cites the instance of
The Australian Dried Fruits Board which has, for many years, been
an active Public Corporation, carrying out a multitude of transactions which presuppose legal personality, 'without having been
equipped with such personality by any legislative or administrative
document'. Again, he refers to 'Sondervermögen' in Germany, a
separate fund without legal personality in the case of both the
Federal Railways and the Federal Post. Professor Friedmann is not
certain if the Soviet State Corporations are independent legal personalities or, being part of the State, they are only treated as such. It
may, however, be mentioned that Friedmann's conception of a
Public Corporation is much wider than the orthodox British conception. The degree of insulation from the parent institution (the
State) is vividly indicated in the Canadian Financial Administration
Act, 1951 (amended in 1955 and 1958), which distinguishes Government Departments, Departmental Corporations, Agency Corporations, and Proprietary Corporations.

3. *Independent Governing Board.* The affairs of a Public Corporation are administered by an independent Governing Board. According to orthodox theory, all the members of this Board should be
appointed by the Government (which generally means the Minister-
in-charge) *without any consideration of class or group interests.*
Specialists may be appointed to the Board, *but not as representatives
of any section.* In the 'twenties it was suggested that public boards
should be composed of representatives of all the interests involved.
This is the type of constitution employed by the Port of London
Authority, on which sit representatives of the shipping companies
and others concerned. This conception was rejected by the Government at the time of the formation of the Central Electricity Board.
Simultaneously, the Labour Movement made a claim for the constitution of public boards from representatives of those employed in
the industry. This so-called workers' control board, which had its
origin in guild socialism, was finally rejected in 1944 in favour of the
so-called efficiency board of persons chosen solely for their ability.
In India, however, these principles have been disregarded on many
occasions. Thus the Employees' State Insurance Corporation was
constituted with representatives of Part A States, Part B States and
Part C States; representatives of employers, employees and the
medical profession; and persons elected by Parliament. In England
(and also in India *in certain cases* like the State Bank of India)
members of the Parliament are disqualified for membership of any

[6] W. Friedmann, *The Public Corporation,* University of Toronto School of
Law, Comparative Law Series, Volume I, 1954, Part IV, 'A Comparative
Analysis', by the Editor.

Governing Board. Further, in England, Ministers do not sit on these Boards. But, in India, they hold *ex-officio* positions in certain cases. Thus the Minister of Labour is the ex-officio Chairman of the Employees' State Insurance Corporation. The Minister for Food and Agriculture and representatives of several Ministries sit on the National Co-operative Development and Warehousing Board. Also in Canada and Saskatchewan (despite earlier protestations), the practice of having a ministerial representative as a member of the Boards of Crown Corporations is now fairly universal.

Professor Sargent Florence, speaking of British Public Corporations, states : 'The mixture of functional *specialists,* supervisory and policy-making *generals,* and part-time business statesmen is at present a model for a Board rather than a regular pattern, but at least two of the elements are usually found on every Board.'[7] But as the Fleck Committee[8] have conceded, however competent individuals may be in their own particular fields, it will be no use appointing them to the Board if their personalities are such that they cannot work as a team.

4. *Respectful relationship with the Minister.*[9] A Public Corporation is responsible to the Government through the appropriate Minister. The powers given to the Ministers by the various Acts are undoubtedly extensive. Mr Brendan Bracken noted during the second reading of the (British) Gas Bill that in twenty-eight places it empowered the Minister to make regulations, in nineteen places it empowered him to give directions, and in twenty places it gave him powers of approval.[10] The powers of the Minister may be divided into three categories: powers which the Minister would exercise whether the industries were nationalized or not (e.g. safety regulations); powers concerning the process of nationalization (e.g. compensation); and powers designed to control the policy of the nationalized Corporations. It is the last category of powers which are really relevant.

The tradition of greater control was built up in England after

[7] P. Sargant Florence, *Present Problems in the Nationalization of British Industries,* Indian Journal of Economics (University of Allahabad), Special Number on Economic Development and the Rôle of the State, July 1956, No. 140, p. 17.

[8] National Coal Board, *Report of the Advisory Committee on Organisation* (Chairman: Dr A. Fleck), London, February 1955, p. 15.

[9] Mr Herbert (now Lord) Morrison used this phrase in his *Socialisation and Transport.* He felt that because both the Board and the Minister would be public servants there can be franker relationships than between the Minister and private railway companies.

[10] Acton Society Trust, *The Powers of the Minister,* Nationalized Industry (2), 1952, p. 2.

1945. Prior to that, the Central Electricity Board, the prototype of the present industrial corporations, was subject to the supervision, not of the Minister, but of the Electricity Commissioners, who were in their turn responsible to the Minister of Transport. The London Passenger Transport Board, as finally constituted, was subject even less to ministerial control.[11] A strange arrangement for the appointment of LPTB members placed the burden on such random functionaries as the President of the Law Society and the Chairman of the London Clearing Bank Committee. Sometimes it is suggested that a Commission may be set up to make appointments to the various Boards. The Minister's power of supervising rates is often transferred to tribunals specially constituted for the purpose. But the dual rôle of the Minister remains—a trustee of Parliament and a spokesman for the Boards. His position can be compared to an Intermediate Holding Company which is 'pulling' as well as 'being pulled'. The Acton Society Trust go to the extent of suggesting that it is a question of effectively combining the contrary rôles of Counsel for the Prosecution and Counsel for the Defence.

5. *Autonomous Working.* Overcentralization has been held to be the root cause of inefficiency in the public undertakings managed on the Post Office model.[12] It was in recognition of this dictum that the management of the Posts and Telegraphs Department was entrusted by the Government of India to a Board (on the lines of the Railway Board—a quasi-corporation) constituted in December 1959. The basic ideology of Public Corporation rests on autonomy in its normal (often described as day-to-day) operations with a view to ensuring the following advantages:

(i) *Freedom from the red tape.* Commercial activities require quick decisions which ordinary Government Departments are either incompetent or unwilling to arrive at. The Public Corporation, as an autonomous unit of the modern Leviathan State, can be more flexible and agile in its operational framework. It can ill afford to be callous towards its clientele in so far as its revenues depend on public satisfaction and are not in the nature of compulsory levies.

(ii) *Freedom from Treasury control.* This will be discussed under 'Self-contained Finance'. Complete freedom in this regard is perhaps neither possible nor desirable. However, there must be reasonable

[11] *Ibid.,* p. 4.
[12] See, for example, Viscount Wolmer, *Post Office Reform,* London, 1932, p. 300. Lord Wolmer refers to 'the changing Postmaster General, Treasury Control, overcentralization, civil service conditions, and the conversion of a communication service into a tax collecting machine.'

opportunities for incurring capital expenditure and for financing expansion of business. Generally, statutory limits are laid down in this regard.

(iii) *Freedom from political dictation.* A Public Corporation is expected to maximize operational efficiency. It is to be guided only by its charter of incorporation or such other formal policy directives which are issued by the Government. Apart from these considerations, it should not get entangled in the political fabric of the country.[13]

However, in several of the nationalizing Acts, an attempt has been made to ensure a happy blending of 'business principles' and 'public interest'. Thus the State Bank of India Act, 1955, lays down that 'the Central Board in discharging its functions shall act on business principles, regard being had to public interest'. In actual practice, however, it has been a Herculean task to make a workable distinction between 'day-to-day business' and 'overall policy'. For example, the State Bank of India may refuse to grant a loan to a small industrialist on the ground that he is unable to furnish adequate security. But this small 'routine' matter could be interpreted to suggest a policy of discrimination against particular types of industries. R. Kelf-Cohen suggests that the 'attitude of Parliament to the nationalized industries can only be described as frustration.'[14] By Parliament he means the back-benchers in the House of Commons and, to some extent, in the House of Lords. These people feel dissatisfied when Ministers refuse to discuss certain matters 'because they were not within their own responsibility, but fell within the scope of "day-to-day" administration'. Further, there is a general feeling of dissatisfaction that, somehow or other, these nationalized industries are removed from the scrutiny of Parliament, so that very inadequate information is obtainable about them. These grievances could be genuine as well as imaginary. But it is true that many a time Ministers try to withhold information, which Parliament can legitimately claim to seek, but which probably is the weak point either of the Ministers or of the Boards.

6. *Self-contained Finance.* It is a corollary to the fifth characteristic. The idea of autonomy remains illusory unless it is accompanied by

---

[13] If nationalized industries 'come to regard themselves as part of the political fabric of the country . . . they will be in danger of losing *the habits of thought and action* on which efficient business depends'.—Ronald S. Edwards and Harry Townsend, *Business Enterprise*: Its Growth and Organizations, Macmillan, London, 1958, pp. 512-13.
[14] R. Kelf-Cohen, *Nationalisation in Britain: The End of a Dogma*, Macmillan, London, 1958, p. 142.

financial independence. Public Corporations should realize that income depends upon economic factors rather than upon the benevolence of the legislature. They should be free from the inordinate delays caused by excessive Treasury control. They should also be free from the lapse system which encourages lavish and imprudent spendings towards the close of the financial year. In India, Public Corporations, which may be said to possess 'self-contained finance', include the Reserve Bank of India, the State Bank of India and the Life Insurance Corporation of India. The Life Insurance Corporation is a giant profitable enterprise with vast investment holdings. Only in the event of a black plague may it be obliged to approach the Government for financial assistance. The State Bank is less lucky because it is, in terms of the statute, required to open 'unremunerative' branches which require subsidization. The Air Corporations in India are also business-earning, but they need to incur vast capital expenditure; they carry the uncertainty of aircraft-crash, and the risk of occasional deficits. The Damodar Valley Corporation needed vast sums of money to build costly dams and ancillary projects with no possibility of earning any revenue during the initial years. Corporations like the Rehabilitation Finance Administration, the National Co-operative Development and Warehousing Board and the Central Warehousing Corporation are very much away from the ideal of self-contained finance. In England, a statutory obligation is imposed on most of the corporations to conduct the undertaking in such a way as to secure a revenue which is not less than sufficient to enable them to meet their current liabilities and expenditure properly chargeable to revenue account, taking one year with another. That is, a Public Corporation must not incur losses year after year, although it can certainly make profits. The airways corporations were not subjected to this requirement, because air transport has hitherto needed subsidies. In India, the principle of imposing such an obligation on Public Corporations has not found favour. The manner in which profits are to be disposed of is, however, sometimes laid down by statute. For example, the Industrial Finance Corporation Act, 1948, lays down: that the Corporation shall establish a Reserve Fund; that so long as the Reserve Fund is less than the paid-up share capital of the Corporation, and until there has been repaid to the Central Government such sums, if any, as that Government may have paid in fulfilment of guaranteed dividend ($2\frac{1}{4}$ per cent) or any other guarantee, the rate of dividend shall not exceed the 'guaranteed rate'; that under no circumstances shall any such dividend exceed 5 per cent; and that when the Reserve Fund becomes equal to the share capital of the Corporation, the surplus remaining after declaration of dividend shall be paid to the Central Government.

7. *Disinterestedness*. The Public Corporation is *not interested* in maximizing the profit, though it must be run efficiently; and in that process, it may make large profits.[15] Mr Herbert (now Lord) Morrison was perhaps a little too optimistic—as the sponsors of all new devices tend to be—when he said that the Public Corporation would quickly absorb the fine traditions of public service, maintaining freedom, at the same time, from corruption 'which characterizes, for example, the Civil Service and the staff of the London County Council'. In India, the same Civil Servants who are Departmental Secretaries are often appointed as members of the Governing Boards of Public Corporations. Sometimes, these Civil Servants step into the Boards without relinquishing their previous offices, i.e. they hold two or more offices concurrently. Thus the Principal Finance Secretary in the Government of India was appointed (concurrently) as the Chairman of a huge organization like the Life Insurance Corporation of India. Whatever advantages of co-ordination may exist in such a scheme, it is clear that it is not a case of disinterestedness, unless we think that a man has a double face or a flexible personality.

8. *No shares and no shareholders*. Professor Friedmann in his article on 'The New Public Corporations' published in *The Modern Law Review* (Volume 10) says: 'The Public Corporation has no shares and no shareholders, either private or public.' Professor Robson supports this contention. He says: 'There are no shareholders and the profit motive has been replaced by the public service motive[16] ... *The equity is owned by the nation*.'[17] It is true that—whether there are *formal* shareholders or not—the nation owns the equity in case of public enterprises. The nation is the entrepreneur, in the ultimate analysis, because it stands to gain (or to lose) from the successful (or unsuccessful) operation of publicly-owned industries. The gain (or loss) may be of a monetary character, i.e. lower prices and reduced level of taxation (or higher prices and increased level of taxation caused by inefficiency). At the same time, the gain or loss may take the shape of 'conveniences' and 'inconveniences'. But in India, many of the Public Corporations have share capital *just like* Joint Stock

[15] See Herbert Morrison, *Socialisation and Transport, loc. cit.*, pp. 156-7. There is the classic statement: 'The Public Corporation must be no mere capitalist business, the be all and end all of which is profits and dividends. ... It must have a different atmosphere at its Board table from that of a shareholders' meeting; its Board and its officers must regard themselves as the high custodians of public interest.'

[16] William A. Robson, *The British System of Government*, published for The British Council by Longmans, Green, 1948, p. 25.

[17] William A. Robson, *Problems of Nationalized Industry, loc. cit.*, Allen & Unwin, London, 1952, p. 29. (Italics ours.)

Companies. In this category we find the Industrial Finance Corporation of India, the Reserve Bank of India, the State Bank of India, and the Central Warehousing Corporation. This is mainly the financial group of Corporations. Moreover, these bodies are (or *have been,* or *are destined to be*) Mixed Corporations. The Reserve Bank of India *was,* up to 1948, a mixed Corporation. The Industrial Finance Corporation of India, and the Central Warehousing Corporation, *are* Mixed Corporations. The State Bank of India *was* and *is destined to be* a Mixed Corporation, though to start with, all its issued capital was held by the Reserve Bank of India, an institution with 100 per cent public ownership. In all these institutions, the State (or organization representing the State, like the Reserve Bank of India) holds a majority interest. There are, however, a number of Public Corporations in India which do not have any share capital. In this category we find the Damodar Valley Corporation, the Employees' State Insurance Corporation, the Rehabilitation Finance Administration, the Indian Airlines Corporation, the Air India International Corporation, the Life Insurance Corporation of India, and the National Co-operative Development and Warehousing Board. Finally, it may be mentioned that the practice of issuing perpetual stock has not been found to be expedient in India. Industries requiring a vast amount of capital expenditure, generally speaking, have not been entrusted to Public Corporations.

9. *Public Monopoly.* Whether a public enterprise takes the shape of a Corporation or of a Departmental Organization, it is customary for the State to declare monopolistic rights for itself in that particular line of business activity. This was the practice followed by ancient kings; and this is the norm of modern Governmental activity. Thus, as early as 1717, the British Post Office enjoyed the monopoly of carrying letters. The same principle has been followed in the matter of giant Public Corporations created in post-1945 Britain. Each of the industrial Corporations (e.g. the National Coal Board) aims at controlling all the units (with minor exceptions) within a particular industry. Some industries, by reason of their size (determining the optimum scale of operation), are suitable for monopolistic operation. Even when working under private ownership, there may be a strong case for amalgamation and monopolistic operation. Thus the Government of India brought about a compulsory merger of the Steel Corporation of Bengal and (into) the Indian Iron and Steel Company with effect from January 1, 1953. Similarly, even though railways may be privately owned, it would be most uneconomical, and indeed wasteful, to permit competing units to lay parallel lines. The same could be said of other public utility undertakings. The British Labour Party, therefore, declared that where monopoly was

inevitable, it should be in public hands.[18] But now they seem to be thinking on different lines. Two Reports, *Public Enterprise* and *Industry and Society*, considered by the Labour Party Conference at Brighton in October 1957, aim at extending the nationalized sector, but not on the old pattern (except the re-nationalization of Road Haulage and Iron and Steel). The Labour Party envisages a steadily increasing holding of equities by the Government. The *Socialist Union* also seem to be dissatisfied with the erstwhile pattern of nationalization. The Socialist Union, founded in 1951 by a group of Labour Party members, emphasize that 'the keynote of socialist realism has always been its emphasis on a transformation of the economic system. This must remain. What has to be rejected is the idea of transformation through total public ownership; that leads only to totalitarianism. . . . A Socialist economy is a mixed economy, part private, part public, and mixed in all its aspects. . . . The private sector of a socialist economy is not there merely on sufferance, to be tolerated only on grounds of political expediency, with the Sword of Damocles hanging over it in perpetual threat. On the contrary, it has a legitimate and indeed a necessary function to perform.'[19]

In England there appears to be a feeling—at least so long as the Labour Party is out of office—that public monopoly has reached the saturation point. In India, however, things are very much different. Since many of the basic industries are still largely in the hands of private enterprise, there is considerable scope for creating giant public monopolies on the British model. It may, however, be mentioned that *public monopoly does not necessarily mean monopoly for each Public Corporation*. Thus, there may be *socialist emulation* between two or more Public Corporations. For example, instead of establishing a single Corporation to manage the entire sphere of air transport, the Government of India preferred to create two Corporations. Although there is a broad allocation of responsibility as between foreign air services and internal air services, it *does* provide an opportunity to analyse comparative efficiency in certain respects.

[18] It has been pointed out that even on the absurd assumption that a socialized industry would restrict output and charge monopoly prices, at least monopoly profits would accrue to the community in the form of reduced prices for something else or reduced taxation, not to the advantage, of any private individual or group—the NSW Fabian Society, *Towards a Socialist Australia*, Pamphlet No. 2, March 1949, pp. 13-14.

[19] Socialist Union, *Twentieth Century Socialism* (The Economy of Tomorrow), a Penguin Special, 1956, pp. 146-7. Recently, a Study Group (Chairman: Mr R. G. Saraiya) has expressed the view that there is 'good scope' for 'Joint Sector Industries' in the newly-formed State of Maharashtra (Government participation ranging between 26 per cent and 49 per cent). Other States in India may propose to embark on similar schemes.

23

Similarly, the Life Insurance Corporation of India, in general, enjoys a monopoly of life insurance business; but the Post Office Life Insurance Fund has not been abolished. The State Bank of India is, for the most part, a commercial bank; but it does not enjoy any monopoly in that regard. Nor do the various Financial Corporations claim any monopolistic status. Even the Warehousing Corporations do not enjoy any statutory monopoly rights regarding the establishment of warehouses. The Damodar Valley Corporation has been entrusted with developmental work in a particular region, but there are comparable organizations—they may not be Statutory Corporations—like the Bhakra-Nangal Project and the Hirakud Dam Project.

10. *Judicial Control.* To guard against the dangers of public monopoly, judicial control is considered necessary. It may be noted that Private Monopolies, particularly in the United States, have a long history of judicial and quasi-judicial control (i.e. through Law Courts, Administrative Tribunals and Regulatory Commissions). The dangers of a Public Monopoly may be less imminent, but they do exist; and legislators generally consider it desirable to provide the necessary safeguards. For example, the Air Transport Advisory Council in England has 'to consider any representation from any person with respect to the adequacy of the facilities provided by any of the three corporations (now only two), or with respect to the charges for any such facilities'.[20]

In India, the Air Transport Council, established under the Air Corporations Act, 1953, does not enjoy that independent judicial status. It is the duty of the Council to consider such matters as are referred to it by any of the Air Corporations—the operation of scheduled air transport services, the routes on which such services should be operated by each of the Corporations, the frequency of such services, the passenger fares and freight rates to be charged, the measures of economy to be adopted, the provision of any services in regard to overhaul and maintenance of aircraft, or any other matter falling within the scope of the functions of either of the Corporations and, generally, in regard to ensuring the fullest co-operation in respect of all such matters. Although statutory bodies like the Air Transport Council may not be strictly judicial, it is clear that the activities, schemes and price policies of Public Corporations are subject to review by independent persons.

Another, and more critical, stage of review is in the hands of

[20] D. N. Chester, *The Nationalised Industries* (An Analysis of the Statutory Provisions), published for the Institute of Public Administration by Allen & Unwin Ltd, London, 1951, p. 36. The approval of 'charges scheme' is an important power of the Transport Tribunal.

Parliamentary Committees like the Estimates Committee and the Public Accounts Committee. This review, it is true, is more or less in the nature of a post-mortem examination; even then, it is extremely useful and necessary. It can be considered judicial in the sense that the administrators of Public Corporations are often required to appear before members of these Parliamentary Committees to tender their evidence and to answer questions which the members of the Committees may consider relevant for the 'post-mortem' examination. The Parliamentary Committees work on non-party basis, since it is supposed to be a matter of common interest to eradicate inefficiency and corruption. Hence these Reports are very close to judicial reviews.

The Law Courts, too, may come into the picture on certain occasions. For example, when a Public Corporation discriminates against a particular individual or Privately-owned Corporation, the Courts may have to examine the question of whether Articles 14 and 15 of the *Constitution of India* can be invoked to grant relief to those who are being discriminated against. On the one hand it is contended that a Public Corporation, because of *insulated personality,* is *not* the State, and that the Constitution only says that 'the State shall not discriminate'. On the other hand, it is argued that a Public Corporation is the shadow of the State and that, as a public body, it cannot be permitted to act in an arbitrary manner. An extreme case of *permissible* judicial control is presented by the London Passenger Transport Board (1933-48). Here the holders of 'A', 'B' or 'L.A.' stock, if not less than 5 per cent of the total amount of that stock then outstanding, could apply to the High Court for 'a receiver' or 'a receiver and manager' if the Board defaulted in respect of the payment on the stock for not less than three months. 'C' shareholders had the same right should the Board fail to pay interest on that stock at the standard rate for three consecutive years, of which the first year was to be not earlier than the one ending on June 30, 1936. Of course, such an eventuality did not arise; otherwise, it would have been an interesting scene to see a Public Corporation in the liquidation court. In India, it is customary to put a legal bar to liquidation in the case of various Public Corporations. The Damodar Valley Corporation Act, 1948, gives a place of honour to judicial control in the matter of certain disputes: '. . . any dispute between the Corporation and any Participating Government regarding any matter covered by this Act or touching or arising out of it shall be referred to an arbitrator who shall be appointed by the Chief Justice of India. The decision of the arbitrator shall be final and binding on the parties.'

Judicial control also comes in with regard to the question of fixing compensation. This is a temporary phase in the life of a Public

Corporation, and is relevant only in those cases where existing industrial units have been nationalized. Further, the Indian Constitution (Fourth) Amendment Act, 1955, lays down that inadequacy of the compensation provided for by the Legislature shall not be called into question in a Court of Law. However, the Air Corporations Act, 1953, and the Life Insurance Corporation Act, 1956, provided for the setting up of a Tribunal of three members (one of them having been a Judge of a High Court or of the Supreme Court). If the amount of compensation offered to an erstwhile owner were not acceptable to him, he could have the matter referred to the Tribunal for decision. Every such Tribunal was to enjoy the powers of a civil court with regard to enforcing attendance of any person, production of documents, receiving evidence and issuing commissions. It may, however, be noted that all the members of a Tribunal were to be appointed by the Central Government.

11. *Commercial Audit.* The Public Corporation was conceived as a device for freeing public enterprises of a commercial or industrial character from the vexatious rules of procedure applicable to Government Departments. The Estimates Committee of the Indian Parliament in their Ninth Report (1953-54) pointed out that every undertaking must prepare its accounts according to well settled commercial principles—paying interest on the capital outlay, income tax and also a percentage of profits to the Consolidated Fund.[21] Paul H. Appleby, in his 1956 Report, puts a strong word against the conventional pattern of auditing : '. . . *the Comptroller and Auditor General is today a primary cause of a widespread and paralysing unwillingness to decide and to act.*'[22] Appleby adds : 'This repressive and negative influence is in considerable part indirect, impinging on the bureaucracy by way of Parliament because of the exaggerated and unselective attention given by Parliament to the *petty exceptions and the inflated pretensions built around the pedestrian function of auditing.*'[23] No doubt auditors have, on many occasions, fallen a prey to the 'Penny Wise, Pound Foolish' practice. They so much engross themselves with petty technical details that they hardly have time (and temperament) to be able to pay attention to broader questions of business efficiency and prudent management. Mr Asoka Chanda (Comptroller and Auditor General) concedes that objections are raised, technical in character, even in respect of schemes

[21] Estimates Committee (Ninth Report), *Administrative, Financial and Other Reforms,* Lok Sabha Secretariat, New Delhi, May 1954, p. 19.

[22] Paul H. Appleby, *Re-examination of India's Administrative System* with special reference to Administration of Government's Industrial and Commercial Enterprises, Government of India, Cabinet Secretariat, Organization and Methods Division, 1956, p. 28. (Italics ours.)

[23] *Ibid.*

and projects which have been executed with competence and expedition.[24]

The Damodar Valley Corporation Act, 1948, lays down that 'The accounts of the Corporation shall be maintained and audited in such manner as may, in consultation with the Auditor General of India, be prescribed.' The Industrial Finance Corporation Act, 1948 (as amended in 1952), provides: 'The affairs of the Corporation shall be audited by not less than two auditors duly qualified to act as auditors of companies . . . one of whom shall be appointed by the Central Government in consultation with the Comptroller and Auditor General of India and the other elected in the prescribed manner. . . .' The Rehabilitation Finance Administration Act, 1948 (as amended in 1953), lays down that the accounts of the Administration shall be audited by the Comptroller and Auditor General, who shall have 'the same rights, privileges and authority in connection with such audit as . . . with the audit of Government accounts. . . .' Thus the RFA is treated on the level of an ordinary Government Department. The Air Corporations Act, 1953, surprisingly, provides for annual audit by the Comptroller and Auditor General just as in the case of the Rehabilitation Finance Administration (i.e. like an ordinary Government Department). The State Bank of India Act, 1955, provides that 'The affairs of the State Bank shall be audited by two auditors duly qualified to act as auditors of companies . . . who shall be appointed by the Reserve Bank in consultation with the Central Government.' An auditor may be a shareholder but no director or member of a Local Board or of a Local Committee or an officer of the State Bank shall be eligible to be an auditor. The auditors are required to report on the following matters:

(a) whether the Balance Sheet exhibits a true and correct view of the affairs (and whether the explanations have been satisfactory);

(b) whether the transactions were within the power of the State Bank;

(c) whether the returns received from the offices and the branches have been found adequate;

(d) whether the Profit and Loss Account shows a true balance of profit and loss for the period covered by such account; and

(e) any other matter which they consider should be brought to the notice of the shareholders or the Central Government, as the case may be.

This is, by and large, a commercial pattern of auditing. The greatest measure of autonomy in the matter of audit is enjoyed by the Life Insurance Corporation of India. The Life Insurance Corporation Act, 1956, lays down: 'The accounts of the Corporation

[24] Asoka Chanda, *Indian Administration,* Allen & Unwin, London, 1958, pp. 252-3.

shall be audited by auditors duly qualified to act as auditors of companies under the law for the time being in force relating to companies, and the auditors shall be appointed by the Corporation with the previous approval of the Central Government and shall receive such remuneration from the Corporation as the Central Government may fix.'

In case of Government Companies, the general practice is to have only one firm of auditors. The auditor is sometimes appointed by the Company itself, sometimes by the Government, and sometimes by the Government *in consultation with the Comptroller and Auditor General*. But the Comptroller and Auditor General has the right to conduct a supplementary or test audit in addition to the usual audit. He can also direct the manner in which the Company's account shall be audited by the (usual) auditors, and give instructions to such auditors in regard to any matter relating to the performance of the audit function. The comments of the Comptroller and Auditor General are communicated to the Government Companies under the signatures of the Director of Commercial Audit. The usual communication runs as follows: [25]

I have to state that this office has no comments upon or supplement to the Auditor's Report under sub-section (4) of section 619 of the Companies Act, 1956, on the accounts of..........................for the year ended on 31st March, 1958.

The results of the Supplementary or Test Audit conducted on behalf of the Comptroller and Auditor General under section 619 (3) (b) will, however, be intimated to the Company separately in due course.

12. *Freedom from Civil Service Regulations.* Professor Hodgetts suggests that one of the privileges most cherished by the managers of a public corporation is their freedom from civil service regulations.[26] This freedom makes for convenience and speed in the process of recruitment and promotion, and liberality in the fixation of remuneration and other conditions (including amenities) of service.

The employment provisions relating to Canadian Crown Corporations fall into two broad categories:

(a) where employees of the Corporation must be appointed 'in the manner authorized by law' or 'in accordance with the provisions of the Civil Service Act'; and

(b) where employees of the Corporation may be appointed by the

[25] Based on a letter dated December 6, 1958, issued from the office of the Director of Commercial Audit, New Delhi, with regard to the accounts of the Hindustan Shipyard.

[26] J. E. Hodgetts, *The Public Corporation in Canada,* Friedmann (Ed.), 1954, *loc. cit.*

Corporation 'nothwithstanding the Civil Service Act'.

The second broad category can be further divided into two groups:

(i) where the corporation may exercise its powers of appointing staff and fixing remuneration, without reference to the Governor in Council; and

(ii) where some or all of the corporation's powers of appointing staff and determining remuneration may be exercised subject to the approval of the Governor in Council, or in accordance with by-laws or regulations which are subject to approval by the Council.

While practices differ very widely, it may be said that Departmental Corporations tend to have their employment policies geared to the Civil Service Act. Proprietary Corporations appear to be the most independent (being required seldom to seek approval of the Governor in Council). Agency Corporations seem to occupy a midway position (usually having powers to make appointments and to fix salaries, but often only with the approval of the Governor in Council). Salaries in the clerical and stenographic grades are comparable to those prevailing in Government Departments, whereas emoluments in the higher ranges resemble those in private employment.[27]

In the United States, the Ramspeck Act, as early as 1940, authorized the application of civil service laws to employees of federally-owned and -controlled corporations (with the significant exception of the TVA) at the *discretion* of the President which has been extensively employed for that purpose.[28] The President was authorized to extend the classified civil service 'from time to time' and 'so far as practicable' in his opinion.

In India, members of the Governing Boards of Public Corporations are very often Civil Servants. Thus, on July 1, 1959, all the three members of the Damodar Valley Corporation were ICS men, serving on the Board as part-time members (including the Chairman). The Corporation paid only their travelling allowance, etc. The Secretary and the Financial Adviser of the Corporation are to be appointed by the Central Government, and the Corporation 'may appoint such other officers and servants as it considers necessary for the efficient performance of its functions'. The pay and other conditions of service of the officers and servants of the Corporation shall—

(a) as respects the Secretary and Financial Adviser, be such as may be prescribed (by rules made by the Central Government); and

[27] A. H. Hanson (Ed.), *Public Enterprise*, International Institute of Administrative Services, Brussels, 1955, pp. 92-3.
[28] Albert S. Abel, *The Public Corporation in the United States*, Friedmann (Ed.), 1954, *loc. cit.*

(b) as respects the other officers and servants, be such as may be determined by regulations (to be framed by the Corporation with the approval of the Government).

The Employees' State Insurance Corporation is required to obtain the sanction of the Central Government for the creation of any post with a maximum monthly salary of Rs500 and above. Every such appointment shall be made in consultation with the Union Public Service Commission. This, however, does not apply to an officiating or temporary appointment for an aggregate period not exceeding one year. In the case of the Rehabilitation Finance Administration, the appointment and the fixation of the salary, allowances and other conditions of service of the Deputy Chief Administrator and such other officers as may be prescribed by the Central Government, shall be subject to the previous sanction of that Government.

The State Bank of India is fully autonomous in this regard. It 'may appoint such number of officers, advisers and employees as it considers necessary or desirable for the efficient performance of its functions, and determine the terms and conditions of their appointment and service.' The Life Insurance Corporation may (with the previous approval of the Central Government) make regulations regarding the method of recruitment of employees and agents and their terms of conditions of service.

13. *Private Law Status.* The Public Corporation is an amphibious institution. It is a public authority inasmuch as it is owned by the State, and is expected to fulfil public tasks on behalf of the Government and Parliament. But the commercial nature of its activities, and its managerial model, greatly resemble the Privately-owned Corporation. This dual nature of the Public Corporation—while it is designed to achieve the best of both the worlds—gives rise to intricate legal questions, e.g.:

(a) To what extent should a Public Corporation be subjected to taxation laws?

(b) Can a Public Corporation be fined, or penalized otherwise, in the event of violation of certain laws of the land?

(c) Is a Public Corporation answerable before the civil courts in all matters which affect contractual rights (damages for breach of contract, etc.)?

(d) Is a Public Corporation liable in torts—damage caused to a third party by an action imputable to the Corporation, or an injury resulting from an act committed by an employee during employment but not imputable to the Corporation (e.g. in case of actions which are beyond the legal capacity of the Corporation)?

(e) Is a Public Corporation endowed with full liberty to alienate its capital assets?

(f) Can the creditors of a Public Corporation carry it to the Liquidation Court?

(g) Can a Public Corporation claim Crown privileges in the matter of realizing its book debts (i.e. whether it can be classed as a Preferential Creditor), and in the matter of acquiring land and other property?

(h) Is a Public Corporation free to practise discrimination in its business activities (as between various citizens and Privately-owned Corporations, e.g. in the award of contracts)?

(i) Should a Public Corporation be permitted (or required) to maintain secrecy about certain aspects of its working on the lines of Customary Law followed by Privately-owned Corporations (e.g. secrecy regarding Bank Accounts or Loans)?

(j) Should a Public Corporation be treated at par with a Privately-owned Corporation in the matter of observing legal or procedural formalities, e.g. when a Government Department is considering applications and issuing licences (or permits) with regard to particular lines of business activity (or commodities)?

(k) Is a Public Corporation bound by Price Control Regulations, Labour Laws (including Workmen's Compensation) and other laws applicable to private enterprises?

It is really the province of the lawyer to find satisfactory answers to such questions. It may, however, be stated that if a Public Corporation is to show its efficiency without any artificial support, it should, *in most of these matters,* be granted Private Law Status. Here we propose to confine our attention to the question of taxation. If public and private enterprises co-exist in a particular industry, any concessions granted to Public Corporations in the matter of taxation (specially indirect taxes) would vitiate the process of judging 'the relative efficiency', and may create a sense of complacency in the public sector. In New Zealand, the principle seems to have been accepted that public corporate enterprises competing directly with private enterprises are liable to full taxation. In the United States, the test at one time was whether the State were exercising Governmental or Proprietary Functions (immunity attaching to the former). The decision in *New York* v *United States* (1946) recast the formula so that now 'immunity attaches if the State's activities *are* of a kind uniquely and peculiarly performed by government but *not* if it is of a kind in which private enterprise *frequently* or *alternatively* engages.' In practice, this means that the State enterprise of a kind which lends itself to *corporate form* gets taxed by the United States. Sometimes, as in the case of TVA, the Congress has provided compensation to the States for the loss of tax revenues.[29]

[29] Albert S. Abel, *The Public Corporation in the United States,* Friedmann (Ed.), 1954, *op. cit.*

In the Soviet Union, Public Corporations are *not* exempt from taxation. On the contrary, they have been subjected to a tax system 'which places the major burden for the conduct of local and central government upon them'. Local Soviets were authorized to tax them in two ways: upon the use of land assigned to them; and upon the value of buildings constructed upon the land. The Central Government imposes *a turnover tax* (Decree of September 2, 1930) and *an income tax* (Decree of September 3, 1931). The turnover tax varies from commodity to commodity; it may aim at encouraging or discouraging the consumption of a particular commodity. Public Corporations are required to pay income tax to the benefit of the All-Union, the Republic or the Local Government, depending upon the source of the Corporation's authority to function.

In Australia, Government Policy has generally favoured exemption of public authorities from taxation, on the view that 'national taxes could only produce unnecessary book-keeping entries when applied to national services'. Section 23 of the Commonwealth Income Tax Assessment Act exempts 'the revenue of . . . a public authority constituted under any Act or State Act'. In case of Commonwealth income tax, an attempt to tax State public authorities would raise the constitutional issue considered in *Melbourne Corporation* v *Commonwealth* (1947). Many of the Corporations have been granted express exemption (completely or to some specified extent) from taxation. In the case of the Commonwealth Australian National Airlines Commission, liability to pay taxes was left to the discretion of a relevant minister. The Commission was 'left free' for several years, but in 1952, to promote 'fair competition' with private air companies, the Minister directed that the Commission be subjected to taxes on the basis applicable to private concerns.

In India, there are three patterns of statutes in this regard; those which specifically provide that Public Corporations will pay the usual taxes; those which grant specific exemption; and those which are silent in the matter. Thus the Damodar Valley Corporation Act, 1948, lays down that 'The Corporation shall be liable to pay any taxes on income levied by the Central Government in the same manner and to the same extent as a company. The Provincial (State) Government shall not be entitled to any refund of any such taxes paid by the Corporation.' Further, in the event of any betterment levy being imposed by a Provincial (State) Government, the proportionate proceeds thereof in so far as they are attributable to the operations of the Corporation shall be credited to the Corporation. The Industrial Finance Corporation Act, 1948, lays down: 'For the purposes of the Indian Income-tax Act, 1922 (XI of 1922), the Corporation shall be deemed to be a company within the meaning of that Act and shall be liable to income-tax and super-tax accordingly on its income, profits and gains.'

The Rehabilitation Finance Administration Act, 1948, provides: 'Notwithstanding anything contained in the Indian Income Tax Act, 1922, or in any other enactment for the time being in force relating to income-tax, super-tax or business profit-tax, the Administration shall not be liable to pay income-tax, super-tax or business profits-tax on any income, profits or gains.' The Employees' State Insurance Act, 1948, treats the ESIC as a preferential creditor.

In the third category, we may refer to the Air India International Corporation which, in its accounts for the year ending March 31, 1958, made a provision for Deferred Taxation amounting to Rs 57.25 lakhs, as against an operating profit of Rs 71.67 lakhs. During the year ended March 31, 1959, the operating profit was only Rs 15.85 lakhs and no provision was made for Deferred Taxation.

14. *Socialization.* It is perhaps the highest ideal of a Public Corporation. Mere nationalization or public ownership is not enough. It is only the beginning of a great experiment. The concept of socialization as enunciated by Mr Herbert (now Lord) Morrison may be said to consist of:

(a) a combination of public ownership, public accountability and business management for public ends;

(b) maximum of public well-being;

(c) the material well-being and the status, dignity, knowledge and freedom of the workers by hand and by brain employed in the undertaking;

(d) setting aside those personal, private and sectional prejudices or interests which are inconsistent with the public good; and

(e) a new consciousness on the part of management, technicians and labour as to their responsibilities to John Bull.[30]

We would like to define a socialized industry as one *which is responsive to the needs and interests of the society.* In order that *responsiveness* may be a reality, it is necessary, first, to have efficient channels of communication and, secondly, to have a desire to utilize these channels in the proper spirit. While some of the Public Corporations have succeeded in building up attractive networks of communication, they have generally failed to generate the proper spirit. The entire fault, however, should not be placed at the doors of Public Corporations. The people, on their part, have sometimes been too political, sometimes too sectarian, and sometimes too indifferent. The Public Corporations, no doubt, have tried to create a halo of

[30] The term John Bull was used by Mr Morrison in his Foreword to *Efficiency in the Nationalised Industries.* Published for the Institute of Public Administration by George Allen & Unwin Ltd, London (1952), p. (i).

secrecy; but when they do offer opportunities for public co-operation, the response is generally disappointing. Sometimes there is an initial spurt of enthusiasm; but sustained interest is generally lacking. There are, however, a good many professional spectators, whose interest is confined to periodical scandals, and who equate their 'negative' interest in the activities of Public Corporations with the highest degree of patriotism.

CHAPTER II

THE RÔLE AND FUNCTIONS OF
STATE CORPORATIONS IN INDIA

A. THE PUBLIC SECTOR IN INDIA:
SOME FACTS AND FIGURES

Political thinking in India, since independence, has not only been quite confused, but it has also been very much at variance with actual practice. For example, there has been so much talk of socialism on political platforms that an unwary person may be constrained to believe that the private sector of the Indian economy had been practically squeezed out. The baselessness of such a belief would be evident if we just care to glance at the employment statistics in the public sector. A recent study undertaken by the National Employment Service of the Labour Ministry to examine the impact of the Second Five-Year Plan on employment generated in the public sector reveals that the number of persons employed in the public sector at the end of March 1959 was 63.74 lakhs.[1] This figure works out to only 4 per cent of the total working population in India. The corresponding percentage was 24.3 per cent in Great Britain and 12 per cent in the U.S.A. in 1950. Out of an increase of 8.6 lakhs in employment in India's public sector, achieved between April 1, 1956, and December 31, 1958, more than half (4.84 lakhs) was accounted for by governmental services. The increase in administrative offices and departments alone amounted to 3.5 lakhs. It is true that in terms of percentages the increase in the number of persons employed in services is not so high. But it should not be lost sight of that since the level of employment in many of the publicly-owned industries was very low in 1956 (the base period), even a small increase in absolute

Percentage of increased employment for various industries and services in India's public sector

Agriculture, Livestock, etc.	20.1
Mining and Quarrying	26.7
Manufacturing	33.7
Construction	30.6
Electricity, Gas and Water	30.0
Trade and Commerce	95.8
Transport and Communications	10.5
Services	19.2

[1] Figures released on March 27, 1960.

numbers was enough to present inflated rates of growth in percentage terms. It is in this light that the preceding table should be judged.[2]

The public sector has presented a paradox in India. On the one hand, she is living in an economic framework which is essentially capitalistic. Many of the basic industries[3] like coal mining, electricity supply, petroleum refining, commercial banking and even iron and steel (until the Government-owned steel plants are able to achieve sizeable output) are largely in the hands of private enterprise. At the 'national' level only two measures of nationalization are worth mentioning—air transport in 1953 and life insurance in 1956. The taking over of the Imperial Bank of India (and renaming it as the State Bank of India) in 1955 is not of much significance because the pre-nationalization Bank had already been working under the patronage of the Government as a Statutory Corporation.[4] Further, this measure must be considered as something isolated and inconsistent with the general attitude of the Government of India towards commercial banks. At the 'State' level, the only noteworthy measure of nationalization relates to road transport.[5]

On the other hand, it is interesting to observe that public enterprise in India has made inroads into consumer goods industries like sugar and paper and has unnecessarily diverted its energies and resources to undertakings like the Oshoka Hotel. The attitude towards nationalization has been allowed to remain conveniently ambiguous. For example, with regard to the coal industry, the Production Minister, Mr K. C. Reddy, informed the *Lok Sabha* on December 12, 1955, that 'no guarantee of non-nationalization for any definite period of time would be given to the existing private collieries as asked for by them'. About a year later, on November 30, 1956, Mr Satish Chandra, Deputy Minister for Production, 'ruled out complete nationalization of collieries on the ground that it was not a practical proposition. He reiterated the Government's policy to run

[2] For example, an increase of 95.8 per cent under the heading Trade and Commerce is only indicative of the fact that before 1956 there was hardly any State trading. Even the State Trading Corporation had not come into existence. An increase of 10.5 per cent in case of transport and communications is disappointing.

[3] The Railways, no doubt, constitute the biggest public enterprise in India. But their public ownership goes back to the pre-independence era.

[4] Again, the nationalizing Act of 1955 permitted 45 per cent ownership for the private sector.

[5] In the field of agriculture, an important measure was the abolition of *Zamindari* system (elimination of land intermediaries). Both transport and land reforms created numerous legal difficulties because the Constitution of the Indian Republic, as it came into force on January 26, 1950, had not provided for so much of socialism as it came to be professed in later years. The Constitution had to be amended several times, very early in its life, to ensure faster economic progress.

36

new coal-mining units by themselves and offer encouragement to existing private collieries to increase their production'.

State Corporations have a special rôle in the context of a mixed economy. Apart from the usual pattern of a mixed economy, where public and private enterprises exist side by side, State Corporations are an ideal device for promoting mixed shareholdings in each enterprise. It is on these lines that the British Labour Party propose to extend the scope of nationalization in future. The ideal of progressive socialization, to which India is wedded, may also be better achieved through the device of State Corporations. Nationalization, through the transfer of shareholdings to the State, is a very convenient device. The nationalized corporations (like the Air India International) may continue to work under the same label without causing any dislocation in working or diminution in goodwill.

B. THE METHODOLOGY OF PROMOTION

The growth of public enterprises, especially since 1945, has presented an amazing diversity. While there is a general tendency to move away from the government departmental type of organization, no single trend can be cited as typical of innovations in organization and control.[6] From the organizational viewpoint the principal forms of public enterprise may be outlined as follows:

(1) Statutory Corporations;
(2) Limited Companies;
(3) Quasi-Corporations;
(4) Departmental Undertakings;
(5) Control Boards;
(6) Commodity Boards;
(7) Commissions; and
(8) Port Trusts and Local Authorities.

Statutory Corporations are established under special Acts of Parliament or State Legislatures. They may be wholly owned by the Central Government, by any of the State Governments, jointly by several Governments, or they may involve financial participation by private interests as well. In the last-mentioned situation they may be termed as Mixed Corporations. The State generally retains the majority interest in shareholdings, i.e. 51 per cent or more, though there are instances of minority participation also. Thus the Reserve Bank of India was a Statutory Corporation even before its nationalization in 1948. Even when doors are left open for the entry of private enterprise, one or more of the following safeguards are often provided:

[6] United Nations: *Some Problems in the Organization and Administration of Public Enterprises in the Industrial Field,* New York, July 28, 1954, p. 3.

(i) that only institutions, e.g. scheduled banks, investment trusts and co-operative societies may purchase the shares of Statutory Corporations;

(ii) that no single individual or institution in the private sector may purchase more than a certain percentage of the shares;

(iii) that there may be restrictions on the transfer of shares in such a manner that no private individual or institution may acquire dominating influence; and

(iv) that even if any individual or institution comes to acquire large shareholdings, the exercise of voting power, and the right of receiving dividends, may be circumscribed.

There are many Statutory Corporations without any share capital. In such cases, the question of mixed ownership does not arise, though it is always open to the State to have non-official Directors on the Governing Boards of such Corporations.

Statutory Corporations, which are often institutions of national importance, are generally exempted from writing the word 'Limited' after their name, even though they invariably enjoy not only the privilege of limited liability but also immunity from being carried to the court of liquidation. Thus the State Bank of India is not required to add 'Limited' to its name, though other commercial banks have to observe that formality.

The period 1944-1950 was marked by the creation of a large number of Statutory Corporations in England, India, Canada, Australia and several other countries of the world. Their growth synchronized with the first flush of post-war economic planning. However, in course of time it was realized by administrators and planners that it meant considerable inconvenience to go to Parliament every time a fresh undertaking had to be established. There was also a desire to maintain secrecy about the working of State enterprises. Hence it became fashionable, particularly in India, to promote Government Companies under the ordinary law of incorporation.[7]

It is interesting to note that most of the Government Companies in India have been registered as Private Companies,[8] where only two persons are required to sign the Memorandum and Articles of Association, where the number of members (excluding member-employees) cannot exceed fifty, where a prospectus *cannot* be issued for raising share capital from the general public, and where shares are not freely transferable. Where the participation of private interests is desired, Government Companies have been registered as Public

---

[7] In certain other countries, like Pakistan, limited companies were floated as subsidiaries of Statutory Corporations.

[8] Private Companies should not be confused with private enterprise. For clarification, see Chapter IV on Government Companies in India.

Companies so that there is no limitation on the number of share-holders, there is no restriction on the transfer of shares and there is no bar to the issue of prospectus for raising share capital from private individuals and institutions.

Since a Private Company needs only two promoters, the usual methodology of promotion employed in India is that the President of India (through some Departmental Secretary) and the Secretary of the Ministry or Department concerned become the first share-holders of the new enterprise. In some cases the same civil servant puts two signatures on the Memorandum and Articles of Associa-tion, first on behalf of the President of India and secondly as Departmental Secretary. In the first capacity he might take (for example) 95 per cent of the shares and in the second capacity he may agree to take the remaining 5 per cent.

We now come to Quasi-Corporations. The most notable example of such an organization is the Railway Board which manages the largest nationalized undertaking in India employing 1,108,529 workers and a capital of Rs 1,169 crores as on March 31, 1958.[9] The Railway Board consists of Functional Members: Chairman; Financial Commissioner; Member, Engineering; Member, Staff; and Member, Transportation. All these members are Departmental Sec-retaries. Thus the Railway Board and the Ministry of Railways are almost synonymous terms (the Ministry, no doubt, being concerned with the supervision of—almost negligible—privately-owned rail-ways also). The Posts and Telegraphs Board was established by the Government of India in December 1959 on the lines of the Railway Board. It was contended that the P. and T. Board would be an autonomous organization—though not formally a corporation—so that it might be able to increase the efficiency of postal services.

There are other Departmental Undertakings like Ordnance Fac-tories, Gold Mines, Salt Works (now entrusted to a Government Company) and Churk Cement Factory (run by the U.P. Govern-ment). Such undertakings are established under executive discretion, the ministerial responsibility being direct (without any intermediary in the nature of a Statutory Corporation or Government Company). Many of the Public Works, Defence Projects and industrial under-takings requiring foreign collaboration or involving any urgency are often established under the direct patronage of the Government. Later on, with a view to exploiting commercial possibilities and reducing the administrative load on the Departments, many of the Departmental Undertakings may be handed over to Statutory Cor-porations or Limited Companies. This has happened with the Damodar Valley Project and the Steel Plants in India.

[9] Report by the Railway Board on Indian Railways for 1957-58, Volume I, 1959, p. (i).

In many cases—particularly for irrigation and power projects—a different method is followed. Instead of handing over a project to a corporate entity, a Control Board is constituted by the Government in order to maintain on-the-spot supervision over that project. Thus the Bhakra Nangal Control Board, the Hirakud Control Board, the Nagarjuna Sagar Control Board and the Chambal Control Board were established in terms of resolutions passed by the Government of India. The Koyna Control Board was established by a resolution of the Bombay Government. The Rihand Dam Control Board and the Kosi Control Board were established under orders of the U.P. and Bihar Governments respectively. The Orissa River Board (to regulate and control the disposal of effluents into rivers by factories) is a statutory body established in 1955 under the Orissa River Pollution Prevention Act, 1953. The Governor of Punjab (in his personal capacity) was appointed Chairman of the Bhakra Control Board, whereas the Chief Minister of Orissa was made the Chairman of Hirakud Control Board. These Control Boards are exclusively composed of officials, the Chairman of the Central Water and Power Commission being one of them. They may be described as Embryonic Corporations.

The Commodity Boards are mixed organizations consisting of, besides Government Officials, representatives of various interests. Thus the Tea Board in India consists of forty-one members, including the Chairman. There are six representatives of the Governments of the principal tea-growing States in India, thirteen members representing owners of tea estates and gardens and growers of tea, seven representatives of persons employed in tea estates and gardens, five representatives of dealers (including exporters and internal traders) and manufacturers of tea, six members representing consumers, and three representatives of Parliament. The Coffee Board consists of thirty-three members, the Rubber Board of twenty-four members, the Coir Board of thirty-four members, the Central Silk Board of thirty-six members, the All-India Handloom Board of fifty-four members, the All-India Handicrafts Board of thirty-two members and the Small Scale Industries Board of fifty members.[10] The Small Scale Industries Board (as reconstituted in September 1958) consists of thirteen Central Government officials; fifteen officers of the State Governments; one representative *each* of the Reserve Bank of India, State Bank of India and State Financial Corporations; one elected representative of each of the State Small Scale Industries Boards; and five non-officials. Many of the Commodity Boards are statutory bodies. Thus the Tea Board administers the Tea Act of 1953, the Rubber Board was set up under the provisions of the

[10] The position as it stood according to the Annual Report of the Ministry of Commerce and Industry for 1958-59.

Rubber Act, 1947, and the Coir Board was established under the Coir Industry Act of 1953. Besides these Boards, there are a number of Offices for the development and regulation of certain industries. Thus we have the Offices of the Textile Commissioner, the Jute Commissioner and the Salt Commissioner.

Regulatory Commissions may be established by executive discretion or under special Acts of Parliament. Thus in India the Tariff Commission is a statutory body established under the Tariff Commission Act, 1951. Similarly, the Forward Markets Commission was created in 1954 under the Forward Contracts (Regulation) Act, 1952. Besides Regulatory Commissions, we have organizations entrusted with development work like the Khadi and Village Industries Commission.[11] Two important characteristics of Commissions are that they are high-powered and they have a small membership. The Khadi and Village Industries Commission possesses both these qualities—it has a membership of only five. As against this, Commodity Boards are not *high-powered* and they have a large membership. Thus, in spite of some apparent similarity in functions, the Khadi and Village Industries Commission does not fall in the category of Commodity Boards.

Finally, we come to Port Trusts and Local Authorities. Prior to the constitutional reforms of 1919, both major and minor ports in India were being administered by the various Local Governments[12] concerned under Local Acts. After 1919, the Central Government became constitutionally responsible for the major ports. However, the Government of India did not actually take over the administrative control of the major ports of Bombay, Calcutta and Madras from the Provincial (State) Governments concerned until April 1, 1937, when the relevant Provincial (State) Acts[13] were suitably adapted to enable the Central Government to discharge its functions in relation to these major ports. Naturally, these Acts were dissimilar in nature and scope, were difficult to interpret and gave rise to administrative anomalies. Hence, when the Port Trusts and Ports Amendment Bill, 1950, was on the anvil, the Parliament Secretariat, in a note dated November 2, 1950, pointed out: 'The objects of the Bill are to

[11] This Commission was established in pursuance to the Khadi and Village Industries Act, 1956, statutorily with effect from April 1, 1957. It replaced the advisory body known as the Khadi and Village Industries Board set up in 1953.

[12] The term Local Government at that time stood for Provincial (i.e., State) Government.

[13] The relevant Acts are: (1) Bombay Port Trust Act (Bombay Act VI of 1879); (2) Calcutta Port Act (Bengal Act III of 1890); and Madras Port Trust Act (Madras Act II of 1905). Besides, there is the Indian Ports Act, 1908, which applies not only to major ports but also to minor ports which now fall in the concurrent field of legislation. It is interesting to observe that the Indian Ports Act and the Port of London Act were passed in the same year.

remove these lacunae, introduce such uniformity as is possible without unnecessary disturbance of the *status quo,* effect a considerable degree of decentralization of authority in the matter of day-to-day administration and introduce a greater measure of Central control and supervision in matters of policy.' Thus, on the one hand, the objective was decentralization of authority; and, on the other hand, there was the (apparently contradictory) aim of achieving greater Central control in matters of policy. It can be inferred that the spirit of Public Corporations was haunting the legislators.[14]

C. THE FUNCTIONAL ROLE OF STATE CORPORATIONS

State Corporations have been entrusted with a wide range of economic activity. However, on the basis of experience gained in certain other countries of the world, their manifestation in the following forms deserves particular notice:

1. *Marketing Boards.* Such organizations have been established even in those countries (like the USA) where public enterprise and socialism are very much at a discount. Their growth may be explained as follows:

(a) Agricultural prices have been found to be much more sensitive than industrial prices. Thus, in a period of boom, agricultural prices may rise to much greater heights and during a depression they tend to fall much more than industrial prices. Hence, agricultural countries —whether they favour or disfavour socialism—find it necessary to stabilize their national income and the level of economic prosperity by interfering in the marketing of farm products.

(b) In those countries (e.g. India) where farmers carry a large voting power, it becomes a part of the political game to assure a fair minimum price in a falling market. Further, even in the advanced countries of the world, agricultural production is not quite independent of rainfall and other climatic factors. As such, farmers' control over the level of supply is less powerful than the control exercised by industrialists over their output. Hence farmers are rightly considered to be deserving of mercy.

(c) Food being a basic necessity of life, any abnormal rise in its price creates hue and cry among the non-agricultural classes, particularly the population living in urban areas, and more especially among the so-called middle-class people. Numerically this section

[14] The Port Trusts in India present an anomalous position. They are neither Public Corporations (like the Port of London Authority and Town Development Corporations in England), nor Departmental Organizations. They are not even autonomous local authorities like Municipal Corporations and Improvement Trusts.

of the population may not be very strong, yet it often represents the intelligentsia of the society capable of being highly critical and vocal in generating opposition. Hence any government which is keen to continue its regime will also try to keep the consumers in good humour.

(d) Violent fluctuations in agricultural prices, seasonally or otherwise, have often benefited not the producers, not even the consumers, but the so-called middlemen (occasionally dubbed as parasites). Hence it becomes necessary for the State to establish Stabilization Boards which can resort to open market operations—buying when the prices are below the lower limit and selling when the prices are above the upper limit. The maintenance of buffer stocks can best be undertaken by State Corporations. Ordinary Government Departments are likely to prove too lazy in the matter. Moreover, the Departments may not be able to take as much care of the stocks as the Corporations may be able to do.

In India, there has been much talk about the stabilization of agricultural prices since 1944, when the Famine Enquiry Commission took stock of the Bengal Famine of 1943 which had caused the death of thirty-five lakhs of people (according to official estimates). The Report of the Co-operative Planning Committee (Saraiya Report), shortly after that, suggested the conversion of wartime military constructions into reservoirs for agricultural produce. About the same time, the Sub-Committee on Agricultural Prices (Krishnamachari Report) favoured the stabilization of agricultural prices to avoid a sudden slump in the post-war period. However, as prices touched new heights, no machinery was created for the purpose of stabilization. During the 1952 recession the problem again presented itself. Thereafter, a record agricultural production during the third year of the First Five-Year Plan, and the successful experiment with the policy of decontrol, strengthened the fears about a falling market. In 1955, minimum prices were fixed in certain cases and open market operations, on an extremely limited basis, were resorted to directly by the Government. However, as the buoyancy in agricultural production was short-lived, prices again began to rise. The following table is indicative of the trend:[15]

	Mid-1953 to Mid-1955	Mid-1955 to Mid-1957
1. General Price Index	−17.6%	+23.4%
2. Manufactured Goods ...	−2.8%	+10.5%
3. Cereals	−34.0%	+51.0%

The Asoka Mehta Report submitted in November 1957 suggested the creation of the following organizations for the successful working of price stabilization measures:

[15] Asoka Mehta Enquiry Committee, 1957.

43

(1) Price Stabilization Board (a policy-making body);

(2) Foodgrains Stabilization Organization (an executive body);

(3) Price Intelligence Division (to collect the relevant data and information on the basis of which policies and actions are to be decided); and

(4) Advisory Council (composed of representatives of all the 'concerned' sections of the public).

It is indeed surprising that in an agricultural country like India, where there is so much talk about the reduction in the inequalities of income, so little attention has been given to the problems of marketing. If about three-fourths of the people derive their livelihood from agriculture (which accounts for nearly half of the national income), it only means that egalitarianism is a hoarse cry unless we are able to develop satisfactory arrangements and institutions for the marketing of agricultural produce.

2. *State Trading Corporations.* They are functional cousins of the Marketing Boards. State Trading Corporations can canalize their activities into several directions:

(a) They can negotiate barter agreements and other package deals with socialist countries where foreign trade is a State monopoly or even with capitalist countries where there are difficulties regarding foreign exchange or settlement of prices (e.g. Indo-Pakistani trade between 1949 and 1955, when the par values of Indian and Pakistani Rupees were different). Thus they may try to solve the problem of hard currencies, the utilization of Sterling credits and the like. They are also suitable agencies for obtaining commodity loans from other countries and repaying them (e.g. rice loans from Ceylon being repaid in rice).

(b) By reducing competition among intending exporters, they can be instrumental in securing better prices and other terms from the importing countries. Likewise, by negotiating for bulk imports, they can secure more favourable terms from the exporting countries. By entering into long-term agreements (e.g. supply of iron ore from India to Japan) and by planning their transactions in advance and on a collective basis, the whole process of foreign trade may move fast and in a smooth way.

(c) The quantum of imports and exports, in relation to the planned economic development, can be better adjusted by State Trading Corporations. Moreover, the abuses prevailing in the issue of import and export licences can be considerably mitigated.

(d) Standardization and quality control can be more conveniently promoted by State Trading Corporations. It has been pointed out time and again[16] that we have lost many export markets because of

[16] See, for example, the Report of the Export Promotion Committee, 1949.

our failure to conform to the specifications indicated by foreign customers. Dirt, dust and foreign matter have also been found in some of the consignments. These low standards of business morality could be substantially raised, at least in the sphere of foreign trade.

(e) The loss of foreign exchange earnings to the State caused by the manipulations of private merchants (e.g. some of the exporters of jute manufactures in 1950 were reported to be showing controlled prices in invoices and getting their accounts secretly credited in foreign countries for the black market balances) and the consequent evasion of income tax, sales tax, etc., can be done away with.

(f) Export promotion programmes can be more economically and conveniently launched by State Trading Corporations. They can resort to regular advertising, establish showrooms and organize exhibitions in collaboration with India's Trade Commissioners in various countries. They can also carry on market researches to study the changing tastes of the foreign customers.

The activities of Marketing Boards are confined to agricultural commodities and they are mainly concerned with the question of price stabilization. State Trading Corporations have a much wider perspective before them. They can be commercial agencies *par excellence*.[17]

3. *Development Corporations*. In underdeveloped countries like India, where there is phenomenal dearth of capital, technical know-how and entrepreneurial ability, Development Corporations are expected to fill a big gap.[18] Even those countries which are ideologically opposed to public enterprise find it a matter of expediency to assign the promotional rôle to State Corporations. Thus the Industrial Development Corporation of Pakistan was started with the avowed objective of following the Japanese pattern of economic development wherein the industries were first established by the State and later on transferred to the private sector. In India this is not likely to happen. Even then, Development Corporations have many important functions to perform:

(a) They can be helpful in giving practical shape to the priorities laid down by the Planning Commission.

(b) They can investigate (and offer solutions for) the factors which are retarding the promotion and development of particular industries.

(c) They can secure the assistance of foreign businessmen and

---

[17] No doubt, certain Marketing Boards have also operated on a world-wide basis (e.g., within the working of the International Wheat Agreements, 1949-53, 1953-56, 1958-59 and 1959-62).

[18] Om Prakash, 'Industrial Development Corporations in India and Pakistan', *The Economic Journal* (Royal Economic Society), March 1957.

world organizations like the International Bank for Reconstruction and Development, the International Finance Corporation and the International Development Association.

(d) They can make available a continuous stream of foreign technicians and business executives wherever necessary on reasonable terms.

(e) They can sponsor training programmes, industrial research and such other schemes of common benefit.

(f) They can establish subsidiary corporations as vehicles for the promotion of new enterprises or for looking after the problems of industrial development on a regional basis.

(g) They can be particularly helpful in the development of cottage and small-scale industries.

4. *Finance Corporations.* Development Corporations also perform the finance function. In fact, development and finance are so closely connected that it is difficult to draw any dividing line.[19] However, in the financial group of corporations we also have:

(i) the Reserve Bank of India (the central bank of the country), concerned with the issue of currency, monetary control, Government banking, foreign exchange regulation, the reorganization of rural credit and co-operative banking;

(ii) the State Bank of India (along with subsidiary State Banks), which plays the triple rôle of a banker to the Government, a commercial bank and a rural bank;

(iii) the Industrial Finance Corporation of India (along with State Financial Corporations), which meets the long- and medium-term financial requirements of corporate undertakings in the industrial field;

(iv) the Central Warehousing Corporation (along with State Warehousing Corporations), which combines the functions of (modernized) storage and finance; and

(v) the Life Insurance Corporation of India, which indirectly finances a large number of industrial undertakings (both public and private) by purchasing their shares and debentures and which also grants loans to policyholders for house building and other purposes.[20]

The existing Finance Corporations are not able to meet the country's requirements regarding industrial finance, rural credit and the like. The resources of many of these corporations are rather

[19] The National Industrial Development Corporation of India has usurped the finance function to a somewhat greater extent, e.g. it is granting loans to Jute Mills for rationalization.

[20] We have not taken into account Co-operative Banks and privately-controlled Finance Corporations, like the Industrial Credit and Investment Corporation, which are also partly State-owned.

limited in the context of the country's size and potential needs. Hence the size of such Corporations will have to be increased and many more Corporations (maybe on regional basis) may have to be established. Further, if and when commercial banking is nationalized, it will have to be entrusted to State Corporations (there may be one Central Corporation with a number of subsidiary Corporations, organized preferably on regional basis).[21]

5. *River Valley Authorities.* Such organizations, to some extent, are in the nature of Development Corporations. But they are concerned with the overall development of particular regions rather than with the promotion and development of particular industries on the basis of a priority list. Moreover, River Valley Authorities are concerned with physical development rather than the promotion of entrepreneurial spirit. The important functions of such Authorities are:

(a) *Flood Control*: This is a non-commercial function, but is most important because human life and property have to be saved from destruction. Regions which are rich in water resources have generally to pay their price through occasional inundations. Moreover, since 1945, maybe due to atomic explosions, the frequency of floods has increased. In the past floods were, no doubt, very destructive, but they used to occur (say) only once in a decade. Now almost every year the major rivers of India threaten to touch danger points. Therefore, unless floods are properly controlled, vast areas of the country would not only be unsuitable for habitation, but also useless for industrial (and even agricultural) activity.[22]

(b) *Health Measures*: In many of the regions which are rich in water resources, there is the problem of controlling malaria and other diseases. This is also a non-commercial function, but contributes substantially to the people's welfare.

(c) *Irrigation*: There is the problem of storing water when it is abundant and making it available in seasons of scarcity, mainly for irrigation purposes. In the context of rapidly increasing population and the difficult food situation, the importance of extending irrigation facilities—bringing the erstwhile barren lands under cultivation and increasing the productivity of the areas already under the plough—cannot be exaggerated.

[21] The Government have repeatedly declared their intention not to nationalize commercial banking. They have even suggested their incompetence to manage it. Hence there is no question of entrusting it to ordinary Government Departments. As the socialist pattern is strengthened, commercial banking will have to be (it may be a surprise announcement like the nationalization of life insurance) entrusted to State Corporations.

[22] It must be confessed that the birth of water projects has not always improved the situation. In certain cases vast areas have actually become marshy and useless for any purpose.

47

(d) *Power*: In a country where the supplies of good quality coal and petroleum are not enough to meet the power requirements of a growing industrial economy, hydro-electricity has to be adequately harnessed. It is true that when the commercial possibilities of atomic energy manifest themselves the importance of River Valley Authorities may decline.[23]

(e) *Miscellaneous Functions*: There are a large number of other functions which these River Valley Authorities can perform—defence, land development, navigation (shipping for commercial ends as well as pleasure boating, ski-ing, etc.) and fishing.

It is generally accepted that multi-purpose projects are best entrusted to Statutory Corporations possessing substantial powers and a high degree of autonomy. However, the Damodar Valley Corporation is the solitary example of a Statutory Corporation managing river valley projects in India. The Hirakud Dam Project was expected to transform itself into a corporation. This did not happen. On the contrary, it was decided to hand over the entire project to the Government of Orissa with effect from April 1, 1960. The cost of maintenance of Stage I (already completed), the revenue accruing therefrom, and interest on capital will be exhibited in the State budget from 1960-61 onwards.[24] Similarly, other big schemes like the Bhakra Nangal Project (expenditure of Rs 142 crores up to November 1959), the Chambal Project (Rs 35 crores up to December 1959), the Nagarjunasagar Project (Rs 26 crores up to December 1959), the Rihand Project (Rs 21 crores up to November 1959), the Kosi Project (Rs 17 crores up to December 1959), the Koyna Project (Rs 17 crores up to December 1959) and the Tangabhadra Project (first stage to cost Rs 13 crores) have *not* been entrusted to Statutory Corporations. There is, however, a good deal of scope in this direction.

6. *Transport and Communication Boards.* The Railway Board and the newly-established Posts and Telegraphs Board are in the nature of Quasi-corporations. At the dawn of the twentieth century, India's Governor-General, Lord Curzon, had pointed out that 'the idea of a Railway Board was, that there should be a body of practical businessmen entrusted with full authority to manage the railways of

[23] If a dam costs Rs 135 crores, its estimated life is 135 years and its net annual income (without deducting the annual depreciation which itself amounts to a crore of rupees) is a crore of rupes, one may ask the question: Is such a dam commercially a sound proposition? But, as we have seen, there are non-commercial functions also like flood control and health measures whose social benefits we must assess before pronouncing any verdict.

[24] Government of India, *Ministry of Irrigation and Power,* Annual Report, 1959-60, p. 21.

India on commercial principles and free from all non-essential restrictions and needlessly inelastic rules'. That ideal still remains to be achieved. Recent changes have only strengthened the bureaucratic pattern. For example, not only the Chairman (who was already the Principal Secretary), but also other members of the Railway Board, are now ex-officio Secretaries to the Ministry of Railways. The Chairmanship of the Railway Board is not a tenure appointment, but an executive promotion depending on political patronage.[25] This is too bad for an organization which is, by and large, a commercial undertaking. Hence it will be desirable to transform the Railway Board into a full-fledged corporation. The P. and T. Board, however, may wait and watch the results of its recent experiment.

In the field of air transport, there are already two Statutory Corporations and there does not appear to be scope for the creation of any new corporation for the time being. For the operation of sea transport we have the State-owned Eastern Shipping Corporation and the Western Shipping Corporation, co-existing with privately-operated services. In course of time there may be scope for further extension in the publicly-operated services.

Road transport offers the best opportunity for the establishment of State Corporations. The development of road transport in rural areas is of the utmost significance in the context of India's economic development. The reorganization of agricultural marketing and the elimination of village intermediaries would very much depend on the availability of reliable, cheap and efficient transport. Many of the States have already nationalized road transport services on the 'paying' routes. But the most significant rôle of State Corporations lies in developing non-paying routes.

Broadcasting has been entrusted to State Corporations in a number of countries. Thus we have the British Broadcasting Corporation (and the Independent Television Authority), the Canadian Broadcasting Corporation and the Australian Broadcasting Commission. Now that television has been introduced in India, it is desirable and opportune that a Radio and Television Corporation be established with a high degree of autonomy. The best guarantee for democracy is the availability of reasonable opportunities for freedom of thought and speech. Broadcasting is such a powerful device of propaganda that any misuse of the same by the party in power can cause incalculable harm to the country. Thus, if on the eve of a General Election, the speeches of Ministers are broadcast because they are Ministers (even though they are speaking as Party leaders) and the Opposition parties are not allowed the use of broadcasting facilities, it may encourage the perpetuation of one-party

[25] Thus Mr K. B. Mathur, who became the Chairman in August 1959, retired from that office in April 1960.

rule.[26] Further, it has been experienced that programmes of a high standard may not be originated adequately. The Estimates Committee in their 12th Report (February 1955) pointed out that out of twenty-two stations of the All-India Radio, only six were broadcasting University programmes. The Committee expressed the hope that 'University broadcasts will improve both in quality and quantity'.

7. *Other Corporations.* Electricity supply companies, when they are nationalized, may be entrusted to State Corporations. The scope of the National Coal Development Corporation will have to be increased considerably. It may be converted into a Statutory Corporation with a large number of subsidiary companies running the various coal mines. In terms of the Industrial Policy of 1956, the future development of the coal industry will exclusively depend on the State. As such, adequate organizational machinery should be devised for the same. Similarly, with the fast development of the steel industry, several corporations will have to be established. New Corporations can be expected in the field of mining, mineral oils, heavy castings, forgings, plant and machinery. The Atomic Energy Commission may have to be given a better status. In the field of social insurance, the activities of the Employees' State Insurance Corporation will have to be considerably extended. Further, if the ideal of the Welfare State is to be translated into practice, a number of State Corporations will have to be established for the efficient performance of social services.

[26] In England proportions of available time are allotted to various parties. In India, before the first General Elections (1951-52), no facilities were offered to opposition parties. On the eve of the second General Elections (1956-57) there were certain proposals which did not prove acceptable to opposition parties. However, one thing is clear. The All-India Radio does not show that tolerance for opposition leaders and criticism of Government policies as is shown in England.

CHAPTER III

PUBLIC CORPORATIONS IN INDIA

BACKGROUND

Public Corporations in India can claim a respectable antiquity. According to the *Arthasastra*, Kautilya's public sector comprised a number of industries like salt, mining, fishing, ferrying and forestry. Kautilya attached great importance to State trading and irrigation projects as well. The *Lavanadhyaksa* was responsible for the manufacture of salt, supplying public demand and fixing the price. Under the *Akaradhyaksa* (highest officer in charge of mining), there were State functionaries like the *Lohadhyaksa* (base-metal manufacture), the *Laksandhyaksa* and the *Rupadarsaka* (coinage and currency), *Swarnadhyaksa* (extracting gold) and the *Khanyadhyaksa* (sea mines). These functionaries in ancient India were either in the nature of Corporations sole or officials presiding over Public Boards.

Here we propose to deal with the Public Corporations as they have developed after 1947, when India got her independence after a long span of foreign rule. The year 1948 saw a bountiful crop of Public Corporations. It will, however, be wrong to suppose that the mere fact of independence resulted in this performance. Some of the legislations which gave birth to these Corporations had already been planned in the pre-independence era. For example, the need for a Damodar Valley Corporation—prince among these Corporations—had 'engaged the attention of the people and the Government since the early years of the last century. . . . In 1863 the Government had explored the Damodar Valley for possible flood control measures and schemes of irrigation and navigation'.[1]

It is of interest to note that a large number of Public Corporations appeared on the scene in a number of countries like England, France, Canada and Australia during the five years (1945-50) immediately following the close of the Second World War. The overwhelming majority secured by the British Labour Party in the General Election of 1945 was a prominent indication of the swing towards the Left in the early post-war years. This event came at a time when Public Corporations had already created a place for themselves—even though, for the most part, as wartime exigencies—in the United States, the traditional land of free enterprise. Moreover, the TVA experiment, which had been started as early as 1933, did really

[1] *Eight Years of D.V.C.*, published by Damodar Valley Corporation, Calcutta, September 1956, p. 5.

receive international approbation when it had completed the first
decade of its eventful existence.

ORGANIZATION

It is difficult to say whether the growth of Public Corporations in
India was inspired more by the American experiment or by the
British pattern of organization. The much-publicized Damodar
Valley Corporation, established in 1948, was, at least in theory, a
replica of the Tennessee Valley Authority. The problems of regional
planning, flood control, development of hydro-electricity, and the
utilization of natural resources in other ways naturally found India
and America closer together. But, while the socialist zeal was absent
in America, it did manifest itself both in India and in England. As
such, the Bank of England and the Reserve Bank of India have had a
similar history, though this in one case is much longer; the Bank
of England had been established in 1694 under Royal Charter, and
was transferred to public ownership in 1946 (though a mere
interpolation of digits, this gap was of 252 years); the Reserve
Bank of India had come into existence on April 1, 1935, under
the Reserve Bank of India Act of 1934, as a shareholders' bank,
and it started its new career on January 1, 1949, under the Reserve
Bank (Transfer to Public Ownership) Act of 1948 (a gap of fourteen
years only).

The Employees' State Insurance Corporation, created in India
under Act XXXIV of 1948, was again in sympathy with the emphasis on Welfare State in England, symbolized by the publication
of the Beveridge Plan a few years earlier, and the subsequent appearance of an elaborate structure of social security. The fact, however,
should not be overlooked that England rejected the corporate pattern
of management for the operation of her National Health Service.
Again, while India did establish a Public Corporation in this sphere,
the composition of the same was poles apart from the British pattern. Thus, under Section 4 of the Employees' State Insurance Act,
the Minister of Labour in the Central Government is the Chairman,
ex-officio, while the Minister of Health, *ex-officio,* is Vice-Chairman.
In this regard, India is closer to the Canadian pattern of Crown Corporations rather than to the British model which aims at keeping the
Ministers in their traditional headquarters. Secondly, the presence
of two persons, elected by Parliament, on the Employees' State Insurance Corporation, is a practice which British tradition does not
permit. Thirdly, the provision that, out of five persons to be nominated by the Central Government, at least three persons shall be
officials of the Central Government, is a departure from the British
practice. Fourthly, a membership of about thirty-five, as in the case

of the Employees' State Insurance Corporation,[2] would be considered too unwieldy in England. Finally, the division of Corporation members into three categories—(1) *ex-officio,* whose term of office is co-extensive with their main office; (2) nominees of the Central and State Governments, holding office at the pleasure of the Government nominating them; and (3) representatives of sectional interests and Parliament, holding office for four years (and even beyond that until the nomination or election of the successor)—tends to undermine the equality of status on the Corporation table, though it has many precedents in England and elsewhere.

The Rehabilitation Finance Administration is an emergency creation of the post-partition period in India and can be compared to the Reconstruction Finance Corporation established in the United States in 1932 to overcome the effects of the Great Depression. Further, in the matter of nomenclature, the RFA is close to the American pattern which abounds with numerous Governmental organizations (*not* really Public Corporations) like the Office of Price Administration. Although the RFA was established as a Statutory Corporation under the Rehabilitation Finance Administration Act of 1948, its composition has been far removed from the British ideal. The Governing Board, as constituted on December 31, 1958, consisted of two Joint Secretaries of the Government of India (Finance and Rehabilitation), two Secretaries of the Assam and West Bengal Governments respectively, two members of the *Lok Sabha,* one member of the *Rajya Sabha* and one member from Bombay.[3] This pattern of composition is very much like the one to be found in the case of Government Companies in India.

The Industrial Finance Corporation of India, which came into existence on July 1, 1948, under the IFC Act of 1948, had derived inspiration from two similar institutions established in England about the close of the Second World War. The British institutions, although functionally in line, were not in the nature of Public Corporations. It may be mentioned that the IFC Bill was introduced in

---

[2] In addition to two Ministers, two Members of Parliament and five representatives of the Central Government, there are five persons representing employers, five representing employees and two representing the medical profession (all nominated by the Central Government), and one person each representing each of the States (including one for the Centrally Administered areas). This regional representation, too, runs counter to the traditional theory of Public Corporation, though even in the United Kingdom it had to be relaxed in the case of the BBC. In a big country like India it may be more difficult to avoid regional representation.

[3] Besides the Chairman, there are eight members of the RFA: four officials appointed by, and holding office during the pleasure of, the Central Government; and four non-officials nominated by the Central Government, but holding office for two years. The Chief Administrator is a whole-time servant of the Administration.

the Indian legislature in 1946 (soon after the British institutions had seen the light); but, owing to constitutional changes in the country, its passage was delayed. It may further be noted that the IFC, at the outset of its career, could not be described strictly as a Public Corporation. At that time, only one-fifth of the share capital was held by the Central Government. With the transformation of the Reserve Bank of India into a fully State-owned Corporation (since January 1, 1949), about two-fifths of the share capital came into the public sector. It was after the nationalization of life insurance business in India (in 1956) that the State was able to control 64 per cent of the share capital of the IFC. The following table indicates the distribution of shares:

	As on June 30, 1959	As originally contemplated
1. Central Government	2,000	2,000
2. Reserve Bank of India	2,054	2,000
3. Scheduled Banks	2,405	2,500
4. Insurance Companies, etc. (Life Insurance Corporation of India holding 2,346 shares)	2,596	2,500
5. Co-operative Banks	945	1,000
Total number of shares issued (each share being of the value of Rs 5,000)	10,000	10,000

Although private individuals are not allowed to become shareholders of the Corporation, the IFC is still a Mixed Corporation with a substantial part of its share capital in the hands of financial institutions in the non-Governmental sector (though here, too, especially in the case of Co-operative Banks, the State can wield indirect influence). Moreover, the pattern of organization obtaining in the IFC is still similar to that prevalent in the case of Joint Stock Companies. Unlike the other Public Corporations established in 1948, the IFC holds its shareholders' meetings for the purpose of election of directors, declaration of dividends and the like. The shares of the Corporation are guaranteed by the Central Government as to the repayment of capital and the payment of annual dividend at $2\frac{1}{4}$ per cent (minimum rate fixed by the Central Government through notification published in the official Gazette at the time of issuing the shares). On this account, the Corporation obtained subventions from the Central Government in the years 1949, 1950, 1951, 1952, 1954 and 1956, the progressive total being Rs 53 lakhs. This, in fact, is an interesting facet of financial administration, since 64 per cent of the shares are now in the public sector.

The Board of Directors of the IFC, besides the Chairman, who is appointed by the Central Government after consultations with the Board, consists of six nominated Directors (four nominated by the Central Government and two by the Reserve Bank of India) and six elected Directors (two each elected by the Scheduled Banks, the Insurance Companies, etc., and the Co-operative Banks). The Chairman[4] shall hold office for three years (or until his successor is appointed, and shall be eligible for reappointment), a nominated Director is to hold office during the pleasure of the appointing authority, whereas the tenure of office in the case of an elected Director is four years, subject to the principle of rotation (i.e. one of the two elected Directors in each of the three categories was to retire at the end of the two years after the first election, the Directors so to retire being determined by lot). An elected Director is to continue in office until his successor has been elected; he is eligible for re-election but 'for not more than two full consecutive terms after the rotation of elected Directors has begun'. This limit on re-election is a peculiarity of the IFC Act.

After an initial spurt, the growth of Public Corporations was at bay for a number of years. It was in 1953 that two new Corporations were created in the field of air transport through a single piece of legislation. It may be of interest to note that even in this sphere, public enterprise had stepped in through the back door (though at the request of private enterprise itself) early in 1948. The Government had entered into an agreement with the Tatas whereby the former subscribed 49 per cent of the capital (with an option available to the Government to increase it to 51 per cent at any time) of the newly-floated 'Air India International Ltd.' The capital of this Company was Rs 2 crores (£1½ million). The Government were to meet the losses, if any, for a period of five years, to be reimbursed out of future profits. It may be added that air transport in this country, as in many other countries, had depended upon Governmental support from the very beginning. The first Indian airline (commercial air transport) established by the house of Tatas in October 1932, and the Indian National Airways, inaugurated in December 1933, were engaged mostly on the carriage of mail and relied for financial support on payments made by Government for this purpose.[5] These services gained strength in 1938 when the newly-introduced Empire Mail Scheme provided a margin of subsidy. Further, the remuneration paid by Government to the existing air companies for various (defence) services rendered by them during the Second World War put them on a somewhat stable basis.[6] Con-

[4] In the light of the Report of the Enquiry Committee dated May 7, 1953 (under the Chairmanship of Mrs Sucheta Kripalani, M.P.) the IFC Act was amended in 1955 so as to have 'a full-time paid Chairman to be assisted by a General Manager' instead of 'an Honorary Chairman and a paid whole-time Managing Director'.

[5] Estimates Committee, 41st Report, 1956-57, Ministry of Communications, Lok Sabha Secretariat, New Delhi, p. 1.

[6] Nationalization of Airlines, Indian Chamber of Commerce, Calcutta, 1955, p. 1.

siderable advance in the technique of flying and radio communication, the availability (at very low price) of a large number of twin-engined Dakota aircraft left behind by American Forces, and the goodwill and support built up amongst the travelling public during these years encouraged a mushroom growth of airways companies in the post-war period. Sir Frederick Tymms, then Director of Civil Aviation, had contemplated the licensing of only three or four airlines. But contrary to the Tymms Plan, the Air Transport Licensing Board, set up in 1946, gave licences to eleven companies within two years. This state of affairs quite naturally resulted in the voluntary liquidation of a few concerns and the statutory transfer of eight undertakings to the Indian Airlines Corporation with effect from August 1, 1953. On the same date, the Air India International Ltd was taken over by the Air India International Corporation as a going concern for the operation of external air services.

Strangely enough, it was the 'flexibility aspect' which hastened nationalization.[7] Flexibility in air transport is a costly affair, generally beyond the capacity of private operators. In 1952 it was calculated that, to replace some of the existing aircraft by more modern machines, the Government would have to advance some Rs 4 crores of capital to the privately-owned companies, in addition to subsidies which by then amounted to over Rs 36 lakhs a year.[8]

The Government preferred to assume full responsibility for scheduled air services, rather than to build a costly 'half-way house'. Towards the capital of the two State-owned Corporations, Government had actually to pay less for the time being.[9] The creation of two Corporations was, obviously, indicated by the British pattern, the Air India International to be the counterpart of the British Overseas Airways Corporation and the Indian Airlines Corporation to be the opposite number of the British European Airways. It was, perhaps, also indicated by the desire not to lump together the 'loss incurring' home services with the 'paying-their-way' foreign services—though this situation could have been met by having two wings within the same Corporation, thereby also causing an economy of Rs 6 lakhs per year in administrative ex-

[7] *The Air Transport Enquiry Committee* (1950), presided over by the late Justice Rajadhyaksha, had remarked: 'A Government organization would not provide such flexibility.'

[8] How the Indian Airlines serve the Nation? Indian Airlines Anniversary—*A Statesman Supplement*—Monday, August 2, 1954.

[9] According to the first Balance Sheet of the Indian Airlines Corporation as at March 31, 1954, capital received from the Government stood at only Rs 23 lakhs (besides Rs 302 lakhs due on compensation)—*First Annual Report & Accounts*, p. 15. In the case of Air India International, capital received from the Government stood at 195 lakhs (besides Rs 285 lakhs due on compensation)—*First Annual Report* (August 1, 1953, to March 31, 1954), p. 30.

penses. However, the existence of two separate entities does provide a vehicle for socialist emulation. Finally, there was the desire to cause the least disturbance to the organization of Air India International Ltd which, during the five years of its existence, had built up some reputation in the operation of external services.[10]

The State Bank of India, created in 1955 as a subsidiary Corporation of the Reserve Bank of India, has had its origin in the three Presidency Banks of Bengal, Bombay and Madras (established in 1806, 1840 and 1843 respectively) merged into the Imperial Bank of India in 1921 (under the Imperial Bank of India Act, 1920). The Report of the All-India Rural Credit Survey (1953-54) had recommended the creation of the State Bank of India for the rapid extension of rural credit facilities. The legislative process was gone through with great speed. The discussion on all the clauses of the State Bank of India Bill was completed within a day and it was passed by Parliament (*Lok Sabha*) on April 30, 1955.

The authorized capital of the State Bank was fixed at Rs 20 crores (£15 million) divided into 20,00,000 fully paid shares of Rs 100 each.[11] The Central Government has the power to 'increase or reduce the authorized capital as it thinks fit so, however, that the shares in all cases shall be fully paid shares of Rs 100 each'. The denomination of shares was to be kept at this 'not-too-high' figure, so that individual farmers or other citizens might also be admitted as shareholders at some later stage. The issued capital of the State Bank was maintained at Rs 5,62,50,000 (divided into 5,62,500 shares)—the same figure as in the case of the Imperial Bank of India —all of which, on the appointed day, stood allotted to the Reserve Bank in lieu of the shares of the Imperial Bank transferred to it. The Central Board of Directors of the State Bank of India may, from time to time, increase the issued capital but no increase therein shall be made in such manner 'that the Reserve Bank holds at any time less than 55 per cent of the issued capital of the State Bank'.[12]

[10] After nationalization, there was no change in name (except deleting 'Ltd' and adding 'Corporation'), no change in the Chairman (Mr J. R. D. Tata) and no change in the sphere of operation. Mr Tata was also appointed as a member of the Indian Airlines. Similarly, Mr B. C. Mukharji, the first Chairman of the Indian Airlines, was a member of the Air India International. Several other members have held concurrent positions from time to time, e.g. Mr P. C. Bhattacharya, Mr M. M. Philip, Mr L. C. Jain and Air Commodore P. C. Pal.

[11] Mr. A. M. Thomas wanted the *authorized* capital to be fixed at Rs 50 crores—and there should have been no objection in accepting that amendment. See *Lok Sabha Debates*, 1955, Vol. IV, No. 53, Column 6977.

[12] The principle of limited nationalization (55 per cent clause) evoked much heat in Parliament on April 30, 1955. Mr Sadhan Gupta, a brilliant Opposition member from Calcutta, felt very unhappy over the situation that starting with full nationalization, the State would transfer 45 per cent

The Central Board of the State Bank of India is considerably bigger than the Central Board of the Reserve Bank of India (the holding Corporation). The Central Board of the Reserve Bank consists of a Governor, two Deputy Governors (there were three Deputy Governors for a period of five years—July 1, 1955, to June 30, 1960), four Directors nominated by the Central Government from each of the four Local Boards, six Directors nominated by the Central Government, and one Government Official to be nominated by the Central Government. This constitution was not found appropriate for the State Bank of India in view of the need to give representation to non-Governmental (i.e. non-Reserve Bank) shareholders, and at the same time to recognize the paternal status of the Reserve Bank of India. Accordingly, the Central Board of the State Bank of India is to be composed as follows:

(a) a Chairman and a Vice-Chairman to be appointed by the Central Government in consultation with the Reserve Bank and after consideration, except in case of first appointments, of the recommendations made by the Central Board of the State Bank;

(b) not more than two Managing Directors, if any, appointed by the Central Board with the approval of the Central Government;

(c) six Directors to be elected by the shareholders, other than the Reserve Bank, whose names are entered in the various branches' registers. But if the total amount of the holdings of all such shareholders on any branch register three months before the date fixed for election is below $2\frac{1}{2}$ per cent of the total issued capital, all the Directors to be elected by the shareholders on that register shall be nominated by the Reserve Bank (such Directors being deemed to be 'elected' for the purposes of the State Bank of India Act);

(d) eight Directors to be nominated by the Central Government in consultation with the Reserve Bank to represent, as far as possible, territorial and economic interests and in such manner that *not less than two* of them have special knowledge of the working of Co-operative institutions and of rural economy and others have experience in commerce, industry, banking or finance;[13]

(e) one Director to be nominated by the Central Government; and

(f) one Director to be nominated by the Reserve Bank.

of the shares back to the private sector. The idea that beneficiaries may as well be owners was amplified by Mr S. S. More, who suggested that some portion of the shares should be allotted for rural areas and particularly to the peasantry for whose benefit the whole measure had been motivated. Although this was not specifically provided, Government can easily enforce Mr More's scheme under the existing Act.

[13] Such positive requirements regarding specialized qualifications in commerce, etc., are a noteworthy feature of the State Bank of India Act. Such requirements were not prescribed even in the case of Air Corporations and the Life Insurance Corporation of India.

On the first constitution of the Central Board of the State Bank of India, all the Directors were to be nominated by the Central Government and all of them (excepting the Chairman, the Vice-Chairman and Managing Directors) were to retire at the expiry of two years from the appointed day. The Chairman and the Vice-Chairman shall hold office for such term, not exceeding five years,[14] as the Central Government may fix when appointing them and shall be eligible for reappointment. The tenure of office for a Managing Director, in the case of the first two appointments, is to be fixed by the Central Government at the time of appointment. In the case of subsequent appointments, a Managing Director shall hold office for such term, not exceeding five years, as the Central Board of Directors of the State Bank may fix when appointing him. A Director elected under clause (c) or nominated under clause (d) shall hold office for four years. As against this, a Director nominated under clause (e) or clause (f) shall hold office during the pleasure of the authority nominating him. The principle of retirement by rotation, compulsorily applicable to at least two-thirds of the total number of Directors in the case of Joint Stock Companies, was incorporated in the State Bank of India Act as well. Out of six Directors elected under clause (c), two were to retire at the end of one year, two at the end of two years and two at the end of three years *from the date of expiration* (the principle being applicable to the Directors elected or nominated *after the expiration of two years* from the appointed day). Out of the eight Directors nominated under clause (d), two were to retire at the end of one year, two at the end of two years, two at the end of three years and two at the end of four years *from such expiration*. The Directors to retire at the end of each year in *both the categories* were to be determined by lot.[15]

After the nationalization of the Imperial Bank, there was the problem of answering the question 'What next?' The Government had repeatedly declared their intention not to nationalize commercial banking.[16] Life insurance business was a more convenient target, capable of ensuring control over long-term (in fact, *irrevocable*) funds with a relatively small amount of compensation[17]—and a

[14] This is quite in line with the British practice.

[15] The constitution of the State Bank of India is indeed the most complicated one among the Public Corporations created in this country. In this connection we have to remember that the State Bank is not only a public institution, it is also the biggest commercial bank and a pioneering rural bank at the same time.

[16] For example, the Finance Minister pointed out on December 27, 1955, that 'as long as there is a private sector, it must be attended to by private banks'. However, this does not exclude the possibility of public and private banks existing side by side.

[17] The paid-up capital of Indian insurers as on December 31, 1953, was

target was also a political necessity on the eve of the General Election to enable the Congress Party to steal a march over certain other political parties which had been professing a greater degree of socialism. There were other important factors which weighed heavily in favour of nationalization. In view of the competitive reduction in the premium rates of life insurance companies, which had gained momentum by 1955 (following better experience in the matter of mortality), it was good strategy on the part of the State to enter the field of life insurance at this moment and to take credit for making it cheaper. This point has been, for obvious reasons, omitted from all public pronouncements. There was, on the other hand, much fuss about the alleged misapplication of some two crores of rupees in the case of the Bharat Insurance Company. Not only this, as many as twenty-five life insurance companies had gone into liquidation during the preceding decade and another twenty-five had so frittered away their resources that their assets had to be transferred to other companies at a loss. The uneconomical working of a large number of privately-owned insurance companies had further manifested itself in the high expense ratio, mainly because of vast duplication in agents and in offices, necessitated by competitive conditions. The ratio of management expenses to premium income stood at 27.3 per cent for Indian companies in 1953.[18] For foreign companies in India, this ratio was 20.7 per cent. In the same year, the expense ratio for US companies was 17 per cent only. For the life insurance companies in the United Kingdom, the expense ratio stood as follows:[19]

1. Average expense ratio for nine companies having total annual premiums between £50,000 and £500,000 ...   ... 19.3 %
2. Average expense ratio for forty-one companies (annual premiums between £500,000 and £5,000,000) ...   . 15.9 %
3. Average expense ratio for nine companies (annual premiums £5,000,000 and over) ...   . 12.0 %
4. All the fifty-nine companies 15.81%

The unsatisfactory working of the privately-owned insurance companies was further indicated by the alarming lapse ratio with regard to policies issued by Indian insurers. In 1953 the new busi-

only Rs 10½ crores. As against this, their assets were of the value of over Rs 300 crores.

[18] As against this, for the years 1948-53, the Mysore State Insurance Department had presented a record low expense ratio of 15.1 per cent—see H. D. Malaviya, *Insurance Business in India,* Economic and Political Research Department, All India Congress Committee, New Delhi, 1956, p. 26.

[19] Jack Johnston and G. W. Murphy, *The Growth of Life Assurance in U.K. since 1880,* Paper read before the Manchester Statistical Society on November 11, 1956, *The Manchester School of Economic and Social Studies,* Vol. XXV, No. 2, May 1957, p. 143.

ness which lapsed stood at over 35 per cent. In the case of one company, this lapse ratio was as high as 55 per cent, while in another case it was as low as 11 per cent. In the case of Oriental, the biggest life insurance company, it stood at 18 per cent. A high lapse ratio gave an exaggerated idea about the progress of life insurance business, and of the efficiency of agents, who were interested in persuading policyholders to get their existing policies paid up and to obtain fresh policies without caring for the long-term consequences of such a short-sighted attitude.

Finally, there was the desire to widen and deepen the channels of public savings, 'with a Second Plan in the offing involving an accelerated rate of investment and development'.[20] The plan of the private sector to raise the total amount of business *in force* from Rs 1,000 crores to Rs 8,000 crores, i.e. from Rs 25 per capita to Rs 200 per capita (ignoring the increase in population) had also allured the Government. This was not an impossible target, the *per capita* insurance in some other countries being as follows: Rs 8,365 in the USA; Rs 6,647 in Canada; Rs 2,544 in Australia; and Rs 1,840 in the UK. Only 5 per cent of the families were covered in India as against 80 per cent in the USA. Annual premiums on some 50 lakh (five million) policies in India amounted to Rs 55 crores, i.e. about $\frac{1}{2}$ per cent of the national income, as against 3 per cent in the UK and Australia, and over 6 per cent in the USA and Canada. The Ordinary Life Assurance Fund in the UK stood at £2,078 million (Rs 2,771 crores), and the Industrial Assurance Fund at £969 million (Rs 1,292 crores) in 1953.[21] *The annual rise of the life fund* in the U.K. (in 1958 over 1957) was of the order of £333 million (Rs 444 crores, i.e. about the total *life fund* in India).[22]

The Agricultural Produce (Development and Warehousing) Corporations Act, No. 28 of 1956, gave birth to two more Corporations at the All-India level. It may be mentioned that, along with the creation of the State Bank of India, the All-India Rural Credit Survey (1953-54)[23] had recommended the establishment of a

[20] Speech broadcast from the All India Radio on January 19, 1956, by the Finance Minister, Mr C. D. Deshmukh. Subsequent events have indicated that there was over-optimism in this regard.

[21] Jack Johnston and G. W. Murphy, 'The Growth of Life Assurance in U.K. since 1880', *The Manchester School,* May 1957, *loc. cit.,* p. 111.

[22] *Commerce,* Bombay, August 15, 1959, p. 270.

[23] The Co-operative Planning Committee (1945), while stressing the need for linking credit with marketing, had suggested the establishment of Licensed Warehouses in suitable areas. One of the useful suggestions made by this Committee was that godowns owned by the Defence Department and other Departments of Central and Provincial Governments might be handed over to co-operative marketing organizations after the war. But, unfortunately,

National Co-operative Development and Warehousing Board, an All-India (Central) Warehousing Corporation, and a number of State Warehousing Companies. Under the Act, which came into force on August 1, 1956, 'agricultural produce' means: (i) foodstuffs, including edible oilseeds; (ii) cattle fodder, including oil cakes and other concentrates; (iii) raw cotton, whether ginned or unginned, and cotton seed; (iv) raw jute; and (v) vegetable oils.

Section 3(1) of the Act reads as follows: 'There shall be established at New Delhi a Corporation by the name of the National Co-operative Development and Warehousing Board, which shall be a body corporate having perpetual succession and a common seal with power to acquire, hold and dispose of property and to contract, and may, in the said name, sue and be sued.' While this incorporation clause is quite similar[24] to those drafted for other Public Corporations, the constitution of the Board is a startling departure from other legislations inasmuch as 'a member of the Board nominated by the Central Government may be nominated by virtue of office'. In fact, under the rules made by the Central Government, and notified on October 16, 1955, the Central Government stall nominate the following ten persons as its representatives on the Board under clause (i) of Section 3(2):

(1) The Minister for Food and Agriculture;
(2) The Secretary, Ministry of Food and Agriculture;
(3) The Joint Secretary in charge of Co-operation in the Ministry of Food and Agriculture;
(4) The Financial Adviser to the Ministry of Food and Agriculutre;
(5) A representative of the Ministry of Finance (Economic Affairs Department);
(6) A representative of the Ministry of Production;
(7) A representative of the Ministry of Commerce and Industry;
(8) A representative of the Ministry of Transport;
(9) A representative of the Railway Board; and
(10) A representative of the Planning Commission.

In addition to these ten representatives, the Board is to consist of the Chairman of the Forward Markets Commission established under the Forward Contracts (Regulation) Act, 1952—ex-officio; one representative of the State Bank, nominated by the Central Government; and nine non-officials, nominated by the Central

many of these godowns began to give way soon after the war was over. Later, the All India Rural Credit Survey favoured State participation in rural credit on a major scale.

[24] The words 'to contract' do not occur in other legislations and are in fact superflous. The specification with regard to 'New Delhi' is also an uncommon phenomenon.

Government of whom (a) one shall be a person who has special knowledge of rural economies, and (b) four shall be persons who have experience for co-operative societies, one being a person who has also special knowledge of co-operative education. This provision regarding the selection of board specialists in 'rural economics and co-operation' is comparable to the qualifications prescribed for certain Directors of the State Bank of India. But, in spite of this redeeming feature, bureaucracy will have full sway over the Board.

The Central Warehousing Corporation was established on March 2, 1957, under the Agricultural Produce (Development and Warehousing) Corporations Act, 1956. Under Section 17, the head office of the Corporation shall be at New Delhi. While there is no share capital in case of the National Co-operative Development and Warehousing Board, the Central Warehousing Corporation has an authorized capital of Rs 20 crores (equal to the authorized capital of the State Bank of India) divided into 2,00,000 shares of the face value of Rs 1,000 each. In the first instance only 1,00,000 shares of the total face value of Rs 10 crores (£7½ million) were required to be issued, the remaining shares to be issued 'with the sanction of the Central Government from time to time, as and when the Central Warehousing Corporation may deem fit'. The proposed distribution of the share capital, under Section 18(2), was as follows:[25]

(a) The Board (National Co-operative Department and Warehousing Board) shall subscribe for 40,000 shares;

(b) on application made before such date as may be notified by Central Government

    (i) the State Bank may subscribe for 10,000 shares;

    (ii) other scheduled banks may subscribe for 12,500 shares;

    (iii) co-operative societies may subscribe for 2,500 shares;

    (iv) insurance companies, investment trusts and other classes of financial institutions may subscribe for 30,000 shares; and

    (v) recognized associations and joint stock companies dealing in agricultural produce may subscribe for 5,000 shares.

A special feature of this legislation is that no institution belonging to clause (ii), (iii), (iv) or (v) can subscribe for more than 25 per cent of the share capital reserved for that class of institution.[26] The shares of the Central Warehousing Corporation shall not be transferable except to the Board, the State Bank and other institutions mentioned in clause (b). Thus even the Reserve Bank cannot directly purchase

[25] The actual position on March 31, 1959, was: Board 40,000; State Bank 10,000; Scheduled Banks 1,501; Co-operative Societies 2,444; Insurance Companies 1,052; Recognized Associations 60; Joint Stock Companies 1. Total 55,108.

[26] This precaution, which aims at preventing concentration of power in the case of Mixed Corporations, was not enacted in the case of the Industrial Finance Corporation of India and the State Bank of India.

the shares of the Corporation, although it can certainly wield indirect influence through the State Bank (which thus becomes an intermediate holding corporation). The capital structure of the Central Warehousing Corporation is very much similar to that of the Industrial Finance Corporation. In course of time, the State Bank of India, too, may present a similar pattern of shareholding.

PERFORMANCE[27]

Public Corporations are expected to function within the framework of autonomy indicated by the various incorporating legislations. Following the pattern set by the British nationalizing Acts, the Government of India have generally retained the residual power to give policy directions from time to time. For example, Section 7 of the Reserve Bank of India Act provides that 'The Central Government may from time to time give such directions to the Bank as it may, after consultation with the Governor of the Bank, consider necessary in the public interest.' The exalted position given to the Governor of the Reserve Bank in this regard was generally denied to the Chairmen of other Public Corporations. However, in the discharge of its functions, the State Bank shall be guided by such directions in matters of policy involving public interest, as the Central Government may in consultation with the Governor of the Reserve Bank and the Chairman of the State Bank, give it'. The status of the Reserve Bank as State Bank's guardian has been duly recognized in Section 18(2) of the State Bank of India Act which provides that all directions by the Central Government shall be given through the Reserve Bank.

The Air Corporations are bound to give effect to any directions which the Central Government may give as to the exercise and performance of their functions. Section (34)2 of the Air Corporations Act provides that the Central Government may, if it is of the opinion that it is expedient in the national interest so to do, after consultation with the Corporation concerned, direct either of the Corporation—

(a) to undertake any air transport service or other activity which the Corporation has power to undertake;

(b) to discontinue or make any change in any scheduled air transport service or other activity which it is operating or carrying on;

(c) not to undertake any activity which it proposes to do.

Such specific directions (which could be positive or negative) were not visualized in the case of any other Corporation. Moreover, if the Corporation satisfies the Central Government that during the

[27] The performance of the Damodar Valley Corporation and the Life Insurance Corporation of India is indicated in Appendices A and B.

relevant year the Corporation has suffered an *overall loss,* along with loss on the particular activity undertaken because of Governmental direction, the 'Central Government shall reimburse the Corporation to the extent of the loss relatable to the operation of the particular service or activity'. Likewise, the State Bank of India was expected to open a large number of branches (to meet the social objective of rural uplift) on a subsidized basis. Of the 384 new branches opened by April 30, 1960, as many as 337 were reported to be working at a loss. In order to partially meet these losses, sums of Rs 8.95 lakhs and Rs 26.37 lakhs were debited during 1959 to the Integration and Development Fund in respect of the years 1957 and 1958 respectively. To this fund, the Reserve Bank credits dividends received on the share capital held by it. Thus, what is paid to the holding corporation is partly reclaimed by way of subsidy.

Public Corporations are expected to bring about a happy combination of 'business principles' and 'public interest'. This aspect received special emphasis in the case of the Air Corporations, the State Bank of India and the Life Insurance Corporation of India.[28] The Air Corporations are 'to provide safe, efficient, adequate, economical and properly co-ordinated air transport services, whether internal or international or both and the Corporations shall so exercise their powers as to secure that the air transport services are developed to the best advantage and in particular, so exercise those powers as to secure that the services are provided at reasonable charges'. Further, Section 9 of the Air Corporations Act points out that 'In carrying out any of the duties vested in it by this Act, each of the Corporations shall act so far as may be on business principles.' As against this, Section 17(2) of the State Bank of India Act provides that the Central Board 'in discharging its functions shall act on business principles regard being had to public interest'.[29] The Life Insurance Corporation of India 'shall so exercise its powers under the Act as to secure that life insurance business is developed to the best advantage of the community'. The phrase *'best advantage of the community',* used for the first time in such legislations in this country, is indicative of the importance attached to social considerations. Section 6(3) of the LIC Act, however, provides that 'In the discharge of any of its functions the Corporation shall act so far as may be on business principles.'

[28] In all these cases the State had assumed business activities which were already being carried out by private organizations. As such, the State was expected to demonstrate its capabilities as an efficient businessman.

[29] In the Parliamentary debate on April 30, 1955, Mr S. S. More suggested that 'business principles coupled with public interest is a sort of contradiction' (*Lok Sabha Debates,* 1955, Vol. IV, No. 53, Col. 7072). Yet it is exactly this happy amalgamation which the Institution of Public Corporation seeks to achieve.

Most of the Public Corporations in India have been established in the field of banking and insurance (financial group). In this category we have the Employees' State Insurance Corporation, the Rehabilitation Finance Administration, the Reserve Bank of India, the Industrial Finance Corporation of India, the State Bank of India, the Life Insurance Corporation of India, the National Co-operative Development and Warehousing Board and the Central Warehousing Corporation. However, the Damodar Valley Corporation is an important exception which falls in the category of river valley projects. Somehow the DVC experiment was not sufficiently encouraging so that other such projects were never transformed into Public Corporations.

The working of the Employees' State Insurance Scheme reveals three distinct periods: the first period, extending up to the end of 1953-54, was one of cautious implementation; the second period, represented by the years 1954-55 and 1955-56, was one of rapid strides; and the third period of four years, 1956-60, was one of slow expansion. Although the ESI Act had been passed in 1948, the ESI Scheme was inaugurated as late as February 24, 1952, in Delhi (40,000 workers) and Kanpur (80,000 workers). For nearly fifteen months the Scheme was confined to two industrial centres only. On May 17, 1953, it was extended to seven small industrial centres in the Punjab covering only 30,000 employees. Again, for fourteen months, there was no addition in the list of industrial centres. The number of insured persons stood at 2,68,272. This rose to 8,71,204 by March 1955 and to 12,92,204 by March 1956. The year 1956-57 saw the setting in of a stagnation, the number of insured persons rising only to 13,74,504 by March 1957.[30]

By the end of the year 1958-59, the total number of workers covered stood at 14.14 lakhs. During 1959-60, the total coverage was only slightly higher at 14.43 lakhs.[31] While the period 1956-60 was one of slow expansion, it witnessed the extension of benefits to the family members of the insured persons in several areas.[32] Further, the Corporation has drawn up a plan for the construction of hospitals exclusively for the use of insured persons as also dis-

[30] *Employees' State Insurance Corporation,* Annual Report, 1956-57, p. 34.

[31] *Ministry of Labour and Employment Report,* 1959-60, p. 34. The figures of 'insured persons' and 'workers covered' are not quite comparable. In the same industrial centre the number of insured persons may rise or fall from year to year. On March 31, 1957, the number of workers covered was 11,52,500, whereas the figure of insured persons stood at 13,74,504.

[32] Medical care, to workers' families, was extended in seven industrial centres of Rajasthan and four of Bihar with effect from October 2, 1958. Shortly after that, this benefit was extended to Bangalore and seven industrial centres of the Punjab. Four industrial centres in Assam obtained this facility on December 28, 1958.

pensaries at various places involving a total capital outlay of Rs 15 crores. The whole programme is likely to be completed during the Third Plan Period. The working of the ESI Scheme was examined by the General Purposes Sub-Committee of the Employers' State Insurance Corporation consisting of the representatives of the workers, the employers, the medical profession and Parliament. The Committee came to the conclusion that the administration of cash benefits was satisfactory in all the six places enquired into. With regard to medical arrangements, the Committee were satisfied insofar as Bangalore, Madras and Madurai were concerned. In the other three places—Calcutta, Howrah and Assam—medical arrangements were not up to the mark. Considering the larger number of workers residing in the three 'unsatisfactory centres', the problem of effecting qualitative improvement assumes serious proportions.[33]

The working of the Rehabilitation Finance Administration has been summed up by the Chairman and Chief Administrator, Mr P. C. Das Gupta, in his review dated July 20, 1957: 'The objective of the RFA to rehabilitate displaced persons in business or industry by giving financial aid has not succeeded to the extent it was originally intended.' With regard to the refugees from East Pakistan he was prepared to accept the statement that 'practically little or no rehabilitation had been achieved till now'. In the Eastern Region, according to him, 'a large proportion of our loans appeared to be either bad or doubtful'. Hence compromises were being entered into with the defaulting loanees 'on more liberal terms'. The Chairman conceded that loans 'were actuated more by considerations other than what are strictly in accordance with commercial prudence'.[34] He, therefore, suggested the conversion of the RFA into a Relief Bank which could give assistance to all displaced persons irrespective of the date of migration. However, a mere change in nomenclature will be of little use. What is required is greater emphasis on commercial considerations and less on political factors.

During the first eleven years of its working, the RFA suffered losses in ten years. Only in 1958 did it make a small profit as indicated by the following table (figures in thousands of rupees):

Year			Loss (−)/Profit (+)	Progressive
1948	...	...	−209	−209
1949	...	...	−958	−1,167
1950	...	...	−1,236	−2,403

[33] Although the workers covered were spread over 86 industrial centres, nearly half the number was to be found at two places: Greater Bombay (4,70,000 workers) and Calcutta City and Howrah District (2,30,000 workers). The working of the ESIC was severely criticized in Parliament during the year 1959. The Government of India, therefore, appointed Dr A. Lakshamanaswami Mudaliar, Vice-Chancellor, University of Madras, as one-man Committee to enquire into the working of the Scheme.

[34] RFA, *Eighth Annual Report*, p. 5.

Year			Loss (−)/Profit (+)	Progressive
1951	...	...	−2,593	−4,996
1952	...	...	−2,307	−7,303
1953	...	...	−2,216	−9,519
1954	...	...	−3,305	−12,824
1955	...	...	−3,369	−16,193
1956	...	...	−257	−16,450
1957	...	...	−376	−16,826
1958	...	...	+77	−16,749

It may be noted that these losses have not taken full cognizance of possible bad debts. The difficulties of the RFA were heightened by the fact that it had started charging 6 per cent interest on the loans, but later on this rate had to be reduced. The working margin, which was originally 3 per cent, was reduced to between $\frac{1}{2}$ per cent and $1\frac{1}{2}$ per cent. Moreover, the RFA had started its organizational network on a somewhat lavish scale. That this structure was top heavy became increasingly evident as the scope of fresh business was circumscribed.

The Reserve Bank of India, in addition to its rôle as the central bank of the country, is the godfather of the State Bank of India, the Industrial Finance Corporation of India and the various State Financial Corporations.[35] Further, the Reserve Bank has played a significant rôle in the development of rural credit facilities. Following the recommendations of the All-India Rural Credit Survey, and in terms of the Reserve Bank of India (Amendment) Act 1955, two giant funds were established to make advances (directly or indirectly) to co-operative credit institutions: the National Agricultural Credit (Long-term Operations) Fund in February 1956; and (2) the National Agricultural Credit (Stabilization) Fund in June 1956. On June 30, 1958, these Funds stood at Rs 25 crores and Rs 3 crores respectively. The increase in the functions of the Reserve Bank of India is indicated by the fact that the number of persons employed rose from 2,574 as on June 30, 1939, to 8,783 as on May 31, 1958. Functional specialization, with adequate co-ordination, is the main feature of the Bank's internal organization. At the top level, it has

[35] The Reserve Bank is rapidly becoming a powerful holding corporation. Besides the entire (initial) capital of the State Bank (with a minimum limit of 55 per cent), the Reserve Bank holds more than 20 per cent of the paid-up capital of the IFC and is entitled to nominate two Directors. The Bank has participated in the share capital of the various State Financial Corporations to the extent of 10-20 per cent and has one nominee on the Board of Directors of each such Corporation. In many instances the Bank has deputed its own officers to work as Managing Directors of these Corporations. The Bank is authorized to conduct the inspection of such Corporations which are required to submit certain periodical statements. Further, it has a statutory right of being consulted in certain matters. The Reserve Bank of India has also contributed Rs 5 crores to the share capital of the Refinance Corporation for Industry (Private) Limited set up on June 5, 1958.

adopted a functional pattern of organization although it was not indicated in the legislation itself. Under the present administrative arrangements, 'one of the Deputy Governors is in charge of matters relating to note issue, exchange control, public accounts, deposit accounts, open market operators, public debt and general administration; another is in charge of banking operations, while the third Deputy Governor looks after the fields of rural credit, banking development and industrial finance'.[36]

That the Reserve Bank of India is 'clothed with the power of Government but possessed of the initiative and flexibility of private enterprise' is clearly brought out by Section 35-A introduced by the Reserve Bank of India (Amendment) Act, 1957:

'(1) where the Reserve Bank is satisfied that

    (a) in the national interest; or

    (b) to prevent the affairs of any banking company being conducted in a matter detrimental to the interests of the depositors or in any manner prejudicial to the interests of the banking company; or

    (c) to secure the proper management of any banking company generally;

it is necessary to issue directions to banking companies generally or, to any banking company, in particular, it may, from time to time, issue such directions as it may deem fit, and the banking companies or the banking company, as the case may be, shall be bound to comply with such directions.'

The Industrial Finance Corporation, too, enjoys many privileges which are not available to any ordinary bank. The IFC may appoint one or more Directors on the Board of Directors of the industrial concern to which financial accommodation is granted. It may also impose such other conditions as it may consider necessary, e.g. restriction on the rate of dividend to be paid by the borrowing concern until the loan is repaid. Under certain circumstances, the Corporation is entitled to recall a loan before maturity. Where an industrial concern (under agreement) makes any default in repayment or otherwise, the IFC (under Section 28) shall have the right to take over the management of the concern,[37] besides the right to

---

[36] The Reserve Bank of India, *Functions and Working*, 1958, p. 5.

[37] Practical experience shows that this prerogative is not always a bed of roses. During the year 1952-53, the Corporation decided to take over the management of Sodepore Glass Works Ltd, under Section 28 of the IFC Act, 1948. The plant did not work satisfactorily and certain modifications had, therefore, to be undertaken. For this purpose the factory was closed on July 20, 1953. The modifications were completed by May 1954. The total amount due from this concern on June 30, 1954, was Rs 103 lakhs, which included Rs 70 lakhs on account of loans (with interest) and Rs 33 lakhs spent after the management had been taken over. The Corporation wanted to get

transfer by way of lease or sale, and to realize the property pledged, mortgaged, hypothecated or assigned to the Corporation.

During the discussion on the IFC (Amendment) Bill 1952, the working of the Corporation was subjected to severe criticism. The principal allegations were of nepotism and favouritism in the grant of loans, particularly to big industries. Accordingly, in December 1952, an Enquiry Committee was set up under the Chairmanship of Mrs Sucheta Kripalani, M.P. The Committee, in its report submitted on May 7, 1953, 'generally exonerated' the Corporation of the charges about partiality. But it did observe—though this view was rejected by the Government—that applications in which the Chairman or other Directors take interest receive more expeditious and liberal treatment. The Committee recommended that the Corporation should publish more informative and comprehensive annual reports and quinquennial reviews disclosing names of all the loanees, setting out the activities and fortunes of individual borrowing concerns and surveying the trend of development in the industries generally. Names of the borrowing concerns, which were kept a closely guarded secret on grounds of banker's propriety, were published for the first eight years in the report for 1955-56; thereafter, annual lists appeared in the reports for 1956-57, 1957-58 and 1958-59. General reviews of industrial development are also being published.[38]

The following table gives an indication of the loans sanctioned and disbursed by the IFC (figures in crores of rupees):

Year			Loans Sanctioned	Loans Disbursed
1948-49	...	...	3.42	1.33
1949-50	...	...	3.77	2.08
1950-51	...	...	2.39	2.38
1951-52	...	...	4.45	1.78
1952-53	...	...	1.43	2.50
1953-54	...	...	5.27	2.82

rid of this white elephant, but the Ministry of Production were not prepared to take over the factory. It was sold to Indo-Asahi Glass Co Ltd, of Tokyo, on May 3, 1957. But this was not the end of the story. On an application made by the Corporation, the Sodepore Glass Works Ltd was ordered to be wound up by the Calcutta High Court with effect from January 17, 1958.

[38] Among other suggestions of the Committee were that the Corporation should conform to the priorities for industrial development as laid down in the plan, that the Government should issue directives to the Corporation regarding guiding principles (specially giving preference to backward areas) and that for the next three years loans exceeding Rs 50 lakhs should be sanctioned with the approval of the Central Government at the ministerial level. The last suggestion could have given rise to further abuses. It was considered enough if loans exceeding Rs 50 lakhs were reported to the Government. Further, the fantastic suggestion regarding the total exclusion of certain industrial concerns (where a Director of the IFC was a Managing Director or a Director/Partner/Shareholder in the Managing Agency concern) from the list of borrowers was not accepted.

Year			Loans Sanctioned	Loans Disbursed
1954-55	...	...	7.34	1.64
1955-56	...	...	15.13	2.20
1956-57	...	...	11.91	9.78
1957-58	...	...	7.79	8.33
1958-59	...	...	3.79	7.48
		Total	66.69	42.32

The annual figures of 'loans sanctioned' present quite a zigzag appearance. The period 1948-52 can be considered as one of medium activity, 1952-56 as one of rising activity, and 1956-59 as one of falling activity. The foreign exchange crisis was, to a considerable extent, responsible for a fall in the amount of loans sanctioned during 1956-59. However, during the last period, actual disbursements exceeded the amount of loans sanctioned. *On the basis of cumulative figures,* the disbursement percentage rose from 39 per cent on June 30, 1949, to 63 per cent as on June 30, 1959. Low percentages have often been the result of delays in the grant of loans.[39] Entrepreneurial enthusiasm being often of a momentary character, many applicants do not accept the loans when they are made available to them. Sometimes other difficulties—like non-availability of capital goods, technical skill or raw material—may compel the applicants to change their minds. In certain cases the loans are not fully disbursed because of the failure on the part of the borrowing companies to make proper utilization of the initial instalment.

The IFC was established for the purpose of making medium and long-term credits more readily available to (corporate) industrial concerns in India, particularly in circumstances where normal banking accommodation is inappropriate or recourse to capital issue channels is impracticable. However, from the standpoint of resources, the Corporation was not initially well-equipped to be able to do justice to this stupendous task. It has tried to augment its resources by issuing debentures, borrowing from the Reserve Bank of India and obtaining foreign credit. But the IFC has given its major attention to consumer goods industries and to those industries which had already shown considerable development. The biggest slice went to Food Manufacturing Industries, mainly Sugar (Rs 20.72 crores), followed by Textiles (Rs 9.73 crores), Basic Chemicals (Rs 7.66 crores), Cement (Rs 6.17 crores) and Paper (Rs 5.72 crores).

The rate of interest charged by the IFC stood at 5½ per cent up to February 1952 when it was raised to 6 per cent. It was further increased to 6½ per cent during 1952-53 and to 7 per cent with

[39] The IFC is not always responsible for such delays. For example, some applications are not supported by the necessary import licences.

effect from April 23, 1957. These increases were, to some extent, in sympathy with the general rise in the rates of interest. But they were largely dictated by the fact that the Corporation was not able to earn enough even to repay the guaranteed dividend of $2\frac{1}{4}$ per cent. Up to 1956, the IFC had to depend upon Government subvention in every year except 1953. In 1957, it could just pay the minimum dividend; and in 1958 and 1959 it could partly repay its liability to the Government previously incurred.

According to Section 16 of the Air Corporations Act, the Indian Airlines Corporation was intended to operate internal air services, and services to adjacent countries like Burma, Ceylon and Pakistan. Long-distance international services were meant for the Air India International Corporation. The two Corporations were formally constituted on June 15, 1953, and they started their career with effect from August 1, 1953. Non-scheduled air services were not nationalized and nine private airlines were still operating during 1956-57.[40] But before operating a non-scheduled flight outside India, a non-scheduled operator was required to obtain a 'No Objection Certificate' both from the Air India International and the Indian Airlines Corporation. The following table gives an idea of the working of the two Corporations during the first six years of their existence:

Year ending March 31				Profits (+) and Losses (−) In lakhs of Rupees	
				INDIAN AIRLINES	AIR INDIA
1954	...	...	...	−79	+7
1955	...	...	...	−90	+14
1956	...	...	...	−119	+4
1957	...	...	...	−109	+38
1958	...	...	...	−103	+72
1959	...	...	...	−91	+16
			Total	−592	+150

(N.B.—Because of approximations, the figures may not 'add up'. The first year of operation consists of eight months only.)

Thus, during this period, internal air services were always run at a loss whereas the external operations have always been profitable. But the average annual loss of the former (roughly a crore of rupees) was nearly four times the average annual profit (Rs 25 lakhs) in the case of the latter. Incidentally, the year of maximum loss for the Indian Airlines, i.e. 1955-56, was also the year of minimum profit for the Air India International. Thereafter, up to 1958, while the losses of the Indian Airlines went on falling, the profits of the Air India International went on rising. But this sympathetic development was disturbed in 1959 when the profit of the Air India International

[40] *Estimates Committee*, 41st Report, 1956-57, Ministry of Communications, Lok Sabha Secretariat, New Delhi, p. 14.

suddenly fell to Rs 15.85 lakhs. If we also take into account non-operating revenues (which fell from Rs 111.68 lakhs in 1957-58 to Rs 2.43 lakhs in 1958-59), the total surplus in 1959 was only Rs 18.28 lakhs as against Rs 183.35 lakhs in 1958.[41]

Before nationalization, the combined losses of the eight concerns inherited by the Indian Airlines Corporation were Rs 110 lakhs in 1949. But they had fallen to Rs 75 lakhs in 1952, which was, incidentally, a period of relatively low prices. The Corporation had to meet a rise of Rs 84 lakhs in the wages bill and higher provision of Rs 27 lakhs for depreciation on account of the introduction of costlier aircraft. Considering these two factors, the Corporation had certainly brought about some improvement in the working of internal air services, though its achievement has not been able to meet the nation's expectations.

Important changes were brought about in the capital structure of the two Corporations in the light of the experience gained during the first few years. The capital of the Indian Airlines stood at Rs 1486.57 lakhs (about £11 million) advanced by the Government of India, and Rs 1.16 lakhs, the face value of Compensation Bonds remaining unredeemed. Originally, the Government of India had granted a moratorium with regard to interest on capital provided by Government for the first five years which ended on July 31, 1958. Thereafter, Government decided to subsidize the losses of the Corporation on the basis of a standard cost and to reorganize the capital structure of the Corporation by writing off the past losses and by treating a part of capital as interest-free. However, even on that portion of the capital on which interest is to be paid, Government have agreed to waive such interest charges until October 1, 1966.[42] The capital of the Air India International stood at Rs 1366.78 lakhs (about £10 million) on March 31, 1959. In accordance with the decision taken during the year 1958-59, half of this was treated as equity capital and the other half as loan capital carrying interest at $4\frac{1}{2}$ per cent. However, as in the case of the Indian Airlines, the moratorium originally granted for five years was extended up to October 1, 1966.

There are two noteworthy features in the working of the State Bank of India during the first five years of its existence—acquiring the business of other banks and establishing new branches. Under Section 35(1) of the incorporating Act, 'The State Bank may, with the sanction of the Central Government, and shall, if so directed by the Central Government in consultations with the Reserve Bank, enter into negotiations for acquiring the business including the

[41] *Air India International Corporation,* Sixth Annual Report, 1958-59, p. 5. Even after providing for Deferred Taxation (Rs 57.25 lakhs) the net disposable balance in 1958 was Rs 126.10 lakhs.
[42] *Indian Airlines Corporation,* Sixth Annual Report, 1958-59, p. 11.

assets and liabilities of any banking institution.[43] The State Bank of India (Subsidiary Banks) Act, passed in September 1959, enabled the State Bank to take over the eight State-owned and State-associated Banks as its subsidiaries. Their position stood as follows on December 31, 1959 :[44]

Name of Bank	Paid-up capital (Rs lakhs)	Total Deposits (Rs lakhs)	Number of Offices
1. State Bank of Bikaner	50	1316	54
2. State Bank of Indore	15	904	18
3. State Bank of Jaipur	50	997	40
4. The Bank of Mysore	50	1957	43
5. State Bank of Travancore	100	697	20
6. State Bank of Hyderabad	50	1879	53
7. The Bank of Patiala	15	958	47
8. State Bank of Saurashtra	100	1657	61

These subsidiary banks continue to retain their separate entity. Thus the State Bank of India has become an *intermediate holding corporation* (controlling certain Banks, and being controlled by the Reserve Bank of India).[45]

The statutory obligation imposed on the State Bank to open 400 new branches within a period of five years was achieved just a month before the stipulated date. The following table gives an indication of the progress made in this direction:

	Number of new branches opened
1. 1955 (July-December)	20
2. 1956 (January-December)	46
3. 1957 (January-December)	91
4. 1958 (January-December)	105
5. 1959 (January-December)	97
6. 1960 (January-May)	40
7. On June 1, 1960	1
	400

Of the 359 new branches opened up to December 31, 1959, 66 branches were opened at towns with a population below 10,000; 182 at places with a population of 10,000-25,000; 86 at places with a population of 25,000-50,000; and only 24 branches were at still

[43] The State Bank of India (Amendment) Act, 1959, seeks to simplify the procedure with regard to the taking over of the actual business of any banking institution.

[44] *The State Bank of India,* Report of the Central Board of Directors for the year 1959, p. 20.

[45] The Board of a Subsidiary Bank consists of (a) the Chairman of the State Bank, ex-officio; (b) an officer of the Reserve Bank; (c) not more than five Directors to be nominated by the State Bank; and (d) two Directors elected by other shareholders. The General Manager is to be appointed by the State Bank with the approval of the Reserve Bank.

bigger places. Actually, at 55 places, no other scheduled, non-scheduled or co-operative bank had a branch or office; and 29 branches were opened at places where no banking facility was available within a distance of 20 miles. The deposits received and advances granted at the 359 new branches stood at Rs 28.29 crores and Rs 11.96 crores respectively on December 31, 1959.[46]

While the State Bank did well in its developmental work, its traditional business did not show any marked progress. The Bank's advances (including bills discounted) rose from Rs 140.16 crores on December 31, 1956, to Rs 173.48 crores as on December 31, 1957. But, thereafter, they fell to Rs 172.06 crores at the end of 1958 and to Rs 166.88 crores as on December 31, 1959. As against this, deposits rose from Rs 242.12 crores at the end of 1956 to Rs 581.17 crores at the end of 1959. This worsened the ratio of advances to deposits from 57.9 per cent in 1956 to 28.7 per cent in 1959.

Again, while gross income was more than doubled (rising from 8.67 crores in 1955 to Rs 18.53 crores in 1959), the expenditure also was more than doubled (rising from Rs 7.11 crores to Rs 16.66 crores). The net profit rose from Rs 1.56 crores in 1956 to Rs 1.87 crores in 1957 and to Rs 1.90 crores in 1958; thereafter it fell to Rs 1.87 crores in 1959. The net rate of dividend, which had been maintained at 16 per cent (income-tax free) up to 1958, was slightly reduced in 1959 when the Bank declared a (taxable) dividend of 20 per cent. (i.e. 14 per cent net). The prospect would be worse when we consider the Chairman's statement 'that the increased earnings of the Bank for the year 1958 were somewhat fortuitous. This continued to be the position in 1959 also. A sizeable portion of the Bank's deposits continued to consist of the United States P.L. 480 Funds.'

The functions of the Central Warehousing Corporation as outlined in Section 25 of the Agricultural Produce (Development and Warehousing) Corporations Act, 1956, are to:

(a) acquire and build godowns and warehouses at such suitable places in India as it thinks fit;

(b) run warehouses for the storage of agricultural produce, seeds, manures, fertilizers and agricultural implements offered by individuals, co-operative societies and other institutions;

(c) arrange facilities for the transportation of agricultural produce to and from warehouses;

(d) subscribe to the share capital of a State Warehousing Corporation;

(e) act as agent of the Board (National Co-operative Development and Warehousing Board) or the Government for the purposes of the

[46] Speech of the Chairman, Mr P. C. Bhattacharya, at the Fifth Annual Meeting of the Shareholders, held in Bombay, March 4, 1960, p. 5.

purchase, sale, storage and distribution of agricultural produce, seeds, manures, fertilizers and agricultural implements; and

(f) carry out such other functions as may be prescribed.

The Corporation had before it a target of constructing 100 warehouses during the Second Plan Period (1956-61). But because 'the Corporation itself was established one year after the start of the Second Five-Year Plan and the organization started working effectively from a much later date and in view of a number of other unforeseen factors'[47] this target of 100 warehouses could not be achieved. During the year 1957-58, not a single warehouse was constructed. But 'as a matter of caution, it was decided by the Board of Directors that before any construction was actually taken in hand, an experimental beginning should be made in a few hired buildings in order to get a fair idea of the potentialities of the place'. The Chairman of the Corporation described the year 1957-58 as 'one of useful exploratory activity'.[48]

In October 1957, personnel for running the warehouses was recruited and a hurried training course was arranged between October 24 and November 21, 1957. In December 1957, warehouses were started at six centres—Amravati, Gondia, Sangli, Davangere, Gadag and Bargarh—in hired accommodation. A warehouse was opened at Warrangal in February 1958, at Moga in May 1958, and at Chandausi in July 1958. Thus, on March 31, 1959, there were only nine warehouses, and these too in rented buildings for which the word 'modern' may not be a suitable description. The total stock at these warehouses rose from 13,340 tons in April 1958 to 1,62,902 tons in March 1959. But the net loss also rose from Rs 1,21,457 in 1957-58 to Rs 4,30,458 in 1958-59. During the year 1958-59, whereas the income from warehousing charges was only Rs 76,195, the establishment expenses, which figured at Rs 425,794, gave an indication of top heavy organization.

---

[47] *Central Warehousing Corporation's* Annual Report and Accounts, 1957-58, p. 9.

[48] Speech delivered by Mr R. K. Damle, ICS, at the First Annual General Meeting held on November 17, 1958.

CHAPTER IV

GOVERNMENT COMPANIES IN INDIA

BACKGROUND

In India and certain other countries of the world like France, Italy, Sweden, South Africa and Canada, the joint stock company has come to be accepted as a vital instrument of the public sector. Since it obviates the necessity of special legislation, and can be registered under the ordinary Company Law, Governments have seen in it a more convenient and less fussy device of promoting State enterprise.

A lot of confusion has been caused in India through the use of the terms 'Public Company' and 'Private Company' in Company Law. With the phenomenal growth of public enterprise and the creation of numerous 'Public Corporations' after the year 1947, it was expected that the terminology employed in Company Law would be adequately rationalized. Far from that, the Companies Act, No. 1 of 1956, has actually made matters worse in this regard.

According to Section 3(iv) of the Companies Act, 1956, 'Public Company' means a company which is not a Private Company. Thus, a negative definition has been offered. According to Section 3(iii), 'Private Company' means a company which, by its articles:

    (a) restricts the right to transfer its shares; if any;

    (b) limits the number of its members to fifty, not including:

        (i) persons who are in the employment of the company, and

        (ii) persons who, having been formerly in the employment of the company, were members of the company while in that employment and have continued to be members after the employment ceased;[1] and

    (c) prohibits any invitation to the public to subscribe for any shares in, or debentures of, the company:

Provided that where two or more persons hold one or more shares in a company jointly, they shall, for the purposes of the definition, be treated as a single member.

The Act does not specify the nature of restriction to be imposed on the transfer of shares in a Private Company. Basically, the idea behind a Private Company is a business carried on by a family or a small group of friends who wish to preserve substantial secrecy about their affairs but who, at the same time, wish to take advantage

---

[1] The concession to ex-members was extended in India in 1956, on the lines of the British Companies Act.

of limited liability. They do not like that their shares should be the object of speculative deals on the stock exchange, or that their affairs shall become the object of public discussion. Free transferability of shares would create both these difficulties. It may enable outside elements to get in as shareholders and to disturb the harmony of that homogenous group. Not only this, unrestricted transfer of shares may also mean violation of the maximum limit of membership. Suppose X is a private company which already has fifty members. One of the shareholders A, who owns two shares, may sell one share to B, and the other share to C. This means that membership has been raised to fifty-one, which is in contravention of law.

In view of the fact that Private Companies enjoy immunity from certain legal provisions, Section 13(1) of the Companies Act, 1956, provides that the Memorandum of Association of every company shall state the name of the company with 'Limited' as the last word in the case of a Public Company and with 'Private Limited' as the last words in the case of a Private Limited Company. All the Private Companies existing on April 1, 1956, were also required to add the word 'Private' (before 'Limited') in their name. The term 'Private Limited' is something like a note of caution, addressed to the people, which we may describe as follows:

'Beware: This is a Private Company, a close preserve of a few individuals on whom the State has conferred the privilege of limited liability along with immunity from public scrutiny. If you deal with this company, be careful, lest you burn your fingers.'

Under this provision, a large number of State-owned companies, which had been registered as private companies, began to be called Private Limiteds, e.g. Sindri Fertilizers and Chemicals (Private) Limited, National Industrial Development Corporation (Private) Limited and Hindustan Steel (Private) Limited. To avoid this anomolous nomenclature, the Hindustan Steel (Private) Limited obtained the permission of the Registrar of Joint Stock Companies to delete the word 'Private'. Accordingly, in March 1959, this word was dropped and the concern was simply called 'Hindustan Steel Ltd.' Other Government Companies have followed suit.

It is thus clear that the terms 'Public Company' and 'Private Company' have nothing to do with the 'public sector' and the 'private sector' of business enterprise. Most of the public companies in India are privately-owned, whereas public enterprise through public companies is a rarity (so far as the Central Government is concerned).

A Private Company enjoys a number of concessions under the Indian Companies Act, 1956. Only two persons can form such a Company, whereas at least seven persons must subscribe their names to the Memorandum of Association of a Public Company.[2] Further, a Private Company need have only two Directors (as against three required in the case of a Public Company); its Directors have not to file their 'consent' and 'contract'; and they are not subject to the principle of retirement by rotation (unless the Private Company is a subsidiary of a Public Company). Again, a Private Company is prohibited from issuing prospectus; it does not require a certificate to commence business; it need not publish the Statutory Report; and it is not required to hold the Statutory Meeting. It is also immune from the restrictions regarding the sale or lease of a company's undertaking, investments, borrowings and contributions to charitable and other funds. The maximum limit on overall managerial remuneration (11 per cent) also does not hold good in the case of a Private Company. Further, Directorships and Managing Agencies in Private Companies (unless they are subsidiaries of Public Companies) are not to be counted for the purpose of maximum limits (twenty Directorships for any person and ten Managing Agency contracts for any Managing Agent) imposed by the Companies Act of 1956. For these reasons, Private Companies have earned popularity in both the public and private sectors of the Indian economy. The following table is quite revealing:

JOINT STOCK COMPANIES IN INDIA[3]

	1916-17	1938-39	1945-46	1954-55	1960-61
I *All Companies*					
No.	2,513	11,114	17,343	29,625	26,108
Paid-up Capital (Rs. Crores)	91	290	424	971	1,725
II *Public Companies*					
No.	2,306	6,859	10,129	10,056	6,745
Paid-up Capital (Rs. Crores)	85	213	323	663	876
III *Private Companies*					
No.	207	4,255	7,214	19,569	19,363
Paid-up Capital (Rs. Crores)	6	77	101	308	849

[2] It would be convenient if a provision for 'Companies Sole' is introduced in the Companies Act so that the President of India may be a single subscriber. The Private Company device is specially suited to wholly Government-owned Companies. For Mixed Companies the prospectus may have to be issued and—also on the basis of other considerations—the Public Company device may be more appropriate.

[3] Figures for the years 1916-17, 1938-39 and 1945-46 obtained from the Report of the Company Law Committee, 1952; figures for 1954-55 from Dr S. K. Basu's 'The Managing Agency System: In Prospect and Retrospect' (1958); and figures for 1960-61 made available by the Department of Company Law Administration, New Delhi. Out of 6,039 new companies registered during the Second Plan Period (1956-61) with an authorized capital of Rs

PERCENTAGE ANALYSIS

	1916-17	1938-39	1945-46	1954-55	1960-61
IV *Public Companies*					
No.	92%	62%	58%	34%	26%
Paid-up Capital	94%	73%	76%	68%	51%
V *Private Companies*					
No.	8%	38%	42%	66%	74%
Paid-up Capital	6%	27%	24%	32%	49%

Under Section 620 of the Companies Act, 1956, the Central Government may, by notification in the Official Gazette, direct that any of the provisions of this Act (other than Sections 618, 619 and 639):

(a) Shall not apply to any Government Company, or

(b) Shall apply to any Government Company only with such exceptions, modifications and adaptations as may be specified in the notification.

But it must be noted that 'Government Company' is *not* a separate class *as such*. A Public Company as well as a Private Company may be a Government Company. According to Section 617, 'For the purposes of Sections 618, 619 and 620, Government Company means any company in which not less than 51 per cent of the share capital is held by the Central Government, or by any State Government or Governments, or partly by the Central Government and partly by one or more "State Governments".'

Section 618 provides that no Government Company formed after the commencement of this Act shall appoint a Managing Agent.

According to Section 619, the auditor of a Government Company shall be appointed or reappointed by the Central Government on the advice of the Comptroller and Auditor-General of India, who shall have power to direct the manner in which the company's accounts shall be audited by the auditor appointed and to give such auditor instructions in regard to any matter relating to the performance of his functions as such. He may also conduct a supplementary or test audit of the company's accounts by such person or persons as he may authorize in this behalf; and, for the purpose of such audit, require information or additional information by general or special orders. The auditor aforesaid shall submit a copy of his audit report to the Comptroller and Auditor-General of India, who shall have the right to comment upon, or supplement, the audit report in such manner as he may think fit. Any such comments upon, or supplement to, the audit report shall be placed before

1,045 crores, the major groupings were as follows: Metals and Chemicals Rs 394 crores; Other Industrial Goods Rs 177 crores; Mining and Quarrying Rs 170 crores; Commerce, Trade and Finance Rs 117 crores; and Processing of Foodstuffs Rs 100 crores.

the annual general meeting of the company at the same time and in the same manner as the audit report.

Section 639 requires that the Central Government shall cause an annual report on the working and affairs of each Government Company to be prepared and laid before both Houses of Parliament, together with a copy of the audit report and any comments upon, or supplement to, the audit report, made by the Comptroller and Auditor-General of India. Where any State Government is a member of a Government Company, the annual report on the working and affairs of the Company, the audit report, and the comments upon or supplement to the audit report, shall be placed by the State Government before the State Legislature or, where the State Legislature has two Houses, before both Houses of that Legislature.

ORGANIZATION

The following table indicates the progress of Government Companies in India during recent years: [4]

Year	No. of Companies	Paid-up Capital (Crores of rupees)
1955-56	61	66.0
1956-57	77	72.6
1957-58	91	256.8
1958-59	103	424.2
1959-60	125	468.4
1960-61	139	498.0

As against these developments, the total number of *all* companies (Public and Private, and in both the sectors) actually declined from 29,874 as on March 31, 1956, to 26,108 as on March 31, 1961. The total number of Private Companies (in both the sectors) fell from 20,299 to 19,363 and that of Public Companies (in both the sectors) from 9,575 to 6,745.[5] The paid-up capital of *all* companies increased

[4] These figures include not only Central Government Companies but also Government Companies owned by State Governments. Figures released by the Department of Company Law Administration. The statistics depict the position at the end of each year (i.e. the year 1960-61 actually means March 31, 1961).

[5] These numbers have fallen in spite of substantial new registrations. Since the enforcement of the new Companies Act with effect from April 1, 1956 (and up to March 31, 1961, i.e. during the Second Plan Period), 6,039 new companies were registered with a total authorized capital of Rs 1,045 crores. Out of these new registrations, there were 447 Public Companies (Rs 390 crores) and 5,592 Private Companies (Rs 655 crores). During the year 1960-61, 1,683 new companies (144 Public and 1,539 Private Companies), were registered. Out of these, eighty-nine bigger companies constituted 68 per cent of the total authorized capital. There were seven Government Companies (all Private Companies) in this 'bigger' category registered during the year 1960-61: the National Building Construction Corporation Ltd (Rs 2

from Rs 1,024 crores to Rs 1,725 crores, i.e. by less than 70 per cent. As against this, the paid-up capital of Government Companies rose from Rs 66 crores to Rs 498 crores, i.e. by over 650 per cent. On March 31, 1956, Government Companies accounted for only 6.4 per cent of the total paid-up capital, but their share was as high as 28.9 per cent on March 31, 1961.

Calculations regarding the average paid-up capital per company are quite revealing. This average for *all* companies comes to about Rs 7 lakhs as on March 31, 1961. The average for all *Public* Companies works out at about Rs 13 lakhs; and, for all *Private* Companies, at about Rs 4 lakhs. As against these figures, the average paid-up capital in the case of Government Companies comes to Rs 363 lakhs. As on March 31, 1956, the average for Government Companies had stood at Rs 108 lakhs. The tremendous increase during 1956-61 is, to a large extent, accountable to the rise of the Hindustan Steel Limited.[6]

There is an almost uninterrupted trend leading to the flotation of Private Companies as Central Government Companies. Among the exceptions to this general tendency we may refer to the Sultania Cotton Manufacturing Company, which had been floated as early as December 23, 1913; the Eastern Shipping Corporation, established on March 24, 1950, by way of joint venture with the Scindias; the Rehabilitation Housing Corporation, created on September 19, 1951, as a semi-Government undertaking with functions like those of an Improvement Trust; the Ashoka Hotel, registered on October 17, 1955, as a mixed enterprise; the National Newsprint and Paper Mills (Nepa Mills), established in 1947 as a private enterprise, later substantially financed by the Government of Madhya Pradesh and, ultimately, the Government of India acquiring majority interest during the financial year ending on March 31, 1959; and the Praga Tools Corporation, set up in 1943 and later, at the request of the Government of Hyderabad (Managing Agents), the Government of India investing Rs 70 lakhs (about 51 per cent in March 1959) to take over its administration. Generally speaking, Public Companies have been found necessary for running mixed enterprises, although the Indian Telephone Industries established on January 25, 1950, jointly by the Central Government, the State Government of

crores); Bihar State Industrial Development Corporation (Rs 2 crores); Hindustan Teleprinters (Rs 3 crores); Hindustan Photo Films Manufacturing Co Ltd (Rs 3 crores); Andhra Pradesh Industrial Development Corporation Ltd (Rs 3 crores); Hindustan Organic Chemical Ltd (Rs 12 crores); and the U.P. State Industrial Corporation Ltd (Rs 5 crores).

[6] The same is also included in the paid-up capital of all Private Companies, which rose from Rs 334 crores as on March 31, 1956, to Rs 849 crores as on March 31, 1961. The rise in the paid-up capital of all Public Companies was small—Rs 690 crores to Rs 876 crores.

Mysore and private interests, is just a Private Company.

The 1948 boom in the creation of Statutory Corporations had spent itself by 1949. The Government of India wanted to create new bodies at a speed faster than that dictated by Parliamentary legislation, and to canalize their momentary enthusiasm into the creation of new entities just according to the convenience of the relevant Minister and his Secretariat. At the same time, Government had realized that the various Departments would not be able to bear the load of 'direct management' of the ever-increasing number of public enterprises. Under these circumstances, time was ripe for the creation of a large number of Government Companies.

At the Central Government level[7] only three Companies had come into existence before 1949. Besides the one Company established in 1913, the year 1940 had seen the creation of two Companies, viz. Government Telephones Board and Hindustan Aircraft. The Indian Mining and Construction Company registered on April 13, 1949, was the first Government Company established after India's independence. Up to June 30, 1959, forty-six Central Government Companies had come into existence, the peak years of registration being 1956 and 1957. However, the popularity of Government Companies had already been heralded by the Sindri Fertilizers and Chemicals Ltd, registered on December 18, 1951.

Since there is no 'Central Registration Office' (it will be worthwhile to have such an office), Central Government Companies had to be registered in the various States. Out of forty-six such Companies, fifteen were registered in Delhi, nine in Bombay, five in West Bengal, four in Mysore, three in Bihar, two each in Madras and Madhya Pradesh, and one each in the Punjab, Himachal Pradesh, Rajasthan, Andhra Pradesh, Orissa and Kerala. In most of the cases the State of registration was suggested by the location of the factory or activity, e.g. Sindri Fertilizers and Chemicals, and the National Coal Development Corporation in the State of Bihar, Hindustan Aircraft in Mysore, and Ashoka Hotels in Delhi. But there is a glaring example of the Hindustan Shipyard, whose registered office was located at Delhi, although Delhi has nothing to do with shipbuilding as such. Further, in the case of Development Companies (having all-India jurisdiction) like the National Research Development Corporation, the National Industrial Development Corporation and the National Small Industries Corporation, Delhi was, in its own right, chosen as the State of Registration.

Out of forty-six companies referred to above, five were jointly owned by the Central Government and private interests (first category); another four represented joint enterprise of the Central and

---

[7] This study is confined to the corporate enterprises falling within the jurisdiction of the Central Government.

the State Government concerned (second category); three companies were jointly owned by the Central Government, the State Government concerned and private interests (third category); and the remaining thirty-four companies were exclusively owned by the Central Government (fourth category). In the first category were created the Sultania Cotton Manufacturing Company (1913), the Rehabilitation Flouring Corporation (1951), the Hindustan Shipyard (1952), the Ashoka Hotels (1955) and the Refinance Corporation for Industry (1958). The second category consisted of Hindustan Aircraft (1940), Indian Rare Earths (1950), Orissa Mining Corporation (1956) and Travancore Minerals (1956). The third category comprised the Indian Telephone Industries, the Nepa Mills and the Praga Tools Corporation.

The control of these Companies was spread over ten Ministries of the Central Government. Twenty-three Companies fell within the jurisdiction of the Ministry of Commerce and Industry; eight within the Ministry of Steel, Mines and Fuel; five within the Ministry of Transport and Communication; two each within the Ministry of Defence, the Ministry of Works, Housing and Supply, and the Department of Atomic Energy; and one each within the Ministry of Scientific Research and Cultural Affairs, the Ministry of Irrigation, the Ministry of Rehabilitation and the Ministry of Finance. The Ministry of Commerce and Industry, which claimed the largest number of enterprises, had inherited many concerns from the Ministry of Production (created in May 1952 and abolished with effect from April 17, 1957). Among the initial responsibilities placed on the Ministry of Production were: (i) Coal; (ii) Salt; (iii) Oil Refineries; (iv) Steel Projects; (v) Sindri Fertilizers Project; (vi) Visakhapatnam Shipyard; and (vii) Bangalore Machine Tool Project. 'The main idea was to concentrate Government effort during the pioneering stage of its entry into the industrial field in a dynamic way.'[8] Thus the Ministry of Production played the rôle of a professional promoter, and after nearly five years of useful existence it was considered unnecessary![9] The Ministry of Production tried to set standards for the management of public enterprises in India, with

[8] *Ministry of Production*, last Annual Report, 1956-57, p. 1.

[9] Chapter I, paragraph 24, of the last Report summarizes the results of experiments during these five years: (1) The Company form of organization has been the most fruitful; (2) Attempts to build up sound conventions for the proper discharge of responsibility from the ground organization right up to Parliament; (3) Special attention to autonomy, decentralization of functions and authority; (4) Constant endeavour to carry full benefits of experience gained both technical and managerial, in the private sector—association of non-official directors and technical experts (including foreign experts and consultants); (5) Labour leaders were appointed Directors on several of the Boards—also special efforts regarding adequate pay scales and amenities; (6) keeping prices low 'in public interest'.

particular emphasis on autonomy. Its annual reports contained the Balance Sheets, Profit and Loss Accounts, Directors' Reports and other useful information about the constituent concerns. Many of these items are not to be found in the reports of successor Ministries. The ten 'autonomous' companies' managed by the Ministry of Production at the time of its liquidation were: Sindri Fertilizers and Chemicals (with an authorized capital of Rs 30 crores); Hindustan Shipyard (Rs 10 crores); Hindustan Cables (Rs 3 crores); Hindustan Machine Tools (Rs 12 crores); Hindustan Insecticides (Rs 1 crore); Hindustan Antibiotics (Rs 4 crores); Nangal Fertilizers and Chemicals (Rs 30 crores); Heavy Electricals (Rs 30 crores); National Coal Development Corporation (Rs 50 crores); and Neyveli Lignite Corporation (Rs 25 crores).

In the case of Government Companies established after January 26, 1950 (when the constitution of the Indian Republic came into force), the promoter's rôle was formally assumed by the President of India. The Companies Act requires that in the case of Private Companies, the Memorandum and the Articles of Association should be signed by at least two persons. To comply with this formality, the documents were signed by the President of India (through some Departmental Secretary) and some other official(s) of the relevant Department. In the case of the Indian Telephone Industries registered on January 25, 1950, under the Mysore Companies Act (XVIII of 1938), the Memorandum of Association was subscribed by the Governor-General through Mr V. K. R. Menon, ICS (for 10,000 shares); Mr V. K. R. Menon as Secretary, Ministry of Communications (for 100 shares); Mr R. Narayanaswami, Ministry of Finance (for 100 shares), and Mr A. F. Bennett for the Automatic Telephone and Electric Co. Ltd, London (for 6,667 shares). Thus the same official may put two signatures on the Memorandum, one on behalf of the President (or the Governor-General) and another as Secretary of the Ministry concerned. The Memorandum of Association of the National Industrial Development Corporation dated October 20, 1954, was signed by three persons. The President of India (through Mr H. V. R. Iengar, Secretary, Ministry of Commerce and Industry) took 9,998 shares. Mr S. Bhoothalingam, Special Secretary, and Mr L. K. Jha, Joint Secretary of the Ministry, took one share each.

Even in the case of Mixed Companies (first and third categories), the Government of India have generally taken care to obtain a commanding position in the ownership. For example, in the case of the Indian Telephone Industries, the capital contribution on March 31, 1958, stood as follows: the Government of India, Rs 3,58,74,500; the Government of Mysore, Rs 31,25,000; and the Automatic Telephone and Electric Co. Ltd, Rs 10,00,500. Thus the Government of India's share amounted to 90 per cent. Beside this, the Company had obtained unsecured loans from the Central Government; these stood at Rs 75,84,200 on March 31, 1958. In the case of the Hindustan Shipyard Ltd, registered on January 21, 1952,[10] the Government (in the name of the President of India) took shares of the value of Rs 208.50 lakhs as against Scindias' share of Rs 104.25 lakhs. Thus the mixed ownership was initially based on 2 : 1 ratio. By March 31, 1959, the shareholdings of the Government had increased (mainly through conversion of Debenture and other loans into share capital) to Rs 413.92 lakhs, whereas the capital contributed by the Scindias remained constant at Rs 104.25 lakhs. Thus, out of a total paid-up capital of Rs 518.17 lakhs, Government's share stood at about 80 per cent.

In the case of Ashoka Hotels, a promoters' Agreement was entered into between the President of India, His Highness the Maharaja Jamsaheb Digvijayasinghji of Nawanagar, and Mr Harbans Lal Chadha of Dehra Dun. The Agreement stipulated the formation of a public limited company with an authorized and fully subscribed capital of one crore of rupees of which the Government was to subscribe and pay for 2,500 Preference Shares of the aggregate face value of Rs 25 lakhs and to exercise voting rights in proportion to its share in the paid-up capital. The Government were to use their good offices for extending all help and facilities regarding promotion, sanctions, permits, etc., and to allot suitable area in Chanakya Puri, New Delhi, for the purpose of the Hotel. The Company was to pay a premium to the Government on account of lease rights at the rate of Rs 50,000 per acre by December 31, 1956, plus an annual rent at the rate of $2\frac{1}{2}$ per cent of the amount of the said premium. Under clause 7 of the Agreement the Government were not (either solely or jointly with any other person directly or indirectly) to carry on (or be interested in) the business of any other Hotel or like concern within the limits of Diplomatic Enclave of New Delhi. Further, the Government were not to 'permit or transfer any other person to commence or start any Hotel or like concern within the said limits'. Thus the joint enterprise was to enjoy immunity from competitive conditions, even though the Government *were* to hold only minority interest. However, by September 30, 1956, the Government had taken up shares to the extent of Rs 76 lakhs out of the subscribed capital of Rs 91,85,100 as on that date. Thus Ashoka

[10] The foundation of the Shipyard was laid in June 1941 by Dr Rajendra Prasad, who was then the President of the Indian National Congress. This venture was pioneered by the Scindia Steam Navigation Company Limited and the work of building ocean-going ships commenced in 1946. The first vessel, ss 'Jalausha', was launched by the Prime Minister, Pandit Jawaharlal Nehru, on March 14, 1948. On the recommendation of the Estimates Committee (1950-51), the Government of India took over the Visakhapatnam Shipyard and entered into a partnership with the Scindias.

Hotels Limited became a Government Company under Section 617 of the Companies Act, 1956. Later on, the balance of the (unissued) capital amounting to Rs 8,14,900 was also taken up by the Government. On July 1, 1959, the authorized and paid-up capital of the Company was increased to Rs 1.5 crores, the Government purchasing all the additional shares. Thus the total Government shareholding rose to Rs 1,34,14,900 (about 90 per cent) as against the private shareholding of Rs 15,85,100.

The Articles of Association of the various Government Companies generally provide that the President of India shall have the right to appoint all the Directors with the exception of the Directors to be appointed by technical consultants or other interests. Thus, in the case of the Indian Telephone Industries, the Automatic Telephone and Electric Co. Ltd shall, during the period of fifteen years from May 3, 1948, under the terms of an Agreement with the President of India, have the right to appoint one Director. In the case of the Hindustan Insecticides (fully State-owned) a representative of the DCM Chemical Works (with whom a six-year agreement was entered into for the supply of raw materials) was nominated on the Board of Directors by the President of India.[11] The Eastern Shipping Corporation, up to August 15, 1956, was in the nature of a joint venture between the Government and the Scindias. Under Article 3 of the Articles of Association, the Corporation was to enter into a Managing Agency Agreement with the Scindia Steam Navigation Company Limited. There was another agreement between the President of India and the Corporation covering the indemnity and refunds in connection with the business of the Corporation. It was specifically provided in the Articles that the Eastern Shipping Corporation being formed on the basis of these Agreements, 'No objection shall be taken to the said Agreements nor shall any Promoter or Director be liable to account to the Company (the Eastern Shipping Corporation) for any profit or benefit derived by him.' This was a major concession to the private industrialists and was inspired by the desire on the part of the Government to take advantage of Scindias' experience, in the initial stages, even at the cost of basic principles. Article 111 empowered the Central Government to appoint or nominate one Director to be known as 'Special Director'. Such Special Directors 'shall be entitled to hold office until requested to retire by the said Government. None of the provisions of qualification, disqualifications, retirement by rotation or removal shall apply to them'. The Scindias were entitled to appoint two

[11] The first Board nominated by the President of India consisted of five Directors: (1) a Joint Secretary, Ministry of Production; (2) a Joint Secretary, Ministry of Finance; (3) Chief Adviser, Ministry of Commerce and Industry; (4) Director, Malaria Institute of India; (5) a DCM man.

ex-officio Directors under Article 112. Originally, this right was based on two conditions: (i) so long as the Scindia Steam Navigation Co. Ltd continue to be Managing Agents; and (ii) so long as they hold not less than 20 per cent of the total *original* issued share capital (and of such further capital as might be issued out of the original authorized capital of Rs 10 crores). But as a result of the amendments effective from August 15, 1956, the first condition was waived. Further, the *ex-officio* Directors were renamed as Scindia Directors who 'shall be entitled to hold office until requested to retire by the said Scindia Steam Navigation Co. Ltd. None of the provisions relating to retirement or removal shall apply' to them.

Article 117 of the Articles of Association of Ashoka Hotels Ltd provides that 'unless otherwise determined by a general meeting, the number of directors shall not be less than seven nor more than twenty-four'. Under Article 119, the President was entitled to nominate two Special Directors. The Jamsaheb (or his successor) was entitled to nominate three Special Directors so long as shares of the aggregate nominal value of Rs 1,50,000 were held by him. Mr Harbans Lal Chadha could nominate two Special Directors so long as his shareholding did not fall below Rs 1,00,000. The Special Directors were not required to hold any qualification shares, and they were not bound to retire by rotation. They were to hold office until removed or required to retire by the person nominating them (or until they themselves retired). Further, under Article 120, provision was made for the appointment of Debenture Directors and Mortgage Directors, both of these not being required to hold qualification shares. For any other Director, the prescribed qualification was the holding of shares of the nominal value of Rs 5,000 (the *maximum* limit prescribed in the Companies Act of 1956). The Directors (other than Debenture Directors and Mortgage Directors) were to be paid a remuneration at the rate of Rs 1,000 per mensem for each Director, 'unless the Company in general meeting otherwise directs'. The remuneration of a Debenture Director or Mortgage Director was to be a sum not exceeding Rs 100 for each meeting attended by him. In addition to fixed monthly payments, Directors could be paid additional remuneration for 'extra service' or 'special exertions'. Thus the provisions regarding Directors' remuneration were made very liberal. The Jamsaheb, after investing Rs 1,50,000, could get a permanent royalty of Rs 36,000 per year (three Directors @ Rs 1,000 p.m.) and Mr Chadha, on an investment of Rs 1,00,000, could draw Rs 24,000 per year (two Directors @ Rs 1,000 p.m.).

Although the Boards of Government Companies are so much under the control of Departmental Secretaries, it is customary to impose restrictions on the decision-making powers of the Directors. Thus, Article 120 of the Articles of Association of the Hindustan

Shipyard Ltd lays down that the Chairman of the Board of Directors shall reserve, for the consideration of the Central Government, any proposals or decisions of the Board in respect of issue of shares and Debentures, capital expenditure exceeding Rs 20 lakhs, borrowings in excess of 25 per cent of the paid-up capital (or at a rate of interest exceeding the Reserve Bank rate by more than 1 per cent), winding up of the company or any other matter which, in the opinion of the Chairman, is an important issue fit to be reserved for the consideration of the Central Government. However, if the Central Government's views be not received within a period of two months, the Directors shall be entitled to act in accordance with the proposal or decision without further reference to the Central Government. Among other restrictions on the Board's powers of management, mention may be made of the following provision: 'Provided, however, that the appointment of any person to a grade the maximum of which is Rs 2,000/- or more per mensem shall not be made without the prior approval of the Central Government.'

There are similar restrictions on appointments and capital expenditure in the case of the National Coal Development Corporation. There are two other restrictions, viz, on 'payment to any person employed by the Company of a commission on the profits of any particular transaction or of a share in the general profits of the Company' and on 'division of profits'. Further, on important issues, no decision shall be taken in the absence of the Chairman appointed by the President. However, the Board of Directors of the Ashoka Hotels Ltd were not subjected to the restrictions normally prescribed with regard to borrowing, capital expenditure, investments, dividends, etc. The credit goes to the Jamsaheb and Mr Chadha for their negotiating skill. The only important restriction was with regard to the appointment of the General Manager (requiring previous approval of the President in writing). But even here the Board of Directors were free to determine the General Manager's remuneration.

In the case of the National Industrial Development Corporation, it was laid down that 'No action shall be taken in respect of any proposal or decision of the Directors reserved for the approval of the President as aforesaid until his approval to the same has been obtained.' As against this, in other cases, the Directors were free to act according to their own decision if no reply had been received from the Government within two months. To add to the powers of the Government, Article 87 of the National Industrial Development Corporation provides: 'Notwithstanding anything contained in any of these Articles, the President may from time to time issue such directives or instructions as he may think fit in regard to the finances and the conduct of the business and affairs of the Company, and the

Directors shall duly comply with and give effect to such directives or instructions.' This provision is on the pattern of Public Corporations.

PERFORMANCE[12]

Government Companies, on the basis of the tasks entrusted to them, could be divided into three categories:

A. *Industrial Companies*, i.e. whose main activity is manufacturing (including repairing) or production as such;

B. *Commercial Companies*, i.e. whose main activity is trading, transportation or the rendering of such other services on commercial basis; and

C. *Development Companies*, i.e. whose main activity is promotional or developmental—to encourage industrial or commercial development in general—including exploration, research and finance.

A. *Industrial Companies*

In the earlier stages, public industrial enterprise was often associated with defence requirements. While many of the concerns were run on departmental basis, there did appear a number of corporate enterprises popularly known as 'Defence Companies'. In this category we have the Hindustan Aircraft Ltd (1940), the Indian Rare Earths (1950) and the Bharat Electronics Ltd (1954). The Hindustan Aircraft Ltd (HAL) was registered as a Private Limited Company on December 23, 1940 (as a joint enterprise of the Government of India and the Government of Mysore). It was run by a comparatively small Board of Directors consisting of six persons, including the Chairman (Defence Secretary) and the Managing Director. The activities of HAL cover a wide range of projects, including designing and manufacture of aircraft, overhaul and repair of various types of airframes, engines and accessories, and manufacture of rail coaches and bus bodies.[13] HAL have sold a large number of prefabricated bus body kits, which can be easily assembled by the operators in their own workshops. These are now serving the major State-owned Road

[12] The performance of the Hindustan Steel Ltd (Industrial Company), the State Trading Corporation of India Ltd (Commercial Company) and the National Industrial Development Corporation Ltd (Development Company) is indicated in Appendices C, D and E.

[13] The design of all-metal rail coaches was based on aircraft construction principles. According to a brochure issued on the occasion of the Industries Fair 1955, over 700 coaches had already been delivered. According to a more recent brochure (undated, but made available in 1958) over 1,100 coaches had been delivered by HAL Railcoach Factory. By the end of December 1958, four semi-completed integral coach shells built at Machinefabric Augsburg Nuernberg (Man) of West Germany had been delivered to the Indian Railways—*Ministry of Defence Report*, 1958-59, p. 35.

Transport Companies. The future programme of HAL is to take steps for the manufacture of jet engines, high-speed fighters and high-speed trainer aircraft. It has developed an ultra-light aircraft, the *Pushpak,* which made its first flight successfully on September 24, 1958.[14] As a Defence Company, the Hindustan Aircraft Ltd presents certain peculiar characteristics. The Indian Air Force being the principal user of the services rendered by the Company, there has been a good deal of hesitation in associating non-official experts (in aviation, steel or aluminium industry) with the organization. Moreover, HAL has been subjected to four different kinds of audit: (a) by Company Auditors; (b) by the Comptroller and Auditor-General; (c) by the Accounts Department of Defence Services (with regard to claims preferred by HAL); and (d) by the Accounts Department of the Indian Railways (with regard to claims preferred by HAL). This has also increased the necessity of analysing costs and keeping them under constant check. The Company has been faced with the problem of obtaining prompt payments from the customers. HAL has also been faced with the problem of rationalizing pay structures, 70 per cent of the total employees being governed by a daily-rated pay system. An attempt has been made to solve the problem of absenteeism by introducing the Attendance Bonus Scheme. Further, the Production Bonus Scheme adopted during the year 1958-59 covered all employees except apprentices, Government servants on deputation, trainees, employees on study leave and casual labour drawing a basic salary of Rs 500/- and below. The profits of HAL figured at Rs 28.02 lakhs in 1955-56, Rs 32.29 lakhs in 1956-57, and Rs 34.16 lakhs in 1957-58. Although this means hardly a return of 3 per cent (the paid-up capital being Rs 10.3 crores—Rs 9.7 crores contributed by the Government of India and Rs 0.6 crores by the Government of Mysore—and Central Government loans standing at Rs 53.85 lakhs on March 31, 1957), we can be happy over the situation that there are no losses, and that the profits have been increased during these years.[15]

The Sindri Fertilizers and Chemicals Ltd, registered on December

[14] During World War II, the Company had handled complete overhaul, repair and conversion of Dakota aircraft from overseas customers like Saudi Arabian Airlines (Jeddah), Arabian American Oil Co (Dhahran), Dir Ceylon (Colombo), Ethiopian Airlines (Addis Ababa) and Union of Burma Airways (Rangoon). HAL has finalized arrangements with Messrs Folland Aircraft and Bristol Aeroplane Company of UK for the manufacture and assembly of Gnat Aircraft and Orpheus Engines respectively.

[15] The Company has been able to make substantial appropriations to several Funds: (1) Plant Rehabilitation and Development Reserve—3s 13.54 lakhs (1955-56), Rs 7.08 lakhs (1956-57) and Rs 8.41 lakhs (1957-58); (2) Research & Development Reserve—Rs 15.51 lakhs (1956-57) and Rs 15.84 lakhs (1957-58); and (3) General Reserve—Rs 3.36 lakhs (1956-57) and Rs 3 lakhs (1957-58).

18, 1951, was the first Government Company to have received widespread public attention. This may partly be due to the urgent necessity of popularizing chemical fertilizers in India after the Bengal Famine of 1943 and general deterioration on the food front.[16] In 1947, the Fertilizers and Chemicals (Travancore) Ltd, popularly known as FACT, commissioned a plant to produce 150 tons of ammonium sulphate and 100 tons of super-phosphate per day. The construction of the Sindri factory had been taken in hand departmentally in 1945, but it went into production on October 31, 1951.[17] The production of ammonium sulphate manifested a consistent increase from 0.35 lakh tons in 1951-52 to 3.34 lakh tons in 1956-57, but thereafter the figure fell to 3.30 lakh tons in 1958-59. The net profit of the Company continued to rise up to the year 1954-55, when it stood at Rs 173 lakhs, as against Rs 47 lakhs in 1953-54. It fell to Rs 164 lakhs in 1955-56; but thereafter it rose to a record figure of Rs 205 lakhs in 1956-57. The net profit fell to Rs 156 lakhs in 1957-58, rising slightly to Rs 159 lakhs in 1958-59.[18] The company declared a dividend of 2 per cent in 1954-55; 4 per cent in 1955-56; 5 per cent in 1956-57; and again 5 per cent in 1957-58. The paid-up capital of the Company being Rs 17 crores (as against the authorized capital of Rs 30 crores), entirely subscribed by the Central Government, amounts by way of dividend figured at Rs 34 lakhs, Rs 68 lakhs, Rs 85 lakhs, and again Rs 85 lakhs respectively. On the whole, the performance of Sindri was well up to 1957, when certain unfavourable tendencies set in—stagnation in production, fall in profits and increase in price.[19]

[16] See 'Rôle of Fertilizer Industry in India's Economic Development' (Specially contributed), *Indian Journal of Economics,* Vol. XXXVI, No. 140, July 1955, p. 111. The first pioneering effort had already been made in Mysore, and a plant to produce 20 tons of ammonium sulphate per day was installed at Belagula in 1939.

[17] 'The Sindri Fertilizer Factory completed at a cost of over 23 crores of rupees is the first major industrial enterprise of the Government of India to come into fruition since independence. It is the largest and most modern fertilizer production plant in Asia and one of the finest specimens of chemical engineering in the world.' (Ministry of Production Report, 1954-55, p. 4.)

[18] This fall 'is mainly accounted for by an increase of Rs 34 lakhs due to railway freight and Rs 17 lakhs due to wealth tax and development reserve, in addition to normal increase in wages, etc.' (*Ministry of Commerce and Industry,* Annual Report, 1958-59, p. 54).

[19] On the recommendation of the Fertilizer Production Committee (report submitted on June 8, 1955) the Government of India decided to augment the production of fertilizers in the following manner: (1) a 60 per cent expansion of Sindri; (2) a nitrogen plant at Nangal with a capacity of 70,000 tons; and (3) a plant at Rourkela, utilizing the gases from steel. The control and management of the Nangal Fertilizer and Heavy Water Project was formally transferred to the Nangal Fertilizers and Chemicals (Private) Ltd on April

We now proceed to examine the performance of five Government Companies where the problem of foreign technical co-operation continued to dominate for a number of years. These are Hindustan Shipyard (1952), Hindustan Cables (1952), Hindustan Machine Tools (1953), Hindustan Insecticides (1954) and Hindustan Antibiotics (1954). The Hindustan Shipyard was taken over on March 1, 1952, at a valuation of Rs 272 lakhs worked out by an Expert Committee appointed for this purpose by the Government of India. Soon after the formation of the Hindustan Shipyard Ltd as a Government Company (with the participation of Scindias), an agreement was entered into in July 1952 with the French firm of shipbuilders, 'La Societe Anonyme des Ateliers et Chantiers de la Loire' (ACL). The ACL was to provide technical advice, establish a fully equipped and competent Designing and Estimating Office at Visakhapatnam, provide training and guidance to Indian personnel in the Shipyard as also in their own organization in France, place their purchasing organization and skill at the disposal of the Shipyard, help in obtaining from foreign countries the necessary priorities for steel, stores, materials and plant, and secure orders for ships from outside India. The ACL was to receive a commission of 4 per cent of the actual turnover of the Company. This commission (before deduction of income tax) worked out to Rs 2.28 lakhs, Rs 4.19 lakhs, Rs 7.44 lakhs, Rs 8.48 lakhs and Rs 10.50 lakhs during the years 1952-53, 1953-54, 1954-55, 1955-56 and 1956-57 respectively. Besides, the Shipyard was to pay for the services of a certain number of French technicians, the total payment for whom was not to exceed Rs 3 lakhs per year. The actual payments during the first five years aggregated Rs 8.72 lakhs. The agreement with the ACL was initially for five years. But it was extended for a year with effect from July 15, 1957. During this extended period, the commission payable was only 2 per cent on such of the turnover as did not exceed the average of the turnover of the previous two years, and 3 per cent on the excess over such average. The contract with the French consultants was ultimately terminated in July 1958. Hindustan Shipyard have since entered into an arrangement with Messrs Lubecker Flenderwerke, of Germany, 'by which they would make available the services of two or three expert technicians to the Shipyard, as and when required. These technicians will be from among those who have actually worked on the design and construction of these ships in the Lubecker shipyard and apart from the remuneration payable to these technicians as may be agreed upon mutually, no other fee or commis-

20, 1956. The authorized capital was Rs 30 crores (the same as that of Sindri) and the paid-up capital stood at Rs 13.30 crores as on October 31, 1959. Recently, these fertilizer factories in the public sector have been entrusted to the Fertilizer Corporation of India.

sion is payable to Messrs Lubecker Flenderwerke. Under this arrangement the German technicians will not be in executive charge of any department of the Shipyard but will only act as advisers.'[20]

The following table gives a comparative picture of the time taken in the building of ships at the Hindustan Shipyard before and after its nationalization:

Name of Ship	Date of laying keel	Date of completion	Time spent (months)
1. *Jalausha* (8,000 d.w.t.)	22.6.46	15.10.48	28
2. *Jalaprabha* (8,000 d.w.t.)	22.8.46	31.3.49	31
3. *Kutubtari* (245 d.w.t.)	23.5.47	19.5.49	24
4. *Jalaprakash* (8,000 d.w.t.)	27.5.48	14.12.49	19
5. *Jalapankhi* (8,000 d.w.t.)	7.1.49	31.3.50	15
6. *Jalapadma* (8,000 d.w.t.)	26.1.50	14.1.51	12
7. *Jalapalaka* (8,000 d.w.t.)	26.1.50	29.3.51	14
8. *Bharatmitra* (8,000 d.w.t.)	28.9.50	28.6.51	9
9. *Jagrani* V.C. 108 (8,000 d.w.t.)	9.5.51	4.6.52	13
10. *Jalapratap* V.C. 111 (8,000 d.w.t.)	9.5.51	31.7.52	15
11. *Jalapushpa* V.C. 112 (8,000 d.w.t.)	26.12.51	30.9.52	9
12. *Bharatratna* V.C. 114 (8,000 d.w.t.)	21.7.52	21.6.54	23
13. *Jalaputra* V.C. 115 (8,000 d.w.t.)	21.7.52	12.8.54	25
14. *Jalavihar* V.C. 116 (7,000 d.w.t.)	1.8.53	14.6.55	22
15. *Jalavijaya* V.C. 117 (7,000 d.w.t.)	30.9.53	17.12.55	27
16. *Vidyut* V.C. 123 (Motor Launch)	19.10.53	18.3.58	53
17. *Jalavishnu* V.C. 119 (7,000 d.w.t.)	16.12.53	16.5.56	29
18. *State of Kutch* V.C. 118 (8,000 d.w.t.)	2.9.54	1.11.56	26
19. *Kort Nozzle* Tug V.C. 124 (242 g.r.t.)	27.9.54	20.9.57	36
20. *Andamans* V.C. 135 (4,000 d.w.t.)	10.8.55	4.12.57	28
21. *State of Orissa* V.C. 120 (8,000 d.w.t.)	8.12.55	31.12.57	25
22. *Jalavikram* V.C. 121 (7,000 d.w.t.)	16.4.56	26.3.58	23
23. *Jalaveera* V.C. 122 (7,000 d.w.t.)	4.8.56	4.7.58	23

With regard to the ships completed before nationalization, the average gap between the date of laying keel and the date of completion was nineteen months. But for the ships completed after nationalization this gap had widened to twenty-five months.[21] It may further be noted that during the three years preceding nationalization the average gap was only twelve months; during the three years *following* nationalization, this gap was seventeen months. The

[20] *Hindustan Shipyard*, 6th Annual Report, 1957-58, p. 9.
[21] The delivery dates for three ships ordered by the Eastern Shipping Corporation were changed a number of times. There was a delay of twenty-nine months (as against the original schedule) in the delivery of the first ship. Another ship, MV *Andamans*, suffered from a deficiency in stability. How subtle can be the comment of one public enterprise on another would be evident from the speech (December 17, 1957) of Mr R. R. Saksena, Chairman of ESC. 'It would be inappropriate for me to comment on the working of the Hindustan Shipyard, but I am sure you would wish to join me in the hope which was also expressed last year that in future the yard will pay greater attention to the construction of vessels and will adhere strictly to delivery schedules.'

Hindustan Shipyard has, generally speaking, been running at a loss. The loss was Rs 15.48 lakhs in 1952-53, Rs 7.66 lakhs in 1953-54, Rs 0.78 lakhs in 1955-56, Rs 3.69 lakhs in 1956-57 and Rs 4.75 lakhs in 1957-58. In the year 1954-55, there was a nominal profit of Rs 1.21 lakhs which was later converted into a loss of Rs 47,348 because the Government did not allow the full subsidy claimed by the company. During the year 1957-58 the company was paid an advance subsidy of over Rs 56 lakhs, and the total advances up to March 31, 1958, exceeded Rs 390 lakhs.

In the case of the Hindustan Cables, Messrs Standard Telephones and Cables Ltd (STC) of London were chosen as technical consultants and a Technical Agreement was signed in November 1949 for a period of twenty years. The STC provided the patent rights, technical know-how, supervision in construction and also training facilities to Indian engineers in their factory in England. For these services, the STC were to be paid as follows:

(i) 6 per cent of the total cost of the factory, plant, fixtures and equipments, subject to a ceiling of £30,000;

(ii) 6 per cent of the total cost of any expansion or improvement to the factory if the Government appoints the STC to undertake such expansion or improvement; and

(iii) 2 per cent of the selling price of all goods produced or sold by the factory payable at the end of each year with a guaranteed minimum payment of £3,000 for the first year and £5,000 for the second and third years. The minimum was to be increased on a percentage basis to allow for the introduction of co-axial and carrier cables—not estimated at that time—so that the guaranteed minimum annual payment shall not exceed £10,000.

It is gratifying to note that the work of technical consultants in this case was found to be satisfactory. Although the factory went into regular production on September 1, 1954 (nearly five years after the date of the agreement), the delay could not be ascribed to the technical consultants. As a matter of fact, this project, like some others, was shelved by the Government for reasons of financial stringency. Construction work was started in 1951 under departmental supervision and a Private Limited Company was created on August 4, 1952. As on March 31, 1959, the Company's paid-up capital stood at Rs 124.97 lakhs. Initially, the Company worked at a loss, which figured at Rs 2.48 lakhs for the year 1954-55. But there was a profit of Rs 6.07 lakhs during 1955-56; Rs 9.93 lakhs during 1956-57; and Rs 10.10 lakhs during 1957-58. The Company declared a dividend of 2 per cent during 1956-57 and a similar dividend during 1957-58. The production during the first six months (September 1954 to March 1955) was only 112 miles of cables. But during 1955-56 it figured at 525 miles as against an annual target of 470 miles. During 1956-57, against the target of 555 miles, the actual production was 592 miles. But the progress of the factory was disturbed during 1957-58 when the production was only 538 miles. However, it improved to 636 miles in 1958-59. The factory which is located at Rupnarainpur near Chittaranjan in West Bengal caters for the needs of the Posts and Telegraphs Department in the matter of tele-communication cables. The imports of paper-insulated, head-covered and armoured telephone cables were costing the country about Rs $1\frac{1}{2}$ crores per year.

The Disposals Utilization Committee set up by the Government of India in 1947 had given the highest priority to the establishment of a Machine Tool Factory. The Government accepted this recommendation and the then Ministry of Industry and Supply started working on it in 1948. On March 29, 1949, a Provisional Agreement was entered into with Messrs Oerlikon of Switzerland who were to render all technical assistance regarding the erection of the factory, the training of Indian personnel and direction and supervision of production in the factory for twenty years. They were to disclose secret processes and manufacturing secrets so that the production of the factory reaches the same standard as that of their factory in Switzerland (with comparable cost). Messrs Oerlikon were to train in India as well as in their factory in Switzerland Indian personnel so that within a period of ten years there would be sufficient number available to hold not less than 85 per cent of the technical posts in the factory. The technical consultants were to take 10 per cent of the shares of the Company, Government having the option to buy these shares at the end of twenty years. A return of 5 per cent was to be guaranteed, for the first five years, on Messrs Oerlikon's investment in shares. Government were to assign, free of payment, 5 per cent of the shares of the Company in consideration of the transfer of licence by the technical consultants for the setting up of the factory and the maintenance of machine tools in the factory. Lastly, Messrs Oerlikon were to receive a royalty on a sliding scale—4 to 2 per cent—on actual sales of the products of the factory over a period of twenty years.

From the date of the technical agreement, it took the Government some twenty months (March 28, 1949, to November 11, 1950) to obtain the approval of the Standing Finance Committee for the project. The Cabinet sanction came in December 1950. The designing work was started in August 1951, but the technical experts took some ten months to arrive at a decision in this regard. In May 1952, the design of lathe was altered from hydraulic-electronomic type to the mechanical type 'as the latter was best suited to the conditions prevailing in India'. In June 1952 it was 'discovered' that the design was more suited for a $10\frac{1}{2}$-inch centre lathe. Thus, lack of foresight and planning resulted in much loss.

Details regarding capital, cost, time-table and organization chart had been completed on July 7, 1952. But there was a waiting period of no less than eight months before the company could be registered on February 7, 1953. The production of component parts was started in October 1954. But, up to December 1955, only twelve lathes could be assembled; and of these, only two could be placed on the market during the year 1955. The first batch of predominantly Indian lathes manufactured by the factory rolled off the assembly line on March 31, 1956. By March 31, 1957, 148 lathes had been manufactured. The factory produced 402 machines (313 lathes and 89 milling machines) valued at Rs $1\frac{1}{2}$ crores during the year 1957-58, 'thus reaching the Second Plan Target of 400 fixed for 1960-61, three years in advance'. During the year 1958-59, production stood at 552 machines (consisting of 240 lathes, 262 milling machines and 50 radial drills). The original price of a lathe manufactured by Hindustan Machine Tools stood at Rs 39,000. This was reduced to Rs 36,000 with effect from June 1, 1957, and further to Rs 29,500 with effect from June 1, 1958. The Company earned a profit of Rs 3.9 lakhs during 1956-57. The profit for 1957-58 (including interest on loans advanced by the Government) stood at Rs 30.7 lakhs; that for 1958-59 figured at Rs 41.96 lakhs.[22]

The Estimates Committee, in their report dated June 29, 1955, noted that the Swiss technicians had already been paid a sum of Rs 20.8 lakhs (Rs 5.3 lakhs as salaries in Switzerland, Rs 12.2 lakhs as salaries in India and Rs 3.3 lakhs as passage for Swiss employees). The Committee saw 'no justification for the payment by the Company of such a huge sum of Rs 5,31,515 towards salaries of certain European technicians'. Further, the Estimates Committee were not convinced regarding the justification of employing eighty-four foreign technicians whose total annual emoluments came to Rs 28 lakhs. The financial participation of the Swiss firm was terminated in 1957 and a fresh agreement was executed whereby all the shares held by them were purchased by the Government of India. On March 31, 1959, the issued share capital of the Company stood at Rs 5.31 crores. On June 9, 1958, the Company signed a technical collaboration agreement with the West German firm of Messrs Herman Kolb for the manufacture of ten types of radial drills. Again, on January 2, 1959, a technical collaboration agreement was signed with the French firm of Messrs H. Ernault Batignolles. The first batch of lathes under this arrangement was completed in June 1959.

The Hindustan Insecticides Ltd was registered on March 11, 1954, to manage the DDT factory established under the Joint Plan of Operations, dated July 19, 1952, drawn by the Government of India,

---

[22] *Hindustan Machine Tools,* Annual Report, 1958-59, p. 5. After providing for interest, the net profit came to Rs 32.98 lakhs.

the World Health Organization (WHO), and the United Nations International Children's Emergency Fund (UNICEF). This was necessitated by the large quantities of DDT required for combating malaria (and the problem of importing the same on account of foreign exchange difficulties). UNICEF was to supply all imported equipment involving an expenditure of $100,000 (Rs 4,76,000); and the Government of India was to arrange for the provision of land, building, steam, power, electricity, etc., at an estimated cost of Rs 22,45,000 (about $450,000). The estimate of the expenditure to be incurred by the Government was later revised to Rs 37,77,000.[23]

The Report of the Ministry of Production for the year 1952-53 had claimed that the factory would go into production before the end of 1953. Later, the Ministry's Report for 1953-54 shifted this target date to September 1954. But the factory actually commenced production on March 25, 1955. The main reasons for the delay appear to have been the protracted negotiations which had to be carried out with the DCM Chemical Works,[24] and the time taken in the preparation of estimates in obtaining approval thereof by Government, and in observing the formalities of inviting tenders, etc.

Under Article V(7) of the Plan of Operations, the Company is required to operate on a non-profit basis. 'It is gratifying that in the first year of working it has been possible to charge, on a no-profit-no-loss basis, a price lower than the price of imported production.'[25] While, for the year 1955-56, a Profit and Loss Account had been published, the Company prepared an Income and Expenditure Account for the year ending March 31, 1957. The excess of income over expenditure amounted to Rs 8,70,480 (including a carry over of Rs 2,976 from the year 1955-56). But this amount was to be refunded to the Malaria Institute due to the excess price charged from that organization.

The Delhi factory produced 284 tons of Technical DDT during 1955-56, 518 tons during 1956-57, 694 tons during 1957-58, and 1,288 tons during 1958-59. Initially designed to produce 700 tons of Technical DDT, the Delhi factory has been expanded to double its output. A generous allocation of $275,000 (Rs 13.09 lakhs out of a

[23] Estimates Committee, 27th Report, 1955-56. Lok Sabha Secretariat, New Delhi, April 1956, p. 16.

[24] It was decided to establish the factory near the Delhi Cloth Mills Chemical Works. The exact location was included as an item in the agreement between the Government of India and the International Organizations even before the negotiations with the DCM Chemical Works had been concluded. This put the latter in a favourable bargaining position. Further, while the ownership of land was in dispute, and while attempts were being made by the Ministry of Health through the Delhi Improvement Trust to obtain land for Government, part payment was made to the Chemical Works on account of lease charges.

[25] Hindustan Insecticides Private Ltd, 3rd Annual Report, 1956-57, p. 4.

total estimate of Rs 21.24 lakhs) for the supply of additional plant and equipment has aided the expansion programme. Further, on October 11, 1955, the Government of India had communicated their decision to place the second DDT factory at Alwaye (Kerala) under the control of the Company.[26] The production was inaugurated in July 1958, and was increased to a record figure of 123 tons of Technical DDT in October 1958, one month ahead of the schedule. Total output at Alwaye, during the year 1958-59, was 812 tons.

The Government of India accepted an offer of monetary and technical assistance for the setting up of a Penicillin Project and a Joint Plan of Operations was signed by three parties—Government, WHO and UNICEF—on July 24, 1951. The agreement visualized the production of (best quality) penicillin most economically as a national enterprise on a sound basis but entirely on a non-profit making basis. It also provided for the production of other antibiotics, the development of research and training in that field, and the free treatment of patients, particularly women and children. The responsibilities undertaken by WHO were taken over by the United Nations Technical Assistance Administration with effect from July 1, 1953. The site of the factory was chosen at Pimpri, near Poona. Its control was transferred with effect from June 1, 1954, to the Hindustan Antibiotics Ltd (registered on March 13, 1954). Whereas the target of full production (750,000 mega units per month) was to be achieved by December 31, 1954, the level was actually reached in February 1956. The production of finished penicillin rose from 0.62 million m.u. in 1955-56 to 16.15 million m.u. in 1956-57, 21.243 million m.u. in 1957-58 and 25.20 million m.u. in 1958-59. The Company's working has shown considerable improvement. During 1955-56, the Company had suffered a loss of Rs 8.03 lakhs,[27] but in 1956-57 there was a nominal profit of Rs 57,608. The net profit rose to Rs 33.43 lakhs in 1957-58 and further to Rs 87.10 lakhs in 1958-59.

B. *Commercial Companies*

The Eastern Shipping Corporation Ltd was the first Government Company to be established in this category. It was registered as a

---

[26] A Technical Agreement was signed with Messrs Singmaster and Breyer of New York with great difficulty. The Company wanted to ensure a shorter delivery period and suitable performance guarantees and bonus penalty commitments (i.e. learning a lesson from the working of the Delhi unit). Two firms which had originally tendered for the Formulating Unit withdrew their offers when they came to know of the difficulties of grinding DDT in the summer months.

[27] The Pimpri factory had actually suffered a loss of Rs 19.83 lakhs. This was considerably reduced because of a substantial earning of Rs 11.80 lakhs made by the Bottling Plant at Bombay.

Public Limited Company on March 24, 1950, with an authorized capital of Rs 10 crores. Its paid-up capital rose from Rs 2 crores as on March 31, 1951, to Rs 6.25 crores as on March 31, 1959. At the outset, the Corporation was in the nature of a joint venture between the Government of India and the Scindias. But the Scindia Steam Navigation Co. Ltd ceased to be the Managing Agent with effect from August 15, 1956, pursuant to Section 325(4) of the Indian Companies Act, 1956 (which provides that where, at the commencement of the Act, a Company having a Managing Agent was itself acting as Managing Agent of any other Company, the term of office of the Company first mentioned as Managing Agent of the other Company would expire on the 15th day of August, 1956). The Sixth Annual Report of the Corporation pays tribute to the important rôle played by the Scindias during this period: 'The Corporation owes a great deal to Scindias' fostering care and guidance and for its record of expansion and its present, in the various trades. It is gratifying to record that Scindias have assured the Corporation of continued advice and guidance notwithstanding the termination of the Managing Agency arrangements.'[28]

The Eastern Shipping Corporation was running the following services (*mainly* East of India) during the year 1956-57:

(1) India/Australia (two ships with two round voyages each);
(2) India/Japan (two ships with three voyages each);
(3) India/East Africa (one ship with eleven voyages);
(4) India/Malaya (one ship with fourteen voyages); and
(5) Mainland/Andamans (two voyages of a chartered vessel).

In November 1958, the Corporation had a small fleet consisting of six cargo steamers and only two passenger-cum-cargo steamers. The total tonnage (G.R.T.) of these eight vessels was 52,892. The inordinate delays caused by the Hindustan Shipyard in the delivery of ships (including defective construction in the case of MV *Andamans*), and the shortage of foreign exchange, have imposed serious limitations on the expansion of this fleet.[29]

Except for the year 1954-55, when there was a loss of Rs 19.01 lakhs, the working of the Eastern Shipping Corporation (up to March 1959) has been a profitable one. The profit figured at Rs 1.38 lakhs in 1950-51, Rs 22.54 lakhs in 1951-52, Rs 12.38 lakhs in 1952-53, Rs 4.07 lakhs in 1953-54, Rs 31.71 lakhs in 1955-56, Rs

[28] *The Eastern Shipping Corporation Ltd*, 6th Annual Report, 1955-56. p. 5.
[29] Another limitation, as pointed out by Mr. R. R. Saksena in his Chairman's speech on December 23, 1958, was the competition between the public sector and the private sector. So long as the Scindias were Managing Agents the ESC could not encroach on Scindia routes. Now it has been emphasized that there should be no encroachment by the private sector on the routes developed by the public sector.

35.12 lakhs in 1956-57, Rs 4.24 lakhs in 1957-58, and Rs 15.32 lakhs in 1958-59.

The Western Shipping Corporation (Private) Limited was registered on June 22, 1956. It has been a wholly Government-owned concern from the very beginning. Out of an authorized capital of Rs 10 crores, the paid-up capital stood at Rs 5.65 crores on March 31, 1959 (10,00,000 Equity Shares of Rs 100 each with Rs 56.50 per share called up). The Western Shipping Corporation was to operate initially in the India/Poland, India/Persian Gulf Trades and eventually in the India/Red Sea and the India/Soviet Services. It was also to operate a tanker service on the coast.[30] To start with, the Corporation purchased a second-hand tanker, *Soya Christina* (since renamed as *Desh Sewak*) of 1950 build, with a d.w.t. of 10,172 and a speed of 12 knots, at a price of £650,000. In December 1958 this was the only vessel in service. There were six vessels under construction—one with the Hindustan Shipyard, Visakhapatnam; two in West Germany; and one each in Italy, Yugoslavia and Japan. The Corporation made a nominal profit of Rs 20,955 during the year ending March 31, 1957; and a profit of Rs 3,48,942 during 1957-58 (after providing for normal depreciation amounting to Rs 6,43,023 and paying a sum of Rs 50,000 to the Eastern Shipping Corporation, being the reimbursement of expenses and the services rendered by them for the year).[31]

None of the policy statements had ever suggested that public enterprise in India should waste its meagre resources over the building up of what is described as 'the largest luxury hotel in the East'. But diplomatic considerations must have dictated the need for establishing a costly hotel in the Diplomatic Enclave of New Delhi on the basis of the promoter's Agreement dated May 31, 1955. The Ashoka Hotels Ltd was incorporated as a Public Limited Company on October 17, 1955. The authorized capital of Rs 1 crore was divided into 2,600 A class Preference Shares of Rs 1,000 each; 2,400 B class Preference Shares of Rs 1,000 each; and 50,000 Ordinary Shares of Rs 100 each. On July 1, 1959, the authorized and paid-up capital was raised to Rs 1.5 crores, Government shareholding being Rs 1,34,14,900 as against the private shareholding of Rs 15,85,100.

The construction work was completed on August 31, 1957, even though the Hotel had been thrown open to the public on October 30, 1956, when 200 rooms were needed for accommodating the delegates attending the UNESCO Conference and the Budha Jayanti

---

[30] *The Western Shipping Corporation (Private) Limited,* 1st Annual Report, 1956-57, p. 2.

[31] *Ibid.,* 2nd Annual Report, 1957-58, p. 2. The profit for the year 1958-59 stood at Rs 2,59,501.

Celebrations. Occupying an area of 21 acres of land, with its canti-levered 'Chhatri' 123 feet from the ground floor, the Hotel has been claimed to be the largest and the tallest building in India. Out of a total of 335 rooms, 195 were planned to be single rooms, 47 double rooms, 58 single suites, 23 double suites and 12 de-luxe suites (four of these being known as Saurashtra, Hyderabad, Kashmir and French suites). During the year ended September 30, 1957, as many as 19,497 guest nights were spent by foreign nationals, which indicates that 73.67 per cent of the clientele consisted of foreigners. The Hotel first concentrated on vast publicity within the country. It appears that much of it went waste. Later, it embarked on in-creased publicity in foreign countries. During the first year ended September 30, 1957, the average occupancy in the Hotel was only eighty persons per day. During the second year it rose to 214 per-sons. In these two years the Ashoka Hotels Ltd suffered losses of Rs 37.76 lakhs and Rs 15.77 lakhs respectively. For the third ac-counting period (October 1958 to March 1959—which constitutes the busy season) the average occupancy stood at 290. It rose to 294 between April 1959 and February 1960.

The Export Risks Insurance Corporation was registered in Bom-bay on July 30, 1957, as a Private Limited Company with an authorized capital of Rs 5 crores, in pursuance of the recommenda-tions made by the Export Credit Guarantee Committee in their report submitted to the Government in 1956. The Corporation offers facilities to the exporters to insure risks in the course of export trade which are not normally covered by commercial insurance companies. The insolvency of and the protracted default in making payment by buyers are the commercial risks and changes in import policy, delay in the transfer of funds stemming from payments diffi-culties of buyers' countries, war and civil war are the important political risks covered by the Corporation. Risks may be covered from the date of shipment (Shipments Policies) or from the date of contract for the sale of goods (Contracts Policies). In certain cases Specific Contract Policies and Consignment for Sale Policies may be issued. With regard to raw materials and consumer goods, risks are normally covered for a period not exceeding six months. Exporters are generally required to insure all their shipments of commodities of allied nature on credit terms. This is designed to secure a proper spread of risks and to keep the premium rates at as low a level as possible. However, exporters of traditional goods have been un-willing to get all their exports insured. They want this facility only for those markets which are not quite safe. In view of this, the Corporation has relaxed its rule by insuring exports to selected markets.

With a view to augmenting its business, the Export Risks

Insurance Corporation reduced the premium rates on an average by 10 per cent (even 20 per cent in certain cases) with effect from October 1, 1959. Further, as an incentive to exporters who make shipments for small amounts, the Corporation decided to charge only half the fee for credit reports in respect of applications received on and after February 1, 1960, for the approval of credit limits not exceeding Rs 20,000. The following table presents a classification of the policies in force on December 31, 1959 : [32]

Policies for	Number	Maximum Liability
1. Rs 50,000 and under	95	Rs 34.75 lakhs
2. Rs 50,000 to Rs 1,00,000	69	Rs 65.32 „
3. Rs 1,00,000 to 5,00,000	54	Rs 154.25 „
4. Over Rs 5,00,000	25	Rs 533.00 „
	243	Rs 787.32 lakhs

Thus, less than 10 per cent of the policies were in the highest bracket, although the same accounted for nearly two-thirds of the liability. The maximum liability of Rs 7.87 crores works out to less than $1\frac{1}{2}$ per cent of India's total exports. Although the Corporation insured exports to ninety-four countries, there were only eighteen such countries where the percentage of insured exports exceeded 5 per cent. In case of two countries only, the percentage of insured exports was higher than 20 per cent. Similarly, although the Corporation issued policies in respect of sixty-seven commodities, only in five cases did the proportion of insured exports exceed 20 per cent. However, in case of one commodity, 91 per cent of the exports had been insured by the Corporation. More significant than this was a 7 per cent hold in respect of a major commodity.

During the first year of its operation, the Export Risks Insurance Corporation suffered a loss. However, during the second accounting period (October 1958 to December 1959) the excess of income over outgoings amounted to Rs 2,60,117. Up to December 31, 1959, the Corporation had paid only four claims aggregating Rs 74,439. Hence the experience so far is not adequate to judge the success of the Corporation.

C. Development Companies

The National Research Development Corporation of India was the first Government Company in this category,[33] registered on Decem-

[32] The Export Risks Insurance Corporation Ltd, *Second Annual Report* (from October 1, 1958, to December 31, 1959). The total number of policies issued during this period was 300 as against 146 in the previous year.

[33] It is noteworthy that Development Companies appeared rather late on the scene (the First Five Year Plan had run for more than half of its period by 1953-end).

ber 31, 1953, in Delhi, as a Private Limited Company with an authorized capital of Rs 1 crore. The paid-up capital of the Company, as on March 31, 1958, stood at Rs 10 lakhs, consisting of 1,000 Ordinary Shares of Rs 1,000 each (fully paid).[34] Any further finance required by the Corporation 'will be provided by Government in the form of a long-dated loan either free of interest during the first few years or carrying a low rate of interest'.[35]

Till the end of 1953, the Industrial Liaison Committee dealt with patents and processes arising out of researches sponsored by the Council of Scientific and Industrial Research (CSIR). The Patents Advisory Committee was concerned with the exploitation of Government-owned patents. Both these organizations were working under the Ministry of Commerce and Industry. However, it was felt that there existed a wide gap between research and development which could be bridged effectively only by a specialized organization devoting itself exclusively to that work. The National Research Development Corporation is to develop and exploit in the public interest, for profit or otherwise, inventions (whether patentable or otherwise) of the CSIR, the Government of India, State Governments, commodity research committees and other statutory research organizations. It may also take up such other patents as may be voluntarily assigned to it by universities, research institutions or individuals. The Corporation is authorized to enter into reciprocal agreements with similar organizations in other countries to exploit Indian inventions in those countries and their inventions in India.[36] It may issue exclusive and/or non-exclusive licences on such terms and conditions regarding payment of premia, royalties, share of profits, etc., as are considered advisable to develop the invention and to ensure commercial production of the products of such inventions. In special circumstances, the Corporation may also reward any particular invention by gifts, rewards, *ex-gratia* payments or in such other manner as may be deemed fit. But it has no statutory powers of compulsorily acquiring patents and inventions; it can do so only by agreement and negotiations.

During the period ending March 31, 1955, 177 inventions were reported by various institutions. This figure fell to seventy-seven during 1955-56, rising to 134 in 1956-57, but again falling to fifty-

[34] *National Research Development Corporation of India,* Fourth Annual Report and Statement of Accounts, 1958, p. 12.

[35] *NRDC*: First Annual Report for the period ending March 31, 1955 (Cyclo-styled), p. 2. In recognition of its non-profit making character, a licence was granted under Section 26 of the Indian Companies Act, 1913, enabling the Corporation to dispense with the word 'Limited'.

[36] By March 31, 1958, arrangements had been finalized with the NRDC of the United Kingdom, the Canadian Patent Department and the Patent Department (T.N.O.) of Holland.

nine in 1957-58. The progressive total stood at 447 on March 31, 1958.[37] However, it is disappointing to find that only sixteen processes were 'licensed and in production' and thirty-three processes were 'licensed but not yet in production'. As many as 138 processes were just in a preliminary stage; and no less than seventy-seven processes had to be abandoned. The total value of commercial production *of all the processes* stood at Rs 2 lakhs only for 1957-58. It was expected to reach Rs 3.25 crores out of a total value of industrial production estimated at Rs 1,380 crores for 1960-61. Even this figure works out at only one-quarter ($\frac{1}{4}$) per cent. The Corporation incurred a deficit of Rs 52,457 during the period ending March 31, 1955; of Rs 64,608 during 1955-56; of Rs 1,19,015 during 1956-57; and of Rs 1,58,000 during 1957-58. Thus the deficits were progressively mounting up, the cumulative figure on March 31, 1958, being Rs 3,94,080.[38]

We may now refer to the National Small Industries Corporation (NSIC) which, along with its four subsidiary corporations, was intended to play a phenomenal rôle in the balanced development of the Indian economy. Pursuant to the recommendations of the Ford Foundation's International Planning Team (April 1954) and of the Shroff Committee (May 1954), the NSIC was registered in Delhi as a Private Limited Company on February 4, 1955.[39] Two years later (February/March 1957) four subsidiary Corporations were registered as Private Limited Companies, with an authorized capital of Rs 10 lakhs in each case (of which share capital amounting to Rs 2.5 lakhs was issued and fully subscribed by the holding Corporation). The names of the Subsidiary Corporations, along with the areas of operation, are given below:[40]

[37] Private individuals had reported only 17 inventions. The remaining 430 inventions were reported by 32 public institutions. The largest number of items came from the National Chemical Laboratory, Poona (63), followed by the Central Leather Research Institute, Madras (42), and the CSIR (32). The Indian Railways had reported only one invention.

[38] The deficits had assumed alarming proportions in the context of the Balance Sheet total which stood at Rs 10,81,486.

[39] The President of India had agreed to subscribe for 1,998 shares; Joint Secretary, Ministry of Commerce and Industry, for one share; and the Development Commissioner for Small Scale Industries, for one share. The authorized capital, originally, was Rs 10 lakhs. But it was raised to Rs 50 lakhs (divided into 50,000 shares of Rs 100 each) vide resolution (i) passed by the shareholders at an Extraordinary General Meeting held on January 7, 1957. On March 31, 1959, the issued, subscribed and paid-up capital stood at Rs 40 lakhs.

[40] *The National Small Industries Corporation Private Limited*, Second Annual Report, 1956-57, p. 4. At the outset, each of the Boards contained four members: two Joint Development Commissioners (one of them being the Chairman), one Regional Director of the Small Industries Service Institute, and the Managing Director of the Holding Corporation.

(1) The National Small Industries Corporation (Bombay) Private Limited—States of Bombay, Madhya Pradesh and Mysore.

(2) The National Small Industries Corporation (Calcutta) Private Limited—States of West Bengal, Bihar, Assam and Orissa, Manipur and Tripura.

(3) The National Small Industries Corporation (Delhi) Private Limited—States of Uttar Pradesh, Punjab, Jammu and Kashmir, Rajasthan, Himachal Pradesh and Delhi.

(4) The National Small Industries Corporation (Madras) Private Limited—States of Andhra Pradesh, Madras and Kerala.

The expression 'Small Industry' was defined as 'an industry ordinarily employing less than fifty persons working with power, or less than 100 persons working without power, and having capital assets not exceeding Rs 5 lakhs'. But these limits could be relaxed by the Corporation with the prior approval of the Central Government. The maximum limit for the grant of a loan by the NSIC to any one particular concern was fixed at Rs 2½ lakhs. Bigger loans could, however, be granted with the approval of the President of India.

The Government Purchase Division was actually 'the nucleus of the Corporation'.[41] In the light of Mr Weddell's recommendation, the Ministry of Works, Housing and Supply, in the Memorandum dated November 21, 1956, laid down that in evaluating tenders, the actual quantum of preference (not exceeding 15 per cent) in favour of small-scale firms was to be decided in each case on merit, in consultation with the Finance Department. During the year 1956-57, the NSIC negotiated for 108 tenders, but was successful in respect of eight tenders only valued at Rs 1,19,353. During 1958-59, out of Rs 161.35 crores worth of contracts placed by the Director-General of Supplies and Disposals, those placed through the NSIC did not exceed Rs 2.56 crores. The Government Purchase Division was also entrusted with the function of developing small-scale industrial units as ancillary to large industrial units like San-Raleigh Industries of India, Premier Automobiles and National Machinery Manufacturers. A number of Government Companies like Hindustan Machine Tools, Hindustan Shipyard, Hindustan Antibiotics, Heavy

[41] *Small Industries Corporation* Administration Report, 1956-57, p. 26. This was in consonance with the pattern visualized by the International Planning Team of the Ford Foundation. Further, Mr Kennard Weddell, Chief of the Small Business Programme in the US Air Force Purchase Organization, who had come to India in February 1956, suggested a fourfold classification of Government stores: (1) items of exclusive interest for the large-scale sector; (2) items with large-scale firms as prime contractors, permitting the purchase of components and parts from small-scale units; (3) competitive items; and (4) items which could be reserved for procurement from small-scale units only.

Electricals, National Instruments, Hindustan Cables, Hindustan Insecticides, Sindri Fertilizers and Chemicals, Hindustan Aircraft and Indian Telephone Industries were contacted in this connection.

The Marketing Division was organized in the light of the recommendations made by Dr Lincoln Clark, a marketing expert whose services had been secured by the Government of India at the suggestion of the Ford Foundation. In view of the 'low margins' in India, he favoured mobile shops which could combine wholesaling, physical movement and retailing in a single operation. The Van Operation Scheme was initiated on December 31, 1955. But after two years' experience it had become clear that the scheme 'could not go very far in solving the marketing problem of the thousands of small-scale units spread all over the country'.[42] During four years (1955-59) on (mobile) sales aggregating Rs 6.13 lakhs, there was a total loss of Rs 10.67 lakhs. The Marketing Division also established an Export Section which supplied $2\frac{1}{2}$ lakh pairs of shoes to the U.S.S.R. during 1957. The orders were received through the State Trading Corporation of India. Subsequently, a number of orders were received from the U.S.S.R., the German Democratic Republic and Poland. Besides the Export Section, a number of Wholesale Depôts were established. But their performance was rather disappointing.[43]

The Hire Purchase Division started supplying machinery and machine tools on hire purchase terms to small industries in March 1956. Up to September 1958, the Corporation had accepted applications for 4,751 machines valued at Rs 3.96 crores. The rate of interest was fixed at $3\frac{1}{2}$ per cent for industrial co-operatives and $4\frac{1}{2}$ per cent for other units, where the value of the machinery did not exceed Rs 15,000. For machines costing more than Rs 15,000, the rates of interest for the two categories of units were 5 per cent and 6 per cent respectively.

The Industrial Estates Division undertook the construction of two Estates at Okhla (near Delhi) and Naini (Allahabad) respectively. The Corporation constituted a Co-ordinating Committee consisting of representatives of the Delhi State Administration, the Delhi State Electricity Board, the Joint Water and Sewage Board,

---

[42] *NSIC*, Third Annual Report, 1957-58, p. 6. During the year 1956-57 the value of sales through mobile vans was ridiculously low—Rs 67,069 for all the four regions. A research directed in the small townships of the Punjab (by the National Council of Applied Economic Research) revealed that the trade name 'Jansevak' (selected for quality marking of shoes) was unknown to the people.

[43] The sales up to October 1959 (about three years) were: Agra (Footwear) Rs 8.36 lakhs; Ranigunta (Glass-beads) Rs 0.82 lakhs; Bombay (Paints & Varnishes) Rs 8.81 lakhs; Khurja (Potteries) Rs 4.62 lakhs; and Calcutta (Hosiery) Rs 3.51 lakhs.

etc.[44] Up to March 31, 1959, an expenditure of Rs 40 lakhs (against a total estimate of Rs 75 lakhs) had been incurred on the construction of the Okhla Estate. The management of the Estate was transferred to Delhi Administration on April 1, 1959.

The Industrial Estate at Naini was estimated to cost Rs 26 lakhs. The actual work of construction was started in November 1956 and completed by February 1958. However, the response from the applicants at Naini was not encouraging. While at Okhla there were 145 applications for thirty-five factories, at Naini there were only thirty applications for thirty-four factories.[45] The Corporation had no doubt succeeded in raising attractive structures within a relatively short period. But when all the factories are in operation, it may appear that the whole atmosphere is rather congested. Further, the rentals fixed for factories, as also for residential quarters, were rather high. It is, therefore, not surprising that only well-to-do businessmen could find a place in *Udyog Nagar*. It also came to light that some entrepreneurs had shifted their venue of operations from Allahabad City to Naini just to take advantage of certain concessions granted by the Government in the new areas. Thus the idea of promoting *new* industries had actually been thwarted in some cases. Moreover, non-availability of suitable raw materials and adequate power appeared to be a serious difficulty. The grievance of some of the allottees was that while all assurances had been given to them regarding the procurement of necessary materials, there developed an attitude of apathy after the actual occupation of the factory and the installation of plants. In one case, it was learnt that an expert had arrived from Germany, but because of the non-availability of raw materials, production could not be started and the expert had practically no work to do. The National Small Industries Corporation should have used their good offices to establish suitable liaison with the various Government Departments and State Undertakings in this regard.

[44] In spite of this, all the water supply mains including the meters had to be installed by the Corporation as the Municipal Committee neither agreed to lay down their own mains nor to supply water at bulk rates. Further, out of 1,000 Kw assured by the Delhi State Electricity Power Control Board, only 100 Kw could be obtained and that also after moving the Minister of Irrigation and Power.

[45] Out of twenty-nine factories occupied by twenty-two allottees, only six allottees (occupying ten factories) were reported to have started production. Rental obligations were generally in arrear, the dues in some cases being quite heavy. The rents ranged between Rs 160 p.m. for B-type Factories (about 2,000 sq. ft.) and Rs 460 p.m. for F-type Factories (5,750 sq. ft.)— *Progress Report of Factories in the Allahabad Industrial Estate* as on August 30, 1959.

CHAPTER V

STATE CORPORATIONS IN OTHER COUNTRIES

A. PUBLIC CORPORATIONS IN GREAT BRITAIN

The British Parliament has been described as the mother of Parliaments; it can also be described as the mother of Public Corporations, especially of the recent pattern of such Corporations. Between 1832-55, only a few Ministries, but numerous Boards, appeared on the scene. The period 1855-1908 was relatively a dull one; it witnessed the creation of only two new Ministries and only two new Boards. Since 1908 there has been a tremendous addition in both types of authorities.

The term 'Public Corporation' was first used in 1926 in a report on British Broadcasting;[1] and in accordance with the empirical tradition of English political institutions, there has been no attempt to formulate a precise definition of the term. The concept was brought to manhood by Herbert Morrison, when he was Minister for Transport in the Labour Government (1929-31), and later through the publication of his *Socialisation and Transport,* which is still a classic in the theory of Public Corporations. The following definition propounded by Mr Ernest Davies[2] suggests that *Public Corporations* are symbolized by *Public Boards*: 'The public corporation is a corporate body created by public authority, with defined powers and functions, and financially independent. It is administered by a board appointed by public authority to which it is answerable. Its capital structure and financial operation are similar to those of the public company. But its stockholders retain no equity interests, are deprived of voting rights and power of appointment of the board.'[3]

Professor P. Sargant Florence describes the British pattern precisely in the following words: 'The trend in the form of government of the industries already nationalized is unmistakable: away from government by Department of State, on the Post Office model; away from municipal organization; and away from mixed boards

[1] W. Friedmann, *The Public Corporation in Great Britain* (A Comparative Symposium), University of Toronto School of Law, Comparative Law Series, Vol. I, 1954.

[2] See also Ernest Davies, M.P., 'National Organization in Britain', article in *The Leader,* November 4, 1947.

[3] Ernest Davies, *National Enterprise: The Development of the Public Corporation,* London, 1946, p. 24.

of representatives—all towards the public corporation with its Board or Executive or Commission.[4] He further observes: 'Public Corporations consisting of the central and regional Boards and their officials, have been substituted for the capitalist sole traders, partnerships or companies.'[5] In a recent publication (1958), Professor Ronald S. Edwards and Mr Harry Townsend have preferred to use the term 'Statutory Corporation'.[6]

There are three Public Corporations in Great Britain which deserve particular mention. The *Port of London Authority*, established under the Port of London Act, 1908, is the earliest prototype of a twentieth century Public Corporation. It was entrusted with the management of a local service of national importance and was, for that purpose, granted a high degree of autonomy. The *British Broadcasting Corporation* was created under Royal Charter issued on December 20, 1926, renewed from time to time for varying periods. It is a national organization of international significance, and enjoys substantial autonomy in the management of its affairs. The *National Coal Board*, established under the Coal Industry Nationalization Act, 1946, is the first example of a truly industrial Public Corporation (though with a relatively low degree of autonomy). It is the earliest manifestation of British socialism under a full-fledged Labour Government leading to nationalization on a nationwide scale.

It is of interest to note that the first Corporation (PLA) was established before the First World War, the second (BBC) during the inter-war period, and the third (NCB) after the close of the Second World War. Of still greater interest, perhaps, is the fact that the three corporations were established under the aegis of the three major parties of Great Britain, i.e. the Liberal Party, the Conservative Party and the Labour Party respectively.[7]

The Port of London Authority was actually constituted in 1909, although the incorporation legislation had been passed in 1908. The Board of the PLA numbers twenty-eight or thirty, depending on whether the Chairman and the Vice-Chairman are elected from within or without the panel of appointed and elected members, a facility permitted by the Act. The appointed members (ten) are

[4] P. Sargant Florence, *The Logic of British and American Industry* (A Realistic Analysis of Economic Structure and Government), Routledge & Kegan Paul, London, 1953, p. 236.

[5] P. Sargant Florence, *The Indian Journal of Economics*, Special Number on Economic Development and the Rôle of the State, Vol. XXXVI, July 1955, p. 29.

[6] R. S. Edwards and H. Townsend, *Business Enterprise: Its Growth and Organization*, Macmillan, London, 1958, pp. 483-4.

[7] For the organization and working of the National Coal Board, see Appendix F.

nominated as follows: (i) by the Admiralty (one); (ii) by the Ministry of Transport (two); (iii) by the London County Council (four); (iv) by the Corporation of the City of London (two); and (v) by the Corporation of Trinity House (one). Of the remaining eighteen members, (i) eight are elected by shipowners; (ii) eight are elected by merchants; (iii) one represents the public wharfowners; and (iv) one represents the owners of river craft. The Board is reconstituted triennially, and there is no restriction on reappointment or re-election of members.[8] Vacancies among elected members arising during the three-year period are filled by co-option. Labour is represented on the Board by two members, the Ministry of Transport and the London County Council being required to appoint one each of their representatives after consultation with such organizations representative of labour as are best qualified to advise them on the matter.

The capital of the PLA is in the form of Port Stock bearing fixed rates of interest. The total amount of money authorized by Act of Parliament to be borrowed is £65 million and the total stock stood at £32.7 million on March 31, 1958, viz.:[9]

3% 'A' Stock, 1929-99 ...	...	...	£8,650,299
3½% Stock, 1949-99 ...	...	...	£1,784,783
3½% Registered Stock, 1965-75	...	...	£12,930,424
3½% Registered Stock, 1960-65	...	...	£2,645,405
3½% Redeemable Stock, 1966-71	...	...	£1,700,000
3½% Registered Stock, 1966-68	...	...	£5,000,000
		Total	£32,710,911

The annual interest obligations aggregated £1,101,630. Financially, the PLA are only concerned to collect sufficient revenue to provide efficient accommodations and services and to pay the annual interest to the stockholders, any excess of revenue over expenditure being available for port improvements or the reduction of port dues and charges. Total revenue, for the year ending March 31, 1958, stood at £18,451,673 (roughly Rs 25 crores), whereas total expenditure aggregated £16,034,549, leaving a balance of £2,417,124. After meeting the items appearing in the Net Revenue Account (£1,980,756) the balance was reduced to £436,368; and after deduct-

[8] There has been a good deal of stability in the membership of the PLA. On March 31, 1958, the following members retired after long association: Mr W. C. Warwick, 23½ years; Sir Eric Miller, 21¼ years; and Mr Geoffrey Hinton, 13 years.

[9] Port of London Authority, Abstract of Accounts for the year ended March 31, 1958. Adding to this figure Port Stock redeemed (£3,970,106), Port Stock purchased and extinguished (£1,626,940), and Stock withdrawn from Stock (Redemption) Funds (£5,485,352), the total figure comes to £43,793,309. Thus the unexercised borrowing powers stood at £21,206,691.

ing Special Appropriations (£450,000) there was actually a deficit of £13,632.[10]

A unique feature of the British Broadcasting Corporation is the practice of issuing Royal Charters from time to time, viz. :

Sl. No.	Description	Duration	Remarks
1.	First Charter	Ten years (January 1, 1927, to December 31, 1936)	After Parliamentary consideration of Lord Crawford's Committee of 1925 (which followed Sir Frederick Sykes's Report of 1923)
2.	Second Charter	Ten years (January 1, 1937, to December 31, 1946)	After Parliamentary consideration of Lord Ullswater's Committee of 1935 and authorizing the BBC to carry on the service 'for the benefit of Our dominions beyond the seas and territories under Our protection'
3.	Third Charter	Five years (January 1, 1947, to December 31, 1951)— Granted by Labour Government	After Parliamentary consideration of Government's White Paper of 1946 and authorizing the BBC to provide broadcasting services for reception 'in other countries and places' outside the British Commonwealth and requiring the Corporation to establish machinery for joint consultation with its staff
4.	Extension	Six months (January 1, 1952, to June 30, 1952)	Future pattern not finally decided, presumably because of change in Government
5.	Fourth Charter	Ten years (July 1, 1952, to June 30, 1962)	After Parliamentary consideration of the Report of Lord Beveridge's Committee of 1949, and of the Government's White Papers of July 1951 (Mr Attlee's administration) and of May 1952 (Mr Churchill's administration), providing for competition, i.e. the grant of a non-exclusive licence to the BBC (another licence being granted, by the Postmaster-General, to the Independent Television Authority set up under the Television Act of 1954)

[10] *Forty-ninth Annual Report* of the Port of London Authority, year ended March 31, 1958, p. 3. The number of vessels which entered and left the Port of London stood at 18,704 in 1910 and 19,827 in 1931, figured at only 18,382 in 1958 (year ending March 31). The net registered tonnage, however, improved from 21.25 million in 1910 to 32.98 million in 1931 and 34.05 million in 1958.

Sir William-Thompson (later Lord) Selsdon, who as Postmaster-General was responsible for the establishment of the Corporation at the end of 1926,[11] made the following remarks in the House of Commons on November 15, 1926: 'While I am prepared to take the responsibility for broad issues of policy, on minor issues and measures of domestic policy and matters of day-to-day control, I want to leave things to the free judgment of the Corporation.' This policy has been endorsed from time to time (including a resolution of the House of Commons in 1938) and has never been seriously challenged in Parliament or elsewhere.

The Broadcasting Committee of 1949 visualized fundamental changes in the organization of the BBC. Their emphasis was on regional autonomy, arrangements for better reception, and the use of new (very high and ultra high) frequencies.[12] For each of the three national regions, they recommended a Broadcasting Commission consisting of five persons appointed by the UK Government. They wanted the number of Governors to be increased to nine (including three Governors with special knowledge of Scotland, Wales and Northern Ireland respectively to act as Chairmen for the three National Commissions). The Committee were of the view that the period of appointment would normally be four years, with powers of reappointment, and with shorter periods so far as necessary at the outset with a view to *staggering* dates of appointment and reappointment. They recommended an annual salary of £4,000 for the Chairman of the BBC, £2,000 for each of the three National Chairmen, £1,000 each for the other Governors, and £500 each for the members of the National Commissions. Mr J. Reeves, in his Reservation, considered these salaries too high for part-time appointments. He described the salary of £4,000 for a part-time Chairman as a 'dangerous precedent'. Mr Reeves felt that to be the Governor of the

[11] The privately-owned British Broadcasting Company was dissolved on December 31, 1926, after an eventful existence. It had come to be widely known as 'The BBC' and was required under licence to provide a service 'to the reasonable satisfaction of the Postmaster-General'. Lord Crawford's Committee of 1925 recommended that the broadcasting service should be conducted by a Public Corporation 'acting as trustee for the national interest'.

[12] They also suggested that 'the position and duties of the Governors should be determined *only by the Charter*'. This is of particular interest to us in India, specially after the great agitation created with regard to the responsibilities of Board members, Departmental Secretaries, and the Minister in the wake of the LIC-Mundhra Deal of 1957. Other recommendations of the Committee were: (1) the Charter should run with no duration specified; however, there should be quinquennial reviews of the finance and work of the BBC; (2) there should be a Public Representation Service; (3) the staff should be given a means of discussing by representative organizations; (4) commercial advertising should continue to be prohibited. The Corporation should receive a definite percentage of net licence income (100 per cent during the first five years) which should not be changed without adequate notice.

BBC meant a great honour which public-spirited persons would welcome for its own sake. Ultimately, the salaries were fixed as follows: BBC Chairman, £3,000; Vice-Chairman and National Governors for Scotland and Wales, £1,000 each; National Governor for Northern Ireland and other Governors, £600.[13] The principle of regional autonomy, too, was not accepted to the extent recommended by the Broadcasting Committee. It was, however, decided that, in addition to meeting in England, the Corporation should meet in Scotland, in Wales and in Northern Ireland at such intervals as may to the Corporation seem appropriate, regard being had to its representative function.

The total revenue of the BBC during the year ended March 31, 1958, stood at £26.2 million. Out of this, as much as £25.3 million (£12 million for Sound and £13.3 million for Television) was obtained from the Postmaster-General. During the year ended March 31, 1957, the Postmaster-General's contribution (£12.1 million for Sound and £11.7 million for Television) stood at £23.8 million out of a total revenue of £25.1 million. With total expenditure rising from £22.5 million in 1956-57 to £24.7 million in 1957-58, the annual surplus was narrowed down from £2.6 million to £1.5 million.

B. CROWN CORPORATIONS IN CANADA

The Crown Corporation form of public enterprise is not a new type of organization in Canada but in recent years, as the work of Government has become more complex, greater reliance has been placed on it as the appropriate instrument for administering and managing many public services in which business enterprise and public accountability must be combined. The most usual practice has been to set up a corporation under the provisions of a special Act of Parliament which defines its purpose and sets forth its powers and responsibilities. However, during World War II, the Minister of Munitions and Supply was authorized to procure the incorporation of companies under the Federal Companies Act, 1934, or under any provincial Companies Act, to which he might delegate any of the powers conferred on him under the Department of Munitions and Supply Act or any Order in Council. Under this legislation, about 28 companies were created to serve a wide variety of pur-

[13] During the interim period of two months (July and August 1952) there were to be not more than seven and not less than five Governors. Thereafter, there were to be nine Governors (as suggested by the Beveridge Committee) but appointed for periods not exceeding five years. A National Governor was to be designated 'in virtue of his knowledge of the culture, characteristics and affairs of our People' in Scotland/Wales/Northern Ireland and his close touch with Scottish/Welsh/Northern Irish opinion.

poses; most of these companies have since been wound up.[14]

In 1946, the Government Companies Operation Act was passed in Canada to regulate the operation of companies formed under the Companies Act.[15] However, it was applicable only to a relatively small number of companies and, in order to establish a more uniform system of financial and budgetary control and of accounting, auditing and reporting for Crown Corporations generally, Part VIII of the Financial Administration Act was enacted in 1951 and brought into operation by proclamation on October 1, 1952. Upon its enactment, the *financial* provisions of the Government Companies Operation Act were repealed.

Professor Hodgetts suggests that 'It cannot be said that any unifying philosophy underlines the use of the public corporation in Canada: the whole development has been piecemeal and pragmatic.'[16] However, the Canadian picture is perhaps more systematized than the Indian one. One reason for this fact may be that a large number of corporations were installed during a short space of time, 1944-48.[17] Secondly, since Crown Corporations in Canada have not been a matter of Party politics, it has been easier to arrive at a systematized classification.

Under the Canadian Financial Administration Act of 1951 there are four schedules:

A. Government Departments.

B. Departmental Corporations.

C. Agency Corporations.

D. Proprietary Corporations.

Under Section 76(1) (c) of the Act, 'Crown Corporation' means a corporation that is ultimately accountable, through a Minister, to Parliament for the conduct of its affairs, and includes the corporations named in Schedule B, Schedule C and Schedule D. Under Section 76(3) the Governor in Council may by order

(a) add to Schedule B any Crown corporation that is a servant or agent of His (Her) Majesty in right of Canada and is responsible for administrative, supervisory or regulatory services of govern-

[14] *Administrative Functions of the Federal Government*, Dominion Bureau of Statistics, Information Services Division, Ottawa, 1958, Section 2, p. 9.

[15] In India, the term 'Government Company' was first used in legal parlance in the Companies Act of 1956—in which a few sections are devoted to the operation of Government Companies.

[16] J. E. Hodgetts, *The Public Corporation in Canada*, Friedmann (Ed.), *loc. cit.*, p. 53.

[17] In England also a large number of Public Corporations were established in about four years' time, 1945-49. While the British Labour Party had a definite logic behind the creation of such Corporations, wide differences were allowed to exist in their constitution. In India, a large number of Public Corporations were established in one year (1948); even then, no attempt was made to ensure uniformity in structure.

mental nature;

(b) add to Schedule C any Crown corporation that is an agent of His (Her) Majesty in right of Canada and is responsible for the management of trading or service operations on a quasi-commercial basis or for the management of procurement construction or disposal activities on behalf of His (Her) Majesty in right of Canada; and

(c) add to Schedule D any Crown corporation that:

(i) is responsible for the management of lending or financial operations, or for the management of commercial or industrial operations involving the production of or dealing in goods and the supplying of services to the public, and

(ii) is ordinarily required to conduct its operations without appropriations.

The great virtue of the Act lies in adopting a functional classification of corporations (though apparently it is just a formal classification). As on July 1, 1959, out of 35 Corporations subject to the Act, 10 were Departmental Corporations, 11 were Agency Corporations and 14 were Proprietary Corporations.[18] There are also certain Corporations like the Bank of Canada and the Canadian Wheat Board which do not fall in any of the above categories. Among Departmental Corporations we find such organizations as the National Gallery of Canada (founded 1880, Act of Parliament 1913, re-enacted 1951), the Agricultural Stabilization Board (formerly known as Agricultural Prices Support Board, 1944), the Atomic Energy Control Board (1946) and the Dominion Coal Board (1947).[19] The list of Agency Corporations, *inter alia*, consists of the National Battlefields Commission (1908), Crown Assets Disposal Corporation (1944), Atomic Energy of Canada Limited (1952), Northern Canada Power Commission (1955) and the National Capital Commission (1959).[20] Among Proprietary Corporations, we may refer to the

[18] Information obtained by courtesy of Mr H. R. Balls, Comptroller of the Treasury, Canada (July 1959). See also H. R. Balls, 'The Financial Control and Accountability of Canadian Crown Corporations', *Public Administration*, London, Summer 1953, pp. 127-43.

[19] The Coal Board reports to Parliament through the Minister of Mines and Technical Surveys. It consists of seven members appointed by the Governor-in-Council who also fixes their salaries. One of the members is appointed Chairman and Chief Executive Officer. The members hold office 'during pleasure'. In July 1959 there were no civil servants on the Board.

[20] The Commission had its genesis in the Ottawa Improvement Commission established by Parliament in 1899 to improve and beautify the National Capital. In 1927 the organization's name was changed to Federal District Commission, its scope of operations being widened to include the adjacent areas. In 1946 the Commission became the Federal agency responsible for carrying out the National Capital Plan. A National Capital Planning Committee was appointed to act as a permanent honorary advisory body to the Commission. The governing statute for the National Capital Commission was proclaimed on February 6, 1959.

116

Canadian National Railways (1923),[21] the Canadian Farm Loan Board (1929), the Canadian Broadcasting Corporation (1936/1958), the Trans-Canada Airlines (1937), the Export Credits Insurance Corporation (1945) and the Cornwall International Bridge Company Limited (subsidiary of the St Lawrence Seaway Authority added by Order-in-Council dated February 26, 1959).

C. STATUTORY CORPORATIONS IN AUSTRALIA

It is worth noting that the term statutory corporation has found much favour in Australia. 'It was thus within the framework of an industry chiefly publicly owned and continually becoming more so that the forces making for co-ordinated electricity supply systems slowly exerted themselves and were finally given official recognition in each State through the establishment of major statutory corporations.'[22] A Statutory Corporation consisting of a Chairman of Commissioners and two Commissioners was established under the Victorian Railway Commissioners Act of 1883. Within two years, the railways which had shown repeated deficits began to earn profits. The model was followed in other states beginning with New South Wales in 1887.

Again, the State of Victoria was a pioneer in constituting *State Electricity Commissioners* as a Statutory Corporation in 1918. In 1920, by an Act of Parliament, the name was changed to the State Electricity Commission of Victoria. The public ownership of generation and distribution is now virtually complete. In 1953-54 'the Commission supplied (directly or indirectly) 98.5 per cent of the electricity consumed in Victoria'.[23] Statutory Corporations have been established in various other states like the Hydro-electric Commission (1930) in Tasmania, the Electricity Trust of South Australia (1946), and the Electricity Commission of New South Wales (1950). The last Commission supplied 93 per cent of the State's total consumption of electricity during 1953-54.[24]

[21] On inception the CNR was managed by 'President and Chairman' and eight members of the Board of Directors. On January 1, 1959, the number of other members was only six. There was no Managing Director as such, the 'Chairman and President' being the active managerial head drawing a handsome salary of $75,000 per annum (i.e. about Rs 30,000 per month). Other members of the Board were being paid $5,000 per month. The term of office was three years subject to renewal. There were five industrialists on the Board, but no functional experts, no civil servants and no Members of Parliament.

[22] E. A. Boehm, 'Ownership and Control of the Electricity Supply Industry in Australia', *The Economic Record,* Vol. XXXII, November 1956, p. 259.

[23] *State Electricity Commission of Victoria,* 35th Annual Report, 1953-54, p. 6.

[24] Report of the *Electricity Commission of New South Wales* for the year ended June 30, 1954, Government Printer, Sydney, 1955, p. 7.

Professor Sawer, however, considers the Electricity Commission of New South Wales as a case falling in the category of Crown Corporations because it is subject in all respects to the control and direction of the Minister. He classifies State Corporations into three categories:

1. Public Corporations proper;
2. Crown Corporations; and
3. Autonomous Statutory Corporations.

But this classification has little relevance for the economist and the political scientist, and is by no means free from overlapping and ambiguity.[25] Professor Sawer seems to base his classification on the degree to which the activities of such corporations are insulated from the direct control of the Crown, the Cabinet or the Minister concerned. Thus Public Corporations are supposed to go farthest in the matter of independent operation, the Crown Corporations the least, and Autonomous Statutory Corporations are to remain on the middle rungs of the ladder. Professor Sawer feels that an activity identified with the Crown almost inevitably becomes a political activity, and this might be either bad for the activity or embarrassing for the administrators. The individuals and private organizations dealing with Crown Corporations may also be in difficulty because of strict limitations on Crown liability in legal actions. Crown property and daily operations may not be managed on business lines because of cumbrous procedures and numerous privileges and immunities.[26]

At the Commonwealth level, there are three Corporations which deserve attention.[27] *The Australian Broadcasting Commission* was constituted in 1932. It consists of seven Commissioners, of whom one must be a woman, one a Treasury Officer, and one a Postmaster-General's Departmental Officer, appointed by the Governor-General.

[25] A. H. Hanson (Ed.), *Public Enterprise* (A Study of its Organization and Management in Various Countries), International Institute of Administrative Services, Brussels, 1955, p. 464.

[26] In Australia, many of the Crown Corporations appear as 'Corporations Sole'. Here a Minister is incorporated under the shield of the Crown. The Attorney General was incorporated as the State Government Insurance Office in Western Australia. The most interesting case is that of the Queensland Fish Board which consisted of four members; even then, it was declared to be a Corporation Sole. Another notable example relates to Western Australia where a Corporation was declared to be 'the permanent head of the Department of Railways'; even then, it was subject to the control of a Minister for Railways, who was himself incorporated as a Corporation Sole.

[27] There are six other 'Autonomous Statutory Corporations' besides the Commonwealth Railways (a corporate entity managed by a single Commissioner), the Commonwealth Bank, the Commonwealth Trading Bank and the Commonwealth Savings Bank. Besides, there are examples of Commonwealth-State co-operation like the Joint Coal Board (Commonwealth/New South Wales, 1946) and the Aluminium Industry Commission (Commonwealth/Tasmania, 1944).

The official members hold office 'at pleasure' whereas the non-official members are in office for three years (removable by the Governor-General for misbehaviour).

The Australian National Airlines Commission was established in 1945 (first of the post-war Corporations). The Commission consists of five Commissioners appointed by the Governor-General, who also names the Chairman and the Vice-Chairman. *The Chairman holds office for five years, the Vice-Chairman for four years, and other members for three years.* The salaries of the Chairman and the Vice-Chairman are fixed by the Governor-General; those of others are provided in the Act. Here also, all the Commissioners are removable by the Governor-General for misbehaviour.

The Snowy Mountains Hydro-Electric Authority (comparable to India's DVC) was established in 1949. One Commissioner, constituting a Corporation Sole, is appointed by the Governor-General for seven years. The Governor-General determines his salary, and may remove him for misbehaviour. The Governor-General also appoints (and may remove) two Associate Commissioners who do *not* constitute the body corporate.

The Joint Stock Company, as a vehicle of public enterprise, has not proved so popular in Australia as in Canada and India. But, at the same time, it has not been so uncommon as in England. Thus, the Qantas Empire Airways Ltd was acquired by the Commonwealth as a going concern. It was an undertaking incorporated under State Company Law. The Commonwealth preferred to retain this form, additional capital being provided as necessary by the purchase of capital stock. As the sole shareholder of the 'Public Company', the Commonwealth enjoys complete control over the appointment of Directors and the general affairs of business. The QEA being an international airline, it was considered advisable not to make any change in its nomenclature. A similar consideration appeared in India when 'Air India International Ltd'—which had built up substantial goodwill—was nationalized.

D. GOVERNMENT SPONSORED CORPORATIONS IN PAKISTAN

The following agencies (in which the Central Government hold substantial investment) were working in Pakistan in 1959 (the figures are in lakhs of Pakistani Rupees):[28]

[28] Table constructed on the basis of *Government Sponsored Corporations*, Ministry of Finance (Economic Affairs Division), Government of Pakistan, Karachi, 1959. As the figures of paid-up capital have been approximated to the nearest lakh, they may not fully 'add up'. Further, in case of the Pakistan Refugees Rehabilitation Finance Corporation, the cumulative figure of eight years' loss (1948-56) has been worked out on the basis of ten years' aggregate loss (1948-58) amounting to Rs 37.60 lakhs, as yearly figures were not available.

GOVERNMENT SPONSORED CORPORATIONS IN PAKISTAN

Name of the Corporation	Year of commencement of business	Authorized capital	Paid-up-Capital			Net Profit (+) or Loss (−) cumulative figures up to 1956
			Govt	Private	Total	
1. Pakistan Refugees Rehabilitation Finance Corp.	1948	300	158	—	158	− 30.08
2. Pakistan Industrial Finance Corporation	1949	300	102	98	200	+ 26.66
3. Pakistan Security Printing Corporation	1949	75	30	20	50	+ 37.14
4. Karachi Electric Supply Corporation	1913/1952	300	175	87	262	+ 85.24
5. Pakistan Industrial Development Corporation	1952	100	50	—	50	—
6. Agricultural Development Finance Corporation	1953	500	300	—	300	− 14.10
7. House Building Finance Corporation	1953	500	450	—	450	+ 5.33
8. Pakistan International Airlines Corporation	1953	500	403	97	500	− 252.30
9. Pakistan Insurance Corporation	1953	100	15	5	20	+ 13.60
10. Small Industries Corporation	1956	100	55	—	55	+ 2.61
11. Agricultural Bank of Pakistan	1957	2,000	200	—	200	—
12. Pakistan Industrial Credit and Investment Corp.	1957	1,500	—	200	200	—
13. Karachi Development Authority	1957	—	—	—	—	—
		6,275	1,938	506	2,444	− 131.52

Out of thirteen Corporations sponsored by the Central Government in Pakistan, authorized capital had been specified in case of twelve Corporations, the average per Corporation being Rs 523 lakhs. For the Karachi Development Authority, the Central Government had advanced Rs 1143 lakhs (Rs 11.43 crores) by June 30, 1959. The average paid-up capital of the other twelve Corporations works out to Rs 204 lakhs. Government contribution, on an average, amounted to Rs 162 lakhs (79.4 per cent) as against private contribution of Rs 42 lakhs (20.6 per cent) per Corporation. In case of six Corporations, there was no private investment at all. However, in case of the Pakistan Industrial Credit and Investment Corporation, the entire paid-up capital came from private sources. Strictly speaking, therefore, it is not a State Corporation. The reason why this Corporation is to be found in the company of State Corporations is the fact that the Central Government had advanced an interest-free loan of Rs 300 lakhs. Taking that into account, public investment amounts to 60 per cent of the capital employed. A similar ratio (with regard to paid-up capital) of public-private investment is to be found in case of the Pakistan Security Printing Corporation. The proverbial ratio of 51:49 is to be found in case of the Pakistan Industrial Finance Corporation.

Out of ten Corporations which had started working by 1956, five had shown overall profit, four had incurred overall loss, and the financial results of the remaining one (PIDC) had not been published, presumably because it is a Development Corporation. The aggregate profits up to 1956 for the five profitable Corporations amounted to Rs 167.57 lakhs, whereas the losses for the four unprofitable Corporations aggregated Rs 299.09 lakhs. Thus, on balance, the Government sponsored Corporations in Pakistan (organized by the Central Government) had suffered a loss of Rs 131.52 lakhs up to 1956. The most uneconomic operation was to be found in case of the Pakistan International Airlines Corporation. If we exclude it, we would be left with an overall profit. Other activities which had proved unprofitable were refugee rehabilitation, agricultural finance and small industries. The Pakistan Refugees Rehabilitation Finance Corporation, during the first decade of its working (1948-58), had never shown any profit. The political element in its activities may be said to have been responsible for this situation.[29]

The most profitable working was represented by the Karachi

[29] It may be added that out of total assistance amounting to Rs 396 lakhs (up to June 30, 1958), East Pakistan had received only Rs 17 lakhs. Karachi, in fact, got the lion's share of Rs 215 lakhs. Further, the problem of refugees was most pressing in the initial years. Up to December 31, 1952 (first four and a half years), assistance amounting to Rs 285 lakhs had been granted, whereas during the next five and a half years, the figure stood at Rs 111 lakhs only.

Electric Supply Corporation which had been established in 1913 as a Public Limited Company in the private sector. Government participation started in 1952 with the purchase of majority shares in the Company. Experience has shown that the decision of Government's participation in this vital public utility service was well justified and highly desirable. The index of units generated (1948 = 100), which stood at 200 in 1952, rose to 566 in 1957. The operating ratio (percentage of generation and other costs to total revenue) declined from 93 per cent in 1952 to 69.7 per cent in 1954. This remarkably low ratio has been achieved in the face of moderate electricity rates, only three annas per unit being charged from ordinary consumers. The Karachi Electric Supply Corporation has been paying a decent dividend of 7 per cent tax free to its ordinary shareholders. The Pakistan Security Printing Corporation had paid to the Government, up to March 31, 1959, Rs 25.8 lakhs by way of dividend against an investment of Rs 30 lakhs. The income tax receipts amounted to Rs 28.32 lakhs up to the assessment year 1957-58. The Corporation has also effected substantial savings in foreign exchange. The Pakistan Industrial Finance Corporation displayed a continuously rising trend in its net profits, from Rs 0.31 lakhs in 1949-50 to Rs 4.20 lakhs in 1952-53. Again, from Rs 4.12 lakhs in 1953-54, the profits showed a continuous rise to Rs 8.01 lakhs in 1956-57. In 1957-58, the figure was slightly lower at Rs 7.96 lakhs. The Pakistan Insurance Corporation, carrying on fire, marine and miscellaneous business, worked so profitably that the minimum limit of dividend fixed at 5 per cent had to be raised to 10 per cent under the Pakistan Insurance Corporation (Amendment) Act, 1958. The net profits of the Corporation had risen from Rs 13 lakhs in 1953 to Rs 634 lakhs in 1957. The House Building Finance Corporation worked at a loss during 1952-53 and 1953-54; in 1954-55 it showed a nominal profit of Rs 1,828; and, thereafter, profits continued to rise, the figure being Rs 7.17 lakhs for 1957-58.

The Pakistan Industrial Development Corporation does not envisage nationalization of industries. On the contrary, the rôle entrusted to it is to encourage, supplement and guide private capital by exclusive or joint investments, wherever necessary, with the ultimate aim of handing over the Projects to the control of private industrialists either by selling them to individuals, or by floating limited companies.[30] The PIDC is perhaps the only (Central) Corporation which has given a good deal of attention to the problems of East Pakistan. However, more and more projects are *now* being established in West Pakistan. The following two tables are revealing (figures of investment are in lakhs of rupees):[31]

[30] PIDC, Second Annual Report, 1953-54, p. 2.
[31] Source: *Government Sponsored Corporations*, 1959.

122

COMPLETED PROJECTS
(December 31, 1958)

	Total	Private	Public
1. East Pakistan	4,089	2,012	2,077
2. West Pakistan	3,339	525	2,814
3. Karachi	1,829	1,219	611
	9,258	3,756	5,502

PROJECTS UNDERWAY
(December 31, 1958)

	Total	Private	Public
1. East Pakistan	3,396	—	3,396
2. West Pakistan	6,516	18	6,498
3. Karachi	150	—	150
	10,062	18	10,044

Thus, whereas in respect of the projects already completed by December 31, 1958, the share of East Pakistan stood at 44 per cent, the same was less at 34 per cent with regard to the projects underway. Further, twenty-one projects had been completed in East Pakistan, twenty-one in West Pakistan and four in Karachi. As against this, only two projects were underway in East Pakistan, as many as fifteen in West Pakistan, and one in Karachi. As the PIDC started its promotional work with jute mills, East Pakistan, in the earlier years, occupied an important position in the Corporation's work. However, after establishing fourteen jute mills in East Pakistan, a halting point was inevitable.

Investment made by the Government in all the PIDC projects rose from Rs 150 lakhs in 1951-52 to Rs 1718 lakhs in 1956-57. The revised estimate for 1957-58 stood at Rs 23.08 lakhs. Investments outside Pakistan (Turkey Jute Mills, Rs 67 lakhs; Iraq Jute Mills, Rs 20 lakhs; Egyptian Jute Mills, Rs 27 lakhs; and Lebanon Jute Mills, Rs 11 lakhs) figured at Rs 114 lakhs in 1956-57 and at Rs 11 lakhs in 1957-58 (revised estimate) giving a total of Rs 125 lakhs.[32] A notable feature is the increasing share of public investment in PIDC projects. In the case of Adamjee Jute Mills Ltd (Nos. I, II and III) the share of private investment was over 83 per cent (Rs 625 lakhs out of a total investment of Rs 750 lakhs). In the Daulatpur Jute Mills, there was 100 per cent private investment. The position was just reversed when in the case of Platinum Jute Mills, Khulna, the entire investment of Rs 300 lakhs was provided by the Government. Private enterprise again asserted itself in the case of Karnaphuli

---

[32] *Government Investments in Finance Corporations and other Institutions in which Central Government have a large financial interest as share capital or loan,* 1958, p. 10.

Paper Mills Ltd when it contributed Rs 488 lakhs out of a total investment of Rs 600 lakhs (i.e. over 81 per cent). But the six other projects in East Pakistan (three sugar mills, one cotton mill, Khulna Shipyard and Narayanganj Dockyard) were exclusively financed by the Government.[33] The same is true of the two projects underway in East Pakistan—the Khulna Newsprint and Paper Printing Factory[34] and the East Pakistan Natural Gas Fertilizer Factory.

E. GOVERNMENT CORPORATIONS IN THE USA

An altogether different nomenclature is in vogue in the USA. The Government Corporations in that country are of 'somewhat limited value' in illustrating their use as a means of managing publicly-owned commercial enterprises.[35] A leading authority on the subject observed in 1941 that 'the Government Corporation as a concept—as a definite and specialized form of administrative organization—is rapidly ceasing to exist'.[36] This writing is a reflection of the trend towards assimilation of Government Corporation into the regular governmental pattern—a trend which culminated in the enactment of the Government Corporation Control Act in 1945.[37]

The Act of 1945 classifies Government Corporations into two categories: (1) 'wholly owned Government Corporations' (section 846)—which V. O. Key calls the 'pure' form of Government Corporation; and (2) 'mixed-ownership Government Corporations'. The second category of Government Corporations is fully dominated by financial institutions (insurance coming collaterally to banking). In the first category also, there are as many as sixteen financial

---

[33] Out of twenty-one projects completed by December 31, 1958, in West Pakistan, there was no private investment at all in eight cases. Among these instances are big projects, like Pak-American Fertilizer Factory, Daudkhel (public investment Rs 805 lakhs, including foreign aid of Rs 413 lakhs); Maple Leaf Cement Factory, Daudkhel (Rs 421 lakhs). Out of the fifteen projects underway in West Pakistan, fourteen had been exclusively financed by the Government. These include the West Pakistan High Tension Electric Grid (Rs 1211 lakhs), the Natural Gas Power Station (Rs 1080 lakhs), and the Natural Gas Factory (Rs 1689 lakhs). Generally speaking, private investment has kept away from basic industries (an important exception being Sui-Karachi Gas Pipeline).

[34] The Khulna Newsprint Mill is now working at full capacity (over 100 tons a day)—'Forward', *PIDC Journal,* April 1960, p. 14.

[35] John Thurston, *Government Proprietary Corporations in the English-speaking Countries,* Harvard University Press, Cambridge, 1937, p. 6.

[36] C. H. Pritchett, 'The Paradox of the Government Corporation', *Public Administration Review,* Chicago, 1941, Vol. I, p. 381.

[37] Under §869 of the 1945 Act, no corporation shall be created for acting as an agency or instrumentality of the United States except by or pursuant to an Act of Congress. Further, no wholly Government corporation shall continue after June 30, 1948, unless it is reincorporated by an Act of Congress.

institutions[38] (including housing corporations), seven dealing with transport and communications, six with supplies and reserves, four with development, three with war production and three of a miscellaneous character (including Prison Industries). The total assets of the Government Corporations and credit agencies amounted to $40,639 million on June 30, 1955; merchandise, supplies and materials to $3,476 million; and the ownership of land, buildings and equipment to $7,821 million.[39] Some of the Government Corporations are comparable to the giant corporations in the private sector, e.g. the Export-Import Bank of Washington has had assets worth $2,827 million as against $3,100 million in US Steel Corporation and $3,700 million in the General Motors Corporation. But the important point to remember is that Government Corporations have generally kept away from industrial production *as such*.

It is interesting to observe that most of the Government Corporations are the children of emergency, though their life has not always ended with the end of those emergency conditions. During the two World Wars and the Great Depression, the Federal Government was compelled to conduct extraordinary activities. 'Pressure for speedy action made the corporate form with its freedom from cumbersome procedures attractive'.[40] Thus, during World War I, there emerged the United States Emergency Fleet Corporation, the United States Grain Corporation, the United States Housing Corporation, the War Finance Corporation, and the Russian Bureau Incorporated. Even the names have carried the stigma of emergency. Except for the Emergency Fleet Corporation, which was transmuted into the Merchant Fleet Corporation in 1927, all the wartime corporations were liquidated at convenient moments.

The next crop of Government Corporations was harvested in the early 'thirties. Even before the era of New Deal, President Hoover had created the Reconstruction Finance Corporation in 1932. In course of time, through the spawning of subsidiaries, it became a huge holding company. The Corporation was to stave off economic disaster by granting loans to banks, insurance companies, railroads and other enterprises. Among other Corporations in this category may be mentioned the Federal Home Loan Banks (1932), Home Owners Loan Corporation (1933), Commodity Credit Corporation (1933), Federal Surplus Commodities Corporation (1933), Federal

---

[38] Counting each item as only one. Actually, there are several corporations in some of the items, e.g. 12 Federal Land Banks, 12 Federal Intermediate Credit Banks, 12 Production Credit Corporations, 13 Banks for Co-operatives and 11 Federal Home Loan Banks.

[39] Gerhard Schmidt, 'Government Corporations in the U.S.A.', *Indian Journal of Economics*, October 1956, pp. 203-4.

[40] V. O. Key, Jr, Government Corporations, in Fritz Morstein Marx (Ed.), *Elements of Public Administration*, Prentice-Hall, New York.

Farm Mortgage Corporation (1934), the Mortgage Corporation (1935—under the RFC), Federal Deposit Insurance Corporation and the Federal Savings and Loan Insurance Corporation (1934). Most of these Corporations became permanent agencies.

The last spurt occurred just after the outbreak of World War II. The year 1940 saw the establishment of the Defence Homes Corporation, the Defence Plant Corporation, the Defence Supplies Corporation, the Metals Reserve Company, the Rubber Development Corporation and the Rubber Reserve Company. With the exception of the Defence Homes Corporations and the Rubber Development Corporation, all the others (along with the Disaster Loan Corporation) were merged into the Reconstruction Finance Corporation (vide Public Law No. 109 dated June 30, 1945). The United States Commercial Company, established in 1942, was already a subsidiary of the RFC. World War II was also responsible for the establishment of several Inter-American Corporations, aiming at promoting 'Good Neighbour Policy', their sphere of action extending to several foreign countries.

There are, however, a number of important Corporations which can refute the charge of abnormal birth. We may refer to the Panama Railroad Company, the oldest Government Corporation of this century.[41] The Railroad Company was incorporated under the laws of New York in 1849. But it became a Government Corporation only after 1903 when the United States acquired the French interest in the canal and in the railroad company. Another example is of the Inland Waterways Corporation formed in 1924, where the corporate arrangement was deliberately chosen because of its advantages *over the then existing departmental structure*. That is, the service of waterways was already under Governmental operation.

Finally, there is the case of the Tennessee Valley Authority, the prince among Government Corporations. Although the Authority is of depression origin (1933), it represents a definite ideology, and was destined to be a permanent institution from the very beginning. There is the oft-quoted observation of President Roosevelt who referred to the TVA as 'a corporation clothed with the power of government but possessed of the flexibility and initiative of a

---

[41] The words *of this century* are important because the first Government Corporation was the Bank of North America, founded in 1781. Then followed the First and Second Banks of the United States (1791-1811 and 1816-36 respectively). In 1846 the Congress set up the Smithsonian Institute as a corporate instrumentality to administer the bequest of James Smithson. The National Academy of Sciences was incorporated in 1863 and the National Soldiers' Home in 1866. After a long gap came the Panama Railroad Company in 1904.

private enterprise'.[42] But, in the United States, the TVA is perhaps the last of the really autonomous corporations. President Roosevelt himself did not retain that enthusiasm till his last days; and after his death, the Government Corporations had quite an unfavourable time.[43]

[42] A. N. Agarwala (Ed.), *Public Corporations*, p. 4.
[43] For the organization and working of the TVA, see Appendix G.

CHAPTER VI

THE GOVERNING BOARDS

A. THE TENURE OF THE BOARDS

The strength of the Governing Board, to a large extent, depends on the period for which it is appointed. The theory of autonomous State Corporations suggests that the Governing Boards should be appointed for reasonably long periods. The Tennessee Valley Authority went far in this respect. In that organization, except for the first two members who were to retire after three and six years respectively, every member is appointed for a nine-year period. In case of the Snowy Mountains Hydro-Electric Authority (Australia), one Commissioner, constituting a Corporation Sole, is appointed by the Governor-General for seven years. In case of the Australian National Airlines Commission, the Chairman holds office for five years, the Vice-Chairman for four years, and other members for three years. The National Coal Board of Great Britain adopted the practice of appointing full-time members for five years and part-timers for three years only. The Uniform Charter for Government Corporations in the Philippines provides that the first members shall serve 'for terms of one, two and three years respectively . . . ; but their successors shall be appointed for terms of three years, except that any person chosen to fill a vacancy shall serve only for the unexpired term of the member whom he succeeds'.[1] Thus, while there are wide differences in the tenures of office, there is a fairly common practice to make these tenures staggered. Of course, where there is only one Commissioner, it cannot be helped. In other cases, an effort is made to see that the terms of office of all the members do not expire on the same date. This aims at ensuring some continuity in thought and action. However, it must be pointed out that staggered terms of appointment violate the strict principle of accountability. That is, no *particular team* of members can be said to have behaved well or ill over a reasonably long period. However, the burden of accountability may be largely placed on the shoulders of the Chairman if he is appointed for a long period, as in the case of the Australian National Airlines Commission.

In India and Pakistan much has been left to executive discretion. For example, the Pakistan Industrial Development Corporation

[1] Executive Order No. 399 by the President of the Philippines, January 5, 1951.

128

Act, 1950, lays down that each Director shall 'hold office for a term of three years unless removed by the Central Government and may be appointed thereafter for a further term or terms of such duration as the Central Government may in appointing him therefor determine'. The Damodar Valley Corporation Act did not prescribe any tenure of office, but under the DVC Rules, 1948 (as amended in 1953), the Chairman, Members, Secretary and Financial Adviser 'shall be appointed for such term not exceeding five years as the Central Government may think fit and shall be eligible for reappointment'. The first DVC Board was appointed for a period of five years. But, thereafter, a period of instability set in. There were frequent changes in chairmanship. The term of DVC Chairman has varied from three months to five years.

The Governor and the Deputy Governor of the Reserve Bank of India hold office 'for such term not exceeding five years as the Central Government may fix when appointing them', certain other Directors hold office for four years, and one Government official nominated by the Central Government holds office during the pleasure of the Central Government. The position is almost similar in case of the State Bank of India, but out of six elected directors 'two shall retire at the end of one year, two at the end of two years and two at the end of three years'. The Chairman of the Industrial Finance Corporation of India holds office for three years and the elected Directors for four years. In case of the Air India International, Mr J. R. D. Tata was appointed as Chairman for a period of three years but he has been allowed to continue thereafter on the basis of extensions. In case of the Rehabilitation Finance Administration, the Officials are members 'during the pleasure of the Central Government' and Non-officials only for two years. The members of the Life Insurance Corporation also hold office for two years only. In case of the Employees' State Insurance Corporation, the Minister for Labour is the Chairman, *ex-officio,* and the Minister of Health is the Vice-Chairman, *ex-officio*. Representatives of the employers, employees, medical profession and Parliament hold office for four years.

In case of Government Companies, the position is worse. Here, as far as Official Directors are concerned, there is generally no fixed tenure of office. For example, the Articles of Association of the National Small Industries Corporation provide that 'the President shall be entitled from time to time to remove any Director'. During the first four years of its existence (February 1955 to February 1959) this corporation had seen five Chairmen. Further, during the first two years, the average duration of office of the representative of the Ministry of Finance on the Board was only three and a half months. In case of the Hindustan Machine Tools, leaving aside the

I   129

Managing Director and the nominees of foreign collaborators, the maximum period for which the same director continued on the board (between 1953 and 1957) was two and three-quarter years; the minimum was one month only.[2] In case of the Sindri Fertilizers and Chemicals, three Managing Directors came into picture during the year 1953-54: one worked in April and (part of) May and again from (part of) June to September; a second one worked in (part of) May and June; and the third one from (part of) September onwards.

In fine, it may be suggested that the members of Governing Boards should be appointed for five, six or seven years so that they may take interest in their work and try to achieve real improvements in their organization.

B. THE FREQUENCY OF BOARD MEETINGS

The effectiveness of the Board's control over an undertaking would, to a considerable degree, depend on the number of times the Board can meet to take stock of the changing situations. Before 1956, there was no provision in this regard in the Companies Act. In that year it was laid down that the Board of Directors must meet at least once in three months. This minimum must, therefore, be adhered to by the Government Companies as well. However, in actual practice, four meetings in a year are likely to prove too inadequate for the job. The Board of the Eastern Shipping Corporation met eight times in 1956-57 and nine times in 1957-58. But the Board of Nahan Foundry met only five times in each of these years.

The Statutory Corporations are not governed by the minimum number of meetings prescribed in the Companies Act.[3] But in actual practice, their Boards have been meeting almost as frequently. The Indian Airlines Corporation met eleven times in the first year of its existence. But in later years the frequency fell to four or five. In case of the Industrial Finance Corporation, the maximum number of meetings (1948-59) was nine during the year 1954-55 and the minimum was five in several of the years. During 1958-59, eight meetings were held, five in New Delhi and one each in Bombay, Calcutta and Madras.[4] The total number of Board meetings during

[2] In case of the National Small Industries Corporation this minimum was eleven days only.

[3] The Reserve Bank of India Act lays down that meetings of the Central Board shall be convened at least six times in each year and at least once in each quarter.

[4] This practice was suggested by Industrial Finance Corporation Enquiry Committee, 1952. The same is intended to bring the Corporation in closer touch with regional problems and to meet the criticism of over-centralization (i.e. New Delhi becoming too important). In theory, this practice has several advantages, but in practice it may be quite inconvenient and even risky. (Since 1952 a similar practice has been adopted by the British Broadcasting Corporation.)

the first decade of the IFC's existence amounted to sixty, giving an annual average of six meetings. The annual average for the Reserve Bank of India comes to 7.4. As against this, the average in case of the Tennessee Valley Authority works out to 14.4.[5] The range of variation was 10-18. The Port of London Authority meets ten times in a year and the annual average in case of the Canadian National Railways is eleven. This is quite near the ideal. We feel that a Board to be really effective should meet once a month, i.e. about a dozen times a year.

C. THE SIZE OF THE BOARDS

It is difficult to lay down any hard and fast rules for determining the optimum or ideal size of a Board. In practice it has been found that there is not much relationship between the size of an undertaking and the size of the Board. In certain cases an inverse correlation is discernible. For example, the Railway Board which manages the biggest public undertaking in India has a strength of five members; the Hindustan Steel Ltd, which comes next, has a Board of ten; and the Life Insurance Corporation of India, which is third in order of merit, has a membership of fifteen.

However, it appears that Finance and Development Corporations tend to have a bigger size of the Board, possibly because of the need to provide representation to various interests, especially financial institutions. The Reserve Bank of India and the State Bank of India have fifteen and twenty members respectively. The Employees' State Insurance Corporation, with thirty-four members, heads the list and the National Co-operative Development and Warehousing Board comes next with twenty-two members. Both these Corporations are dominated by Government officials, many of them being *ex-officio* members.

Whether the size of a Board should be big or small is linked up with the question of giving representation to sectional interests or to various Ministries. When such representation is provided for, the size of the Board is swelled up with every possible danger of encouraging disharmonies. Again, the size of a Board also depends on whether there are full-time members, part-time members or a mixture of the two. The size of full-time Boards, as in case of the TVA, the DVC (up to April 1958) and the Indian Railway Board, is likely to be smaller than part-time or mixed Boards. In the USSR and People's China, the Single Directorship system is quite common.

[5] The TVA met 17 times in 1949, 18 times in 1950, 16 times in 1951, 15 times in 1952, again 15 times in 1953, 14 times in 1954, 11 times in 1955, 12 times in 1956, 10 times in 1957 and 16 times in 1958. Figures made available by courtesy of the Director of Information, TVA.

This method can be followed in many of the small-sized enterprises in India. From the viewpoint of accountability, such a system is ideal. However, in case of corporations falling in the financial group, public opinion, for fear of personal patronage and heavy loads of responsibility on one person, may not favour the introduction of Single Directorship system. Moreover, in case of operative under-takings, where there are diverse and highly technical activities to be supervised, it may be necessary to have a Board containing some functional experts. However, even in such cases a big Board may not be conducive to efficient operation. A small Board with three to seven members is likely to feel an adequate sense of responsibility which may make for quick disposal of business and harmonious working. Besides the classic example of the TVA, small-sized Boards are to be found in a number of countries. The Pakistan Industrial Development Corporation Act lays down that there shall be five Directors. The Uniform Charter for Government Corporations in the Philippines (1951) lays down that the corporate powers of the corporation shall be vested in and exercised by a Board of Directors of not more than seven or less than five members as may be fixed by the President of the Philippines, consisting of a Chairman and six or four members appointed by the President of the Philippines with the consent of the Commission on Appointments. The Boards in Ceylon are relatively small, with four to six members.[6] In case of the Japanese National Railways, the Board of Directors is com-posed of a President, a Vice-President and five to ten Directors.[7]

Most of the State Corporations in India have moved away from the ideal of a small Board. The DVC Act of 1948, no doubt, clearly laid down that the Corporation shall consist of a Chairman and two Members (all the three being appointed on whole-time basis).[8] But the Rehabilitation Finance Administration Act passed in the same year (1948) provided for a strength of seven, raised to nine by Act I of 1950. The Industrial Finance Corporation Act, 1948, provided for a Board of twelve members (raised to thirteen by Act XXVIII of 1955). The Employees' State Insurance Act of 1948 stipulated a giant Board whose membership would vary with the number of States. The Air Corporations Act, 1953, was a considerable improve-ment because it provided for 'not less than five but not more than nine members', but in practice the maximum became the minimum.

[6] *Some Problems of Organization and Management of Public Industrial Enterprises: A Case-study on Ceylon,* by the ECAFE Secretariat, December 1959, p. 15.

[7] H. Nakajima and K. Yamamura, *Management of Public Industrial Enterprises in Japan,* December 1959, p. 12.

[8] The DVC Amendment Act of 1957 did not disturb the size of the Board, but it gave discretion to the Government to appoint part-time or full-time members.

The State Bank Act of 1955 and the Life Insurance Corporation Act of 1956 stipulated much bigger Boards.

In case of Government Companies, the number of Directors is often left to be determined, from time to time, by the President of India. But in certain cases, the Articles of Association prescribe the minimum and maximum number of Directors, e.g.:

Government Company	Minimum	Maximum
1. The Eastern Shipping Corporation	4	11
2. Hindustan Shipyard	6	14
3. The National Industrial Development Corporation	15	25
4. Hindustan Antibiotics	2	Not prescribed
5. Ashoka Hotels	7	24

D. THE COMPOSITION OF GOVERNING BODIES

The following table gives an idea regarding the composition of the Boards of Public Corporations in India:

	Officials	Non-Officials	Total
1. Damodar Valley Corporation	3	0	3
2. Rehabilitation Finance Administration ...	5	4	9
3. Industrial Finance Corporation of India ...	7	6	13
4. Employees' State Insurance Corporation ...	22	12	34
5. Reserve Bank of India	5	10	15
6. Indian Airlines Corporation	5	4	9
7. Air India International	6	3	9
8. State Bank of India	6	14	20
9. Life Insurance Corporation of India ...	9	6	15
10. National Co-operative Development and Warehousing Board	13	9	22
11. Central Warehousing Corporation	10	4	14
Total ...	91	72	163

Thus the average size of the Board in 1957 was 14.8, with 8.2 Officials and 6.6 Non-officials. Non-officials were in a majority in case of the Reserve Bank of India and the State Bank of India. The DVC provides the only instance of an exclusively official Board. The Airways Corporations which are commercial organizations, *par excellence,* have encouraged non-official participation. The Air India International has had a non-official chairman during all these six years (1953-59)—Mr J. R. D. Tata, who was also the Chairman of the Air India International Ltd, before nationalization. Out of seventy-two non-official Directors, thirty were Businessmen, seven were Trade Union Leaders and seven were Members of Parliament. A number of persons were holding several Directorships.

In March 1959, the position stood as follows with regard to

fourteen Government Companies falling within the jurisdiction of
the Ministry of Commerce and Industry:

	Officials	Non-Officials	Total
1. National Industrial Development Corpora-tion	8	9	17
2. National Small Industries Corporation ...	6	4	10
3. Indian Handicrafts Development Corpora-tion	3	4	7
4. Nangal Fertilizers and Chemicals	6	2	8
5. Heavy Electricals	9	2	11
6. Sindri Fertilizers and Chemicals	6	4	10
7. Hindustan Machine Tools	7	1	8
8. Hindustan Cables	8	3	11
9. Hindustan Antibiotics	7	4	11
10. Hindustan Insecticides (March 1958) ...	6	3	9
11. Nahan Foundry	9	1	10
12. National Instruments	6	2	8
13. State Trading Corporation	11	1	12
14. Export Risks Insurance Corporation ...	3	4	7
Total ...	95	44	139

Here the average size of the Board was 9.9, with 6.8 Officials and
3.1 Non-officials. Thus Government Companies had not only a
smaller size of Board (as compared to Public Corporations), but
they had also a smaller percentage of Non-officials. Similar trends
are to be observed in case of Government Companies belonging to
other Ministries. Under the Ministry of Steel, Mines and Fuel,
Hindustan Steel had a Board of ten with seven Officials and three
Non-officials. The Official Directors included the Chairman, the
Deputy Chairman, three General Managers of the three Steel Plants
(Rourkela, Bhilai, and Durgapur), the Joint Secretary of the Ministry
and the Chief Industrial Adviser. Formerly, Mr S. Bhoothalingam,
ICS, Secretary, Ministry of Steel, was the Chairman. Later on Mr G.
Pande, Deputy Chairman (and ex-Chairman of the Railway Board),
was raised to the office of Chairman. It is usual for each of the
Government Companies to have a labour leader and one representa-
tive of the Ministry of Finance on its Board.

The appointment of Departmental Secretaries on the Boards of
Government Companies has caused a great deal of instability. We
have seen that the average tenure of the representatives of the
Ministry of Finance in certain cases was only three and a half
months. This means that they can attend only one or two meetings, and
sometimes none. Every new representative must take some time to
grasp the situation. Moreover, the Departmental Secretaries depend
upon the dictates of their respective Minister-in-charge. When the
Secretaries come to the Board meetings they are not armed with

full powers to take decisions, specially if certain new points crop up during the course of discussion. Sometimes they do not get time even to go through the papers sent to them in advance. In such a situation they cannot obtain briefs from the Minister concerned. The result is that Board decisions are deferred and there is an insurmountable craving to get matters postponed. Since Departmental Secretaries belonging to several Ministries assemble at Boards, there is no harmony and no unifying spirit. This is specially so when the several Ministers are at loggerheads—every boss taking pleasure in making the work of others difficult. Further, when Ministers (like civil servants) fly from department to department like homeless birds, it is clear that abiding interests cannot develop, and that their responsibility for efficient management is more illusory than real.[9]

Not only the Government Companies, but even Public Corporations to a large extent, are at the mercy of Departmental Secretaries. The Minister and Departmental Secretaries tend to take an air of superiority in their dealings with the Boards. This superiority complex reaches its height when the relevant Act of Parliament provides that members are to hold office 'at the pleasure of Government' (Government generally meaning the Minister-in-charge). In such circumstances the Sword of Damocles naturally hangs over the heads of the members. Further, in many cases, Departmental Secretaries get themselves appointed as members of Public Corporations, thus *holding concurrent positions.* For example, the Principal Finance Secretary was appointed as the first Chairman of a giant organization like the Life Insurance Corporation of India.[10] The Principal Finance Secretary left the Chairmanship after nine months but his influence did not leave. The second Chairman was a civil servant who, according to his own confession, had no experience of running business. He went away after the Mundhra Deal. The third Chairman, again a civil servant, appeared within two years of the inception of the Corporation.

On the question whether a Board should be a Policy Board or an Executive Board, there was an interesting discussion in a Seminar organized by the Indian Institute of Public Administration in December 1957. An experienced businessman suggested at this Seminar that a Board which is involved in the day-to-day functions 'becomes so much interested in its own success or failure that it

[9] Om Prakash, 'The Problem of Entrepreneurship in Socialist Economy', *Indian Journal of Economics,* Special Number on Problems of Socialist Economy, Vol. XXXIX, No. 152, July 1958, p. 68.
[10] It would appear that he was operating the Corporation with one hand and scrutinizing its activities with the other. The subordinates found it extremely difficult to distinguish between his two rôles.

will never be able to assess objectively and correctly all that is happening'.[11] Another participant observed: 'I do not think the Board of Directors ever run a concern. The Board of Directors consists of a group of men who have fairly wide experience and whose general advice is valuable.'[12] One of the members suggested that 'the most important function of the Board of Directors was to ask intelligent questions'. Thus there was general consensus of opinion on this point. Various suggestions were made that the executive functions be entrusted to a Managing Director or a Standing Committee or a Board of Management (or a Sub-Board on the Burmese model).

One of the members, however, asserted that 'Here in a public enterprise the policy-making authority is not really the Board at all. It is rested somewhere between the Ministry at the top level and the representatives of the Ministry on the Board, and therefore the idea that the Board of Directors must be the policy-making body does not meet the situation.'[13] The Estimates Committee also reject the idea of a Policy Board. They recommend that the management of an undertaking should be entrusted to a Managing Director or a Board of Managing Directors depending upon the size of and importance of the undertaking—usually when a Board of Managing Directors is constituted, it should consist of three or four members, one of whom may be the Chairman; the Chairman and members of such Boards should work collectively and on a functional basis.[14]

The Committee feel that there should be an Advisory Body to advise the Managing Director from time to time. The Body will be composed of representatives from business, labour or workers, consumers and Parliament or Local Legislatures. The Advisory Body will only render advice and will have no powers to decide matters of policy or to give orders to execute any of their directions. It will invariably send a copy of their report to the Minister concerned for information. The Advisory Body will have the right of asking or calling for information on all matters excepting those which have been specified by the Minister as being of a secret nature. It will also have the right of unlimited criticism and will offer advice on any matters they deem fit. The Advisory Body will be kept informed

[11] *Administrative Problems of State Enterprises in India,* Report of a Seminar, December 1957, Indian Institute of Public Administration, New Delhi, p. 22.
[12] *Ibid.,* p. 21.
[13] *Ibid.,* p. 20.
[14] Estimates Committee, Sixteenth Report, *Organization and Administration of Nationalized Industrial Undertakings,* Lok Sabha Secretariat, New Delhi, June 1955, p. 3. The Committee further recommended direct relationship between the Minister and the Board (without any intrusion of the Secretariat).

by the Managing Director through progress reports, balance sheets, development plans and any other schemes which the management may have in view.[15]

Now the Estimates Committee seem to aim at (*though they have not mentioned*) killing three birds with one stone. On the one hand they are trying to transplant the German pattern of organization on Indian soil. German corporate organization has long been based on a twofold system—a Board of Management (*Vorstand*) and a Council of Supervision (*Aufsichtsrat*). Privately-owned companies have worked on that basis. State Corporations—which are not many in West Germany—have followed a somewhat similar pattern. Thus the *Deutsche Bundesbahn* (Federal Railways), under the Statute of December 18, 1951, has a Governing Board (*Vorstand*) and an Administrative Council (*Verwaltungsrat*) which is a compromise between the genuine Supervisory Council to be found in case of commercial companies, and the merely advisory council as it existed under the Nazi regime.[16] The Administrative Council has a *reserve power* and it can decide any question of general importance, besides preparation of annual economic plans and laying down policies with regard to personnel and finance.

Secondly, the Estimates Committee perhaps intend to give a trial —in an indirect manner—to the tripartite composition of Boards as found in France. Professor Robson suggests: 'At best a factious board, or one which cannot agree, may be by-passed by an energetic Director-General; but this is scarcely a tribute to the principles on which the board is founded!'[17] Further, a first-hand study by a student of the London School of Economics and Political Science has shown that *tripartism* has so weakened and divided the Board and it is, in any case, so large and non-homogenous a body, that instead of playing the counterbalancing rôle between Minister and Director-General (one might have expected it to play) it leaves the field even more wide open for closer interplay between the two.[18]

Thirdly, the Estimates Committee appear to be laying down the foundation for a Parliamentary Committee on Nationalized Industries whose members may sit on the Boards of various Public Corporations and Government Companies. However, the Advisory Body as suggested by the Estimates Committee would not satisfy

[15] *Ibid.*, p. 4. The Krishna Menon Report on State Undertakings (November 1959) finds 'little merit' in such Advisory Boards.

[16] W. Friedmann and H. Hufnagel, *The Public Corporation in Germany*, Friedmann (Ed.), 1954.

[17] William A. Robson, *Nationalization in Britain and France*, Ed. 1952, p. 263.

[18] Margaret Finnegan, 'Ministerial Control of *Electricité de France*', *Public Administration*, London, Winter 1954.

137

Parliament. Whether the Minister would like to place sufficient reliance on such a Body is again very doubtful. There appears to be a twofold danger: either the Advisory Body may become a defunct organization like many of the Advisory Committees; or it may develop into a spy system over the head of the Board, depriving the latter of initiative and independent judgment. It may make the Board-Parliament relationship still more complicated through the addition of one more 'tier' in the administrative structure.

Mr A. D. Gorwala rightly suggests[19] that there is no place on the board of an autonomous authority for the representatives of interests. Such a board is not a forum for the settling of points of difference among various interests each of which pulls its own way; its purpose being good management in the public interest, its responsibilities are not to any sectional groups but to the public as a whole.[20] Mr Gorwala feels that even when, in exceptional cases, a subsidy has to be given to an autonomous undertaking, that should not be made a ground for departmental representatives participating in internal control.[21]

Mr Paul H. Appleby is prepared to give greater latitude to civil servants. But he concedes that a Departmental Secretary cannot be an effective chairman of a large number of Boards—it depends on 'his ability to think and act one way for a Corporation and another way for the Ministry proper. . . . Two hats are not likely to be worn *with grace if they are too extremely unlike'*.[22] The American expert adds that the parent Minister, his Secretary and the Managing Director are the crucial trio; they will not get the scope they should have unless they are strong, imaginative, insistent upon results, and skilful in winning support, and then diligent in the practice of delegation.[23] The dangers involved in the bureaucratization of the Boards were visualized earlier by the Estimates Committee.[24]

[19] *Report of the Efficient Conduct of State Enterprises,* by A. D. Gorwala, Government of India, Planning Commission, 1951, pp. 19-20.

[20] *Ibid.* To avoid overlapping of responsibility and to maintain integrity of political life, Ministers and Members of Parliament should not be members of such Boards.

[21] There is, however, a loophole in Mr Gorwala's report. He concedes that in certain cases (e.g. where the Department represented is the main customer), the departmental representative may attend Board meetings; but he should not be a member and should have no vote.

[22] *Re-examination of India's Administrative System with Special Reference to Administration of Government's Industrial and Commercial Enterprises,* by Paul H. Appleby, Government of India, Cabinet Secretariat, Organization and Methods Division, New Delhi, 1956, p. 39.

[23] *Ibid.*

[24] Estimates Committee, Ninth Report, *Administrative, Financial and Other Reforms,* Lok Sabha Secretariat, New Delhi, May 1954, p. 17. If a proposal is not acceptable to a Departmental Secretary he may get the whole thing shelved or vetoed when it comes to the Ministry for a decision.

The organization of the Damodar Valley Corporation was attacked by the Estimates Committee as early as March 1952. Comparing it with the TVA, the Committee opined: 'The DVC has followed the form but lost the spirit.'[25] The P. S. Rau Committee did not accept the above view: 'Members of a functional corporation, being executive heads of their departments are, as a rule, unable to devote undivided attention both to the numerous problems of the Corporation as a whole and to the day-to-day administration of the departments under their charge. Besides, this combination of functions deprives the members of their detachment. In the functional set-up there is over-centralization and a distinct danger of *vertical compartments with divided loyalties* being formed inside the organization with the functional member at the head of each. We would, however, add that *whatever method we may adopt, in the ultimate analysis it is the quality of the members that counts.* On the whole we are doubtful whether a corporation composed of executive heads as envisaged by the Estimates Committee would be the best. Having regard to all the circumstance, we consider that the policy-making corporation is in every way better than a functional board.'[26] The Estimates Commiteee, in their Eighth Report, reiterated their earlier stand: 'There appears to be some confusion in the presentation of facts by the Rau Committee. The Policy whether a river valley scheme has to be undertaken and, if so, at what cost and on what technical data, has to be determined by the Government of India. Once this policy decision is taken, all that remains to be done is that the scheme has to be executed in accordance with the decisions taken by the Government. The latter alone is the business of the DVC.'[27] But it is not so simple as that. The Government of India are expected to lay down only the broad policy. Within that ambit the Corporation has to take numerous policy decisions; and this process is a continuous one.[28]

The above issue was examined in Great Britain by two important Committees: Report of the Advisory Committee on Organization,

[25] Estimates Committee, Fifth Report, *The Central Water and Power Commission and Multi-Purpose River Valley Schemes,* Parliament Secretariat, New Delhi, March 1952, p. 25. The main grievance of the Estimates Committee was that there was no engineering expert like Dr Arthur Morgan of TVA. The first DVC Board consisted of a civil servant, a legislator and a food technologist.

[26] *Report of the Damodar Valley Corporation Enquiry Committee,* June 3, 1953, Government of India Press, New Delhi, 1954, p. 83. (Italics ours.)

[27] Estimates Committee, Eighth Report, *Damodar Valley Corporation,* Lok Sabha Secretariat, New Delhi, May 1954, p. 12.

[28] The Gorwala Report on *The Efficient Conduct of State Enterprise* suggests that the policy Board is likely to be more effective at least in regard to undertakings that have to be given the Joint Stock Company form.

National Coal Board, February 1955 (*Fleck Report*); and the Report of the Committee of Inquiry into the Electricity Supply Industry, January 1956 (*Herbert Report*). Whereas the Fleck Committee had recommended the principle of an executive board at national level, the Herbert Committee wished to see the Central Authority stripped of its executive functions and left merely with supervisory powers. The Central Electricity Authority was to approve such items as capital and revenue budgets, tariffs, research and labour relations, but its executive responsibility for generation and transmission was to be relinquished (to a new statutory corporation called the Central Electricity Generation Board and by a reduction in its authority over the areas). The Central Authority was to inspire, but in no case was it to exercise coercion. Whereas the Fleck Committee had emphasized the managerial nature of the Divisional Board and recognized that part-time members would weaken its authority, the Herbert Committee recommended an Area Board composed exclusively of part-time members (including the Chairman). It was suggested that the establishment of a full-time Board would tend to subordinate local management to functional control, and to attract power to the centre. Part-time members, it was felt, would be less likely to usurp the authority which was best exercised by lower formations.[29]

The dispute between the 'functional' Board and the 'policy' Board cannot be finally settled, because public enterprises differ so widely in their purposes and characteristics and in the external influences to which they are subjected.[30] The functional Board, consisting of experts in charge of particular departments, permits the existence of a small Board because, generally speaking, functional experts will be employed on whole-time basis.

Further, each functional head will put in his best so that he may not have to face an awkward position at the Board meeting. That is, the functional pattern encourages a sense of responsibility because each member may be held strictly accountable for the performance

[29] Alan E. Thompson, 'Organisation in Two Nationalised Industries', *Scottish Journal of Political Economy,* Vol. IV, June 1957, No. 2, pp. 95-6. Footnote 35 in that article is rather misleading. Fleck Report's suggestion that 'normally, therefore, the industry will have to breed its own full-time members' has been interpreted as 'a policy of career appointment held until the normal age of retirement'. The Fleck Committee never suggested that 'Once a member of NCB should always be a member of NCB.' They only appreciated the fact that, the entire coal industry being nationalized, technical experts could only be procured internally (gradually rising from the bottom).

[30] Mr A. H. Hanson has a preference for the 'policy' type of Boards for enterprises in underdeveloped countries. See his *Public Enterprise and Economic Development* (pp. 403-10) and his Basic Discussion Paper, *Management of Public Industries,* Seminar on Management of Public Industrial Enterprises, New Delhi, December 1959, p. 35.

of his department. It also ensures better supervision and closer contact between top management and the point of actual operation. Finally, it is better placed to understand technical problems and to bring about technological improvements.

The case for a policy Board,[31] on the other hand, is that functional experts have often been found to be bad administrators. They interfere too much with the work of their subordinates and tend to become vindictive and short-sighted. Moreover, functional experts are often at loggerheads. They refuse to be considerate and accommodating. Hence they cannot easily bring about that teamwork and harmony which are so necessary for the successful functioning of a Board. The functional Board may lack the necessary prestige and popular support (both within and outside the organization) because it gets involved in petty details and fails to take a broad view of the situation. As against this, a policy Board may be better suited for promoting workers' participation and for conducting public relations. A policy Board may also be in a better position both to take commands and to issue commands. Finally, it may be better placed to interpret and to execute the policy instructions of the Government.

Thus, while technological considerations go in favour of the functional Board, sociological considerations suggest the superiority of the policy Board. In the ultimate analysis, sociological considerations may triumph. However, in case of industrial corporations, due place must be given to functional experts. They may not be formally put in charge of particular departments; but their presence at Board meetings will dispel much ignorance from which laymen are bound to suffer. In case of commercial and social service corporations, the rôle of functional experts may be less important; even then, it will be quite significant. While a policy Board is, on the whole, preferable, the ideal of a small-sized full-time Board should not be given up. Moreover, in the interest of proper accountability, Departmental Secretaries and Members of Parliament should not be made Members of the Governing Boards.[32] Private industrialists and business executives can be appointed to the Boards provided they are prepared to serve in a full-time capacity. Similar considerations will apply to members of learned professions and other eminent personages. As a rule, State Corporations should be kept clear of active politicians.

[31] Various interpretations may be given to the term policy Board. It may mean a Board of laymen, or a Board of all-rounders, or a Board representing the various sections of the society. It may also mean a Board of outsiders, i.e. those who have not been bred within the organization.

[32] This viewpoint has been supported by the Krishna Menon Committee (November 1959).

E. EMOLUMENTS AND AGE

With regard to the salaries payable to members of Public Corporations, the position stood as follows in England: [33]

	Annual Salary £
Chairmen	
1. British European Airways, Road Passenger Executive, London Transport Executive, Road Haulage Executive, and Docks Executive	5,000
2. Hotels Executive (part-time, drawing no salary but entitled to)	2,000
3. Gas Council	6,000
4. Railway Executive	7,000
5. British Overseas Airways Corporation	7,500
6. British Transport Commission, National Coal Board, and British Electricity Authority	8,500
Deputy Chairmen	
1. London Transport Executive, and British Overseas Airways Corporation	3,500
2. British European Airways (part-time, drawing no salary but entitled to)	1,500
3. British Transport Commission, National Coal Board, Gas Council, and British Electricity Council	5,000
Full-time Members	
1. British Transport Commission, National Coal Board and Railway Executive	5,000
2. British European Airways	3,000
3. Other Boards	3,500
Part-time Members	
1. British Electricity Authority	1,000
2. British Transport Commission	750
3. Other Boards	500

The maximum annual salary in these giant national undertakings is £8,500 (about Rs 9,500 per month) which pales into insignificance when we are told about the fabulous salary of £12,500 (about Rs 14,000 per month, but in terms of the pre-war purchasing power of the rupee at least Rs 56,000) fixed for the Chairman of the London Passenger Transport Board. The TVA established in the same year as the LPTB (1933) paid only $10,000 per year to its Chairman, as also to the other members. According to the pre-devaluation (1949) rate of exchange the TVA scale would amount to Rs 2,750 per month; according to the pre-war purchasing power it would be still Rs 11,000 only. The position stood as follows in July 1959:

[33] The Acton Society Trust, *The Men on the Boards,* Nationalized Industry, Research Paper 4, 1951, p. 13.

Tennessee Valley Authority				Annual Salary
				$
1. Chairman ...	...	...	...	20,500
2. Other Members	...	...	...	20,000
3. General Manager	...	...	...	19,000
4. Office and Division Heads	...		...	14,600 to 18,500

Canadian National Railways[34]				
1. 'Chairman and President'	...		...	75,000
2. Other Members	...	...	...	5,000

In terms of Indian rupees the TVA members are receiving about Rs 8,000 per month—a very moderate salary according to American standards. On inception, the Chairman and other TVA members were on equal footing. Today, the Chairman stands nominally upgraded. The most covetable salary is of the 'Chairman and President' of the Canadian National Railways—about Rs 30,000 per month. But considering the changes in the purchasing power of the Indian rupee, even he would be worse off than the Chairman of the pre-war London Passenger Transport Board. The Acton Society Trust rightly observe that 'the most striking thing about these figures is that salaries do not seem to have been allotted on any consistent principle'.

In India salaries are generally paid not according to the undertaking which a Member is required to serve but according to his personal status. None of the Acts lays down the salary of the Members of Public Corporations. In England, too, specific salaries are generally not mentioned. But the salaries of the Governors and Directors of the Bank of England and of the BBC are laid down in the Charter.[35] The TVA also prescribes specific salaries. The Damodar Valley Corporation in India started with high ideals, with three full-time Members (including the Chairman). The Chairman was paid Rs 4,000 per month and the other two Members Rs 2,500 each. The high idealism, however, disappeared in 1957 when the DVC Act was amended to permit the appointment of Part-time Members. In July 1959 all the three Members were ICS men working on part-time basis. They received their usual salaries from the Government of India (i.e. the salaries payable to them according to their personal grade, length of service, etc.). The DVC paid only their travelling

---

[34] Information made available by courtesy of the Director of Public Relations, Canadian National Railways, July 1959.

[35] *For Bank of England*: Governor, £2,000; Deputy Governor, £1,500; each Director £500 (Governor, Deputy Governor and not more than four directors giving their exclusive services to the Bank may receive additional payments and a pension or capital grant). *For BBC*: Chairman, £3,000; Vice-Chairman, National Governors for Scotland and Wales, £1,000 each; National Governor for Northern Ireland and other Governors, £600 each. The Broadcasting Committee had suggested considerably higher salaries. The BBC salaries are substantially lower than those obtaining in several other Corporations.

allowances. The two Part-time Members were appointed for a period of two years with effect from April 12, 1958. The Part-time Chairman was appointed for only three months with effect from April 12, 1959. This period was extended for another three months with effect from July 12, 1959. These part-time arrangements were made 'due to reduced pressure of work'.[36]

The civil servants themselves being the managers of most of the public enterprises, the problem of fixing salaries has not been seriously discussed in India. At any rate, no attempt has been made to pay salaries higher than those of senior civil servants, because private industry has *not* been a serious competitor in attracting the best brains. The Director General of Indian Posts and Telegraphs (who manages an important Departmental enterprise—now converted into a semi-autonomous Board, on the lines of the Railway Board, with the Director General as Chairman) was receiving in July 1959 a salary of Rs 3,500 per month. He was a senior ICS man aged fifty. About the same salaries are paid to full-time members of the Public Corporation. In England such salaries have exceeded the salary of the top men in Government. Such a situation does not exist in India.

The average age of Members of the TVA as in July 1959 was 58. In Great Britain, the average age of the 12 Chairmen was 61; the youngest being 53, and the oldest 68. The average of the Board members exclusive of the Chairmen was between 56 and 57; the youngest being 36 and the oldest 67. The average age of the part-time members was between 55 and 56. The Gas Council (51), and the Air Corporations (54), fell in the younger age group; whereas the old age group included the National Coal Board (58), the British Electricity Authority (60), the Railway Executive (60) and the British Transport Commission (62).[37] Out of 47 full-time Members, only 4 were drawn from the Civil Service. There were 13 Company Directors, 10 Managers and Engineers, 9 Trade Unionists, 3 Accountants, 3 men from Armed Forces, 2 Solicitors, 1 drawn from the Co-operative Movement, 1 Scientist and 1 who had been 'an aircraft designer, journalist, airman, civil servant, and business executive'.[38] This pattern is much better than the Indian model but it has been criticized on the ground that 'Ministers are being driven more and more to play safe and to appoint technical experts from inside the industries.

[36] However, when the present writer met the Full-time Chairman of the DVC in September 1957, the latter was found to be extremely busy, with a huge pile of paper work to be disposed of.

[37] Acton Society Trust, *The Men on the Boards*, 1951, pp. 4-5. In case of Port of London Authority (not included in the Trust's study) the minimum age was 50, and maximum 60 (information made available by courtesy of the Chief Information Officer, Port of London Authority, August 1959).

[38] *Ibid.*, p. 6.

The result is to make the industries more and more into close corporations, consisting on the one hand of Boards and management and on the other of the trade unions. This development will mean that the nation, either as consumer or taxpayer, will have little say in the policy of the industries. The nation may own the industries, but, so far, it has enjoyed the liabilities rather than the benefits of ownership.'[39] These remarks seem to overstate the defects of the British pattern.

The Krishna Menon Committee have suggested that the Chairman of a Board of Directors normally, at the time of his appointment, should be between thirty and forty years so that it does not become the practice that 'the Chairmanship of Boards is a kind of "berth" for retiring civil servants or others, who are appointed to a post as part of a reward for any services they might have rendered to a political party'.[40] While the objective which the Committee have in view is laudable, the lower limit is really of no use because it is very difficult to find a Chairman younger than thirty.[41] The upper age limit, no doubt, is relevant as we do not want the Boards to become the abodes of retired persons. In view of our thesis that a Chairman should be appointed for not less than five years,[42] the maximum age limit of fifty years at the time of appointment would ensure that he would retire almost at the same age as any other civil servant.

This age limit, however, would create one anomaly. Directors of corporate undertakings registered under the Indian Companies Act, 1956, can continue in office up to the age of sixty-five years (and even after that, if specially exempted by the shareholders). In fact, before 1956, there was no limit at all. Hence even the limit of 65 years was opposed on the ground that India is short of managerial talent.[43]

[39] R. Kelf-Cohen, *Nationalisation in Britain: The End of a Dogma,* Macmillan, London, 1958, p. 209.

[40] *Parliamentary Supervision over State Undertakings,* being the Report of the Sub-Committee of the Congress Party in Parliament, November 1959, p. 12.

[41] The idea may be that civil servants or members of the newly introduced Indian Economic Service may not be entrusted with Chairmanship unless they have put in (say) ten years' service. If maturity of mind is aimed at, thirty-five years will be a safe lower limit.

[42] The Krishna Menon Committee do not accept this position. They suggest a three-year tenure for the Chairman and two-year term for other Board members. As the terms are renewable, will the maximum age limit apply at the time of every renewal? Suppose a man was appointed as Chairman at forty-nine. At the end of his first term he will be fifty-two. Should he be reappointed? If he is again appointed the age limit is violated. If he is not reappointed merely on the ground of age, he is worse off than ordinary civil servants who may retire at fifty-five or about that.

[43] A more forceful ground for opposing such a limit in the private sector is the commonly accepted practice that there is no maximum age limit for elective offices. If there is no age bar for Members of Parliament and for

However, we have already found a solution to meet this shortage, viz. the Boards should be small-sized; even the Single Dictatorship system can be accepted for certain undertakings and the Government Companies can be exempted from the minimum limit of two or three directors applicable to private and public companies respectively.

Ministers why should such a bar exist for Company Directors? Moreover, if lawyers, doctors and private shopkeepers can continue to practise their profession or trade till the last day of their life, why should the Company Directors (in the private sector) be deprived of their means of livelihood?

CHAPTER VII

INDUSTRIAL RELATIONS

A. WORKERS' PARTICIPATION IN MANAGEMENT

State Corporations have to show greater concern for workers' co-operation than Privately-owned Corporations because:

(1) State Corporations are often running essential services and any breakdown in these may paralyse the whole life of the nation.

(2) Where Public Corporations have emerged as a result of nationalization programmes, the working class expect their status to be raised fundamentally—the slogan 'mines for the miners' still creates considerable enthusiasm.

(3) In recent years, leading Corporations in the private sector—maybe in their own selfish interest—have instituted schemes of workers' participation. As such, State Corporations have not to lag behind in this race. They must be one step ahead.

In support of the first criterion we present an analysis of strikes which the Port of London Authority had to face during a decade:[1]

Details of Strikes, 1949-59 (Year ending March 31)

June 14-29, 1948	Unofficial strike—19,000 men and 50 ships affected.
April 11-16, 1949	Unofficial strike—11,000 men and 61 ships affected.
June 27-July 23, 1949	'Canadian Seamen's Strike'—State of Emergency declared by H.M. Government on July 11, 1949. Military labour handled 139,129 tons of goods.
April 19-May 1, 1950	Military labour employed.
May 1950	Three weeks' strike of lightermen.
February 1951	Token strikes up to 6 days in protest against: (a) pay settlement (b) criminal proceedings taken against seven dockers.
1952, 1953, 1954	Nil.
October 1954	Overtime dispute lasting greater part of the month. Court of Inquiry set up.
May 23-July 2, 1955	National Amalgamated Stevedores and Dockers Union. 6,000 men involved affecting 50 per cent of the shipping.
January 1957	Tally Clerks at Tilbury Docks.
August 1957	Unofficial action taken in sympathy with the Covent Garden Market dispute.

In India, too, strikes of dockworkers have assumed serious proportions. Among corporate enterprises in the public sector we can refer

[1] Information made available by courtesy of the Chief Information Officer, Port of London Authority, July 1959.

to the March 1960 strike in the State Bank of India—a strike which lasted for several weeks and was aimed at exercising coercive pressure on the Government at a time when the financial year was about to close. However, the strike was withdrawn a week before the close of the financial year, even though the demands of the strikers had not been accepted. The idea was that the employees of the State Bank should not lose the sympathy of the Government.[2]

The Damodar Valley Corporation has faced considerable difficulty in maintaining harmonious relations with workers. The troubles were heightened by the fact that a large number of workers were employed on a temporary basis; and both the management and the employees did not consider it necessary to devise suitable machinery for ensuring lasting harmony. Another problem which the DVC had to face was that the bulk of labour working in various constructions did not belong to the region. A decennial review of the DVC (1948-58) suggests: 'As far as possible, accommodation with facilities of water and electricity has been provided to employees. But the magnitude of the problem of accommodation has been so great, that it cannot be claimed to have been adequately solved.'[3] However, since major constructions were completed by 1958, the DVC should now have a peaceful time.

A classic illustration of the second criterion for workers' participation is to be found in Great Britain. The Labour Party, before its ascendancy to power in 1945, had promised 'higher wages' and 'less work' for the working class. Shortly after the elections, Mr Clement (now Lord) Attlee, in course of a tour, came upon a worker who had the cheek to say: 'We have begun to work less on *our* part. But what about *your part* of the promise? You have not given us higher wages.' In India, the nationalization of Life Insurance resulted in a prolonged agitation of field workers on whom the business of the LIC largely depends. Many field workers, belonging to particular companies, still remember the 'good old comforts' of the pre-nationalization era. Under the Life Insurance Corporation Field Officers' (Alteration of

[2] In January 1960 the pilots of Air India International went on strike. This would have completely paralysed air transport services but for the co-operation extended by Indian Airlines Corporation and certain foreign airlines.

[3] *DVC In Prospect and Retrospect*, Damodar Valley Corporation, Calcutta, 1958, p. 22. The DVC Report for 1954-55 gives an idea of the seriousness of labour unrest which started early in 1955 as 'go-slow' movement. The workers struck work on April 26, 1955, without notice. As the work at Maithon Dam had reached a critical stage, troops were called in for assistance. Even then, the time schedule was delayed by three months. Further, large-scale retrenchments (e.g. 2,660 employees during the year ended March 31, 1957) resulted in strikes and hunger-strikes. However, with the active assistance of the Government, 90 per cent of the retrenched workers were re-employed.

Remuneration and other Terms and Conditions of Service) Order, 1957, and the Life Insurance Corporation Field Officers' (Fixation of Pay and Allowances of Field Officers) Regulations, 1958, 3,644 Field Officers received increase in their remuneration, 221 suffered a cut, 257 were transferred to the administrative side, and the services of 136 were terminated.

The third criterion is explained by certain developments in India. An experiment in workers' participation was started by an Ahmedabad Textile Mill in August 1955. Later, the Tata Iron and Steel Co Ltd, Jamshedpur, and the Tata Workers' Union signed an agreement on January 8, 1956, which provided for the progressive association of the employees with the management in the working of the industry 'at various levels and by gradual stages'. This increased association was considered desirable—

(i) in promoting increased productivity;

(ii) in giving the employees a better understanding of their rôle in the working of the industry; and

(iii) in satisfying 'the urge for self-expression'.

A number of State Corporations have established management-labour organizations in India, e.g.:

(1) *Air India International Corporation*—Labour Relations Committee (February 1956)[4] consisting of six nominated representatives of the management and six elected representatives of the employees.

(2) *Indian Airlines Corporation*—Labour Relations Committee (May 11, 1956) consisting of ten representatives of the management and ten of the employees, the latter elected on an occupational basis. Six meetings of the Committee were held during the year 1956-57 and eight meetings during 1957-58.

(3) *Hindustan Antibiotics Ltd*—Works Committee (January 1958) consisting of five representatives from the management and five from among the workers. The Committee has been meeting at least once in every month. The recommendations of the Committee go to the Managing Director who is expected to take suitable action thereon.

(4) *Hindustan Machine Tools Ltd*—The Company was selected as the first unit in the public sector for the introduction, on an experimental basis, of workers' participation in management. A Joint Council of Management with equal representation for management and labour was inaugurated by Mr Manubhai Shah, Minister of Industry, on June 30, 1958. Subsequently, an agreement was signed on September 12, 1958, with the Employees' Union defining the

---

[4] It was required to be established under the Air Corporations Act, 1953—an Act which was passed much before the TISCO Agreement. However, the latter might have expedited the establishment of the Labour Relations Committee (to replace the *ad hoc* Advisory Committee) since Mr Tata has been the Chairman of TISCO as well as Air India International.

constitution of the Joint Council of Management, its scope and functions.

(5) *Hindustan Insecticides Ltd*[5]—An agreement was made on September 30, 1959, between the Company and the Hindustan Insecticides Employees' Union (Registered No. 447) for a period of two years (the agreement being terminable through three months' notice in writing on either side). The agreement provided for a Joint Council consisting of six members, three being representatives of the Company and three of the employees for the time being. The functions of the Council of Management established in the Hindustan Machine Tools Ltd, and the Joint Management Council of the Hindustan Insecticides Ltd,[6] have been cast in the same mould.

It is a great practical necessity to draw a dividing line between the functions of Joint Councils and Trade Unions and also between the activities of Joint Councils and Works Committees where both exist side by side.[7] The agreement dated September 30, 1959, in the Hindustan Insecticides provides that 'All matters relating to wages, bonus, etc., which are subjects for collective bargaining shall be excluded from the scope of the Council. Individual grievances shall also be excluded from its scope.' Taking the question of individual grievances first, it can be argued that they should be excluded from

---

[5] A notable example of workers' participation among non-corporate enterprises in the public sector is to be found in the case of the UP Government Cement Factory, Churk. A Works Council consisting of eight representatives of workmen and a similar number representing the management was established. (Date not mentioned—see the brochure *Churk Cement, UP Government Undertaking, 1959,* p. 17.) It is the biggest cement factory in this country.

[6] The Council's functions are fourfold—promotive, consultative, informative and operative. The second and third categories manifest the rights of the Council, whereas the first and fourth categories are in the nature of responsibilities. In the *first* category (general objectives to be promoted) we have productivity, employees' suggestions, labour laws, sense of participation and channels of communication. *Secondly,* the Council shall be consulted regarding the administration of standing orders, introduction of new methods and reduction. *Thirdly,* the Council have the right to receive information and discuss the general economic position (including accounts, reorganization schemes, etc.). *Fourthly,* the Council shall be entrusted with the administration of welfare measures, supervision of safety measures, training schemes, working hours, rewards for suggestions and any other matter agreed upon.

[7] The Seminar on Labour-Management Co-operation, held at New Delhi on January 31 and February 1, 1958, opined that since Joint Councils are working at the policy level, they can function separately without encroaching upon the functions of the Works Committee. The Seminar recommended that where Works Committees are already working in units where Joint Councils are to be set up, the Works Committees shall continue. However, we do not see any merit in the multiplication of agencies and we do not accept that the Joint Councils will merely lay down the policy.

the purview of Joint Councils, because such grievances may demean the Councils. But the question still remains as to how these grievances are to be settled. Shall we depend on Governmental machinery (e.g. labour courts) in this regard? Individual grievances are often the cause of major agitations. For example, 10,000 workers of the Rourkela Steel Project resorted to a strike on June 8, 1960, because of the dismissal of a single worker. Why should we not appoint Sub-Committees of such Councils to deal with such grievances? If we feel shy of settling such disputes, it is extremely doubtful if workers' participation can rest on any solid foundation.

Workers are generally keen to maintain the sanctity of Trade Unions so that there may be a forum where they can still speak out their heart and mind fearlessly and which may be canalized as a powerful force in times of emergency. More keen than the workers are outside leaders to maintain the strength of Trade Unions. These leaders have the Trade Unions within their grips, but they are not likely to command much influence over the Joint Councils.[8] Moreover, there may exist rival Trade Unions within an organization and they may like to pursue different political ideologies. When Joint Councils are formed, the question of recognizing one of these Unions as a representative Union becomes a difficult problem. To overcome this difficulty either workers' representatives may be chosen from several Unions (though to decide the relative strength of rival Unions is again not very easy) or the principle of Trade Union representation may be abandoned. At the Seminar on Administrative Problems of State Enterprises (December 1957) it was suggested by one of the participants that 'Trade Union nominees have no place on Joint Councils. First of all, most trade unions are not representative in our country. To give them a monopoly of representation on the Joint Council is to disfranchise a number of workers. The principle of election by departments or categories is the only one on which Joint Councils should be constituted. Thereby you create a domestic forum of the concern and its employees.'[9]

Whether we accept this system of election or not, there is at least one thing which we should be able to decide, i.e. workers' participa-

[8] The New Delhi Seminar on Labour-Management Co-operation (1958) recommended that 'Employees' representatives should be employees themselves; but, if the trade union so feels, it can appoint non-employee members to the extent of not more than 25 per cent of its quota. If the employers have no objection, the number of non-employee members may be raised to two.'

[9] The dangers of such a system of election may be twofold: on the one hand, Trade Unions may still meddle with the elections; on the other hand, if the Unions fail to get success, they may try to make failure of the Joint Councils. Of course, the danger of Trade Union representation is that it may put too much power in the hands of Union leaders. They may misuse their position and get things done for their friends and favourites.

tion must start from the lowest level. We have to avoid excessive centralization of decisions. When top leaders of management and workers negotiate matters on unit basis, industry basis and sometimes on all-India basis (what the managers of public enterprises say being subject to ratification by Government, and what the workers' representatives hold depending upon the approval of all-India labour organizations) workers' participation will lose the real spirit. Dictation from the top, even from the same interests, is likely to mar the enthusiasm and initiative of the men on the job.

In this context we may examine the feasibility of putting workers' representatives on the Boards of Directors of State Corporations. The wisdom of such representation has been doubted even by Guild Socialists.[10] Trade Union leaders, firstly, may not be welcome to the erstwhile managers of nationalized industries. When the proposition was put before the Managing Director of quite a large concern, he is reported to have said: 'Certainly it is a very good idea, but will you please find some other Managing Director first?' He was not prepared to upgrade workers' representatives because he (probably) felt that the same would make it difficult for him to enforce labour discipline. Let us hope that this hurdle is only a temporary one. To take a very old example, when the railways were started in India, the high caste people detested the idea of sitting beside the low caste people. In course of time, that reaction subsided.

However, there are bigger hurdles in the way of Trade Union representatives. By agreeing to serve on the Boards of Directors they are likely to be put in an anomalous position. If they continue to adopt a negative and oppositionist attitude at Board meetings they may be outvoted (unless we give them—what may not be easily acceptable even to a Socialist Government—a 50 per cent or greater share). Thus, instead of making any positive contribution, the presence of Trade Union representatives may only add insult to injury. On the other hand, if the Trade Union Directors adopt a compromising attitude, they may be dubbed as Quislings and turncoats. Such a situation will not only mar the future of those persons as Trade Union leaders; it may, in fact, demoralize the entire labour movement. State Corporations, both in England and India, seem to have acted wisely in not encouraging direct representation of the Trade Unions. No doubt, they have generally chosen some experts in labour matters (often belonging to other enterprises or organiza-

[10] The late Professor G. D. H. Cole in one of his last publications observes: 'The case for workers' participation in control is not a case for turning representative Trade Union leaders into either directors or managers of businesses, whether the businesses are privately or publicly owned. It is a case for giving every worker, at any rate after a short probationary period, the status of a partner in the enterprise for which he works.' (*The Case for Industrial Partnership*, Macmillan, London, 1957, p. 15.)

tions—e.g. Mr Michael John of Tata Workers' Union in case of Air Corporations) to serve on the Boards of Directors. In course of time, when workers get better educated and enlightened, and Trade Unions are freed from the influence of outsiders, the question of putting Trade Union representatives on the Governing Boards of State Corporations in India can be reconsidered. Meanwhile, we must put in every effort to make success of workers' participation at the lower and intermediate levels.

A noteworthy example of workers' participation at the top level is to be found in Yugoslavia. In every enterprise there are three organs of management—the Workers' Council, the Managing Board and the Director of the enterprise.[11] The Workers' Council is elected by all the workers and office employees on the basis of adult franchise through direct and secret voting. Workers from the basic activity of the enterprise must account for at least two-thirds of the members of the Workers' Council. Its term of office is two years and its strength of membership varies from fifteen to sixty. The Yugoslav Constitution entirely prohibits enterprises which are not managed by the workers and office employees. The Workers' Council is the top organ of the enterprise. It elects the Managing Board (consisting of three to fifteen members) which, in its turn, controls the work of the Director. However, the Director has the right and obligation to prevent enforcement of any resolutions of the Workers' Council and the Managing Board which are against law. This may certainly lead to conflicting decisions and overlapping of authority which may necessitate Governmental interference. The Workers' Council, however, has a big sweep. It conducts the economic and personnel policy of the enterprise and issues all the fundamental acts of the enterprise—its statute, pay scales, rules on labour relations, safety precautions, etc. It allocates the net receipts, issues the economic (annual and long-term) plans, establishes the balance sheets and statements of accounts. Thus the points on which the Joint Councils in India expect to receive information are actually controlled by the Workers' Councils in Yugoslavia.

In the USSR, where all the workers of an establishment join only one trade union (while each trade union unites the factory and office workers of one or several branches of the national economy), the participation of workers and office employees in the management of State enterprises is greatly facilitated. Broad sections of the workers take an active part in the elaboration of collective agreements. These agreements include rationalization proposals, preparation of new workers, engineers and technicians, raising the qualification of workers, labour protection and safety measures, and housing

[11] Nikola Balog, *Some Experience in the Management of Yugoslav Industrial Enterprises*, December 1959, p. 20.

and workers' welfare. Copies of the collective agreements are distributed to the workers so that they may be able to keep abreast of its fulfilment. The section and department executives periodically report on the fulfilment of the collective agreements at the workers' meetings. A total of 76,000 meetings and conferences of the workers and office employees were held in 1958 throughout the USSR at which results of the fulfilment of the collective agreements were checked.

The Regulation of Rights of Factory and Plant Committee approved by the Presidium of the Supreme Soviet of the USSR in July 1958 creates for Trade Unions most favourable conditions for discharging their duties. In accordance with the Regulation, Trade Union Committees take an active part in drafting production and capital construction plans, in organizing socialist emulation, in summing up results and in moving suggestions before the higher economic and Soviet bodies. The Trade Union Committees enjoy extensive rights in setting up work rates, norms and wages. The Factory and Works Committee is also invested with broad authority to supervise labour protection and observe labour legislation. It has its representatives in the acceptance committees when new workshops and sections are put into operation. The management cannot dismiss workers or office employees without the consent of the Trade Union Committee.[12] Moreover, the Factory Fund (which is built out of 4 to 6 per cent of planned profits and of 20 to 50 per cent of profits in excess of the planned figure) can be spent by the management only with the consent of the Trade Union Committee.

A growing technique of workers' participation in the USSR is the device of Production Conferences which have turned into permanently functioning bodies. These Conferences work with the active participation of workers, engineers, technicians, office employees, representatives of management, Trade Unions and other public organizations. Members of Production Conferences are elected annually by an open ballot at general meetings of the personnel. They report on their work to the general meetings of factory workers and office employees not less than once every six months. The Production Conferences are concerned with raising the productivity of labour, increasing the output, improving the quality, achieving technological progress and lowering production costs. In 1958, Production Conferences accepted more than 2.5 million suggestions on how to improve work; two-thirds of them have been realized. The Production Conferences, in their turn, have the right to listen to the regular reports of the management on draft production and housing plans and on the fulfilment of State Plans. The participation of broad sections of workers in such a control is a

[12] This is a very important power. Professor G. D. H. Cole considers it as the essence of partnership.

most striking evidence of the full rights of factory workers and office employees in the management of State enterprises. The workers exercise vigilance with regard to the strict observance of State discipline by revealing shortcomings in the country's economic activity. If such a sense of responsibility could be developed in India's public enterprises, the problem of discipline, instead of being aggravated, could be actually solved through the device of workers' participation. An improvement in the quality of Trade Union leadership and the elimination of outside political influences would pave the way for workers' participation in India.

B. RECRUITMENT, TRAINING AND PROMOTION

A fundamental change in labour relations would, no doubt, be an achievement in itself; but the ultimate determinant of success could be nothing but the capability of State Corporations to induce their employees to put in better work than the standard set by the private sector of the economy. Hence there are three facets of the problem. First, there is the necessity of recruiting the best available personnel; secondly, the competence of the persons so recruited has to be maintained and enhanced; and thirdly, these competent persons have to be retained at suitable places within the public sector.

The Hindustan Steel Ltd is the biggest State Corporation in India.[13] Before April 1, 1957, when the Bhilai and Durgapur projects were directly under the Ministry of Iron and Steel, recruitment of engineers was made through the Union Public Service Commission. The Hindustan Steel, however, recruited the personnel required for the Rourkela Steel Plant. This anomaly came to an end in 1957. The Hindustan Steel now invites applications for the three plants by advertisement and through employment exchanges and the selection is made by a Selection Board of the Company, experts from outside also being associated with it. Two Selection Committees in London and Washington have also been selecting Indian engineers in the UK, the Continent and the United States. There has

---

[13] The Railways are the biggest national undertaking. They have been making direct recruitment to fill Class IV posts through local officers of Division/Region/District concerned, the residents of the area receiving 'full consideration'. The posts are notified to the linked Employment Exchanges and notices are also exhibited on the notice board of the Office concerned. In Class III, vacancies for posts carrying a salary of less than Rs 300 per month are advertised in newspapers circulating in the States served by the Zonal Railway concerned, higher posts being advertised in 'all-India' newspapers. There is no recruitment to Class II service : the employees in Class III who show 'intelligence, initiative and ability' are promoted to Class II on the recommendation of Selection Boards. In Class I direct recruitment is made through the Union Public Service Commission (like Class I services of various Government Departments).

been an acute shortage of experienced technical men, particularly to man the senior operational posts in the new Steel Plants.[14] Hindustan Steel have obtained about eighty-five experienced officers from the private sector, but still a large gap has to be filled. Many of the senior posts *had* to be manned by foreign experts. Under the programme of training 2,000 engineers in foreign steel works, the position stands as follows according to the Annual Report of the Department of Iron and Steel for 1959-60:

	ENGINEERS		OPERATIVES	
	Sent	Returned	Sent	Returned
USA	387	295	4	—
USSR	328	285	355	336
UK	200	135	15	—
West Germany ...	119	107	2	2
Australia	45	28	7	—
Canada	1	1	—	—
	1,080	851	383	338

In the matter of providing training facilities within the country, the assistance of the private sector undertakings has been obtained. Arrangements have been made with the Tata Iron and Steel Works to train 450 operatives per year. In future, the 'senior' plants in the State-owned sector will be able to help the new undertakings in this regard. For example, the Sindri Fertilizers and Chemicals Ltd offered training facilities to the Hindustan Chemicals and Fertilizers Ltd.

State Corporations in India have generally their own system of recruitment and little effort has been made at consolidation in this regard. The services offered by these Corporations are often quite attractive—offering the advantages of both public and private employments. Moreover, the tests prescribed for many of the selections are often less comprehensive than those prescribed for comparable positions in the civil service. But the Corporations have, generally speaking, failed to create confidence, in the minds of the candidates and of the people in general, that the appointments are made on merit. The result is that many deserving candidates never apply for these posts. Adequate publicity is not given on all-India basis to many of the jobs because of the 'cost factor'. There are widespread fears that regional and sectarian considerations and personal prefer-

[14] The four Railway Service Commissions in India have similar experience. The number indented for 'Non-technical categories' and 'Technical categories' (for the year ending March 31, 1958) stood at 32,757 and 5,455 respectively. Applications received figured at 630,399 and 37,209; the number called for interview at 147,392 and 12,475; and the number selected at 33,768 and 3,852 respectively.

ences get the upper hand in these selections. It may be pointed out that *freedom from civil service procedure should not mean licence.* Such freedom is justified only if it enables the building up of a more rational and disciplined procedure for recruitment. Further, in many cases Departmental Officers are dumped on these Corporations, with the result that they carry with them unimaginative tendencies to organizations which are expected to develop the 'flexibility of private enterprise'. In order that recruitment at the lower level may be done on the basis of knowledge of commerce and industry, it is necessary that the top officials should be carefully chosen.

The organization of a 'State Enterprise Service' under the aegis of a State Enterprises Personnel Commission is a matter worth consideration.[15] This Commission may have two Wings: an Administrative Personnel Wing and a Technical Personnel Wing. There may be some common members of the two Wings (especially the Chairman). Besides, the first Wing should contain members who have had experience of industry and commerce. In the second Wing there should be top engineers and technicians who should be responsible for procuring technical skill not only within the country, but also from abroad. We have seen that much dislocation was caused to the schedule of work in case of DVC because the Corporation could not find a suitable Chief Engineer for the first two and a half years of their existence. There was a lot of vacillation and indecision. The State Enterprises Personnel Commission should be given adequate authority to determine the emoluments of highly qualified personnel, specially when they are procured from foreign countries. This Commission can also be asked to organize training facilities on the basis of anticipated requirements and to examine the drafts of various Technical Agreements entered into by the Government of India from time to time with foreign firms or Governmental organizations. This would mitigate the maladies which have tarnished the initial career of many of the State Corporations.[16]

The United Nations Report on Rangoon Seminar (1954) suggests that success at the top level of management may depend to a large degree on the selection of the right individuals to intermediate posts, where they will serve the training and experience necessary to

---

[15] Such a Commission is of special importance for India because of indiscriminate growth of public enterprises, particularly in the shape of Government Companies. Many of the organizations are too small to offer suitable opportunities for recruitment and promotion.

[16] The Estimates Committee, in their 16th Report on 'Organization and Administration of Nationalized Industrial Undertakings' (June 1955), suggest recruitment of unskilled labour on the basis of local preference but 'officers and staff should be representative of every part of the country', the postings of officers being made on a tenure basis for four or five years.

undertake the highest responsibilities a few years later.[17] Another United Nations Report, published in 1955, observes that 'Even if new industries are developed under government ownership, the basic social problems of enterprise and management may not be very different. Experience has shown, indeed, that, in under-developed countries moving from semi-feudal agrarianism to urbanized industrialism, government ownership may be associated with *nepotism, with arbitrary action towards the working class, with special upper-class privileges for the managerial class and even with extreme secrecy regarding knowledge and technology.*'[18] A more recent Report (1958) of the United Nations suggests that many aspects of the problem of training are related to selection and recruitment. It stresses the need for *liaison* between industrial enterprises and academic institutions. The Report observes: 'There appears to be a need for developing suitable devices to facilitate impartial screening and selection of candidates for managerial posts from among students and graduates of engineering schools, universities and business schools. Recruitment of candidates would be facilitated if they were systematically informed of existing openings; the establishment of an appropriate register of vacancies might also be considered. As to the composition of screening boards, these should include individuals appointed by academic institutions and industry, and independent persons of high calibre.'[19]

The real solution of the problem lies in having *man-power planning* in India. While there is a general dearth of technical hands in India, we have seen that in certain lines of activity so many technicians are being turned out by training schools that they cannot be absorbed by the existing enterprises. This means not only waste of resources but also a great disappointment to the trainees. Another source of embarrassment to many a young man is that often technical degrees and diplomas are not given suitable recognition by the prospective employers. It is necessary that the State should permit only those technical courses to be run which are framed in consonance with practical requirements; and once a candidate has fulfilled such a training he should not be unnecessarily harassed at the time of recruitment.

[17] United Nations, *Some Problems in the Organization and Administration of Public Enterprises in the Industrial Field,* Sales Number, 1954. II H.1.

[18] *Processes and Problems of Industrialization in Under-developed Countries,* United Nations, Department of Economic and Social Affairs, New York, Sales No. 1955. II B.1, p. 20. (Italics ours.) Further, in under-developed countries, the educational system is not geared to the needs of economic development, there being a tremendous pressure on white-collar jobs.

[19] *Management of Industrial Enterprises in Under-developed Countries,* United Nations, Department of Economic and Social Affairs, New York, 1958 (Sales No. 58 II B.5), p. 11.

It is, of course, necessary to have three types of training: training in educational institutions; training within the enterprises; and refresher training on 'industry level' or 'national level'. The first type of training must be geared to the requirements of industrial enterprises; the second type of training will vary from firm to firm; and for the third type of training we may have institutions like the *Ecole d'administration publique* of France and the Administrative Staff College of the United Kingdom (Henley-on-Thames). The latter selects its trainees from industry, candidates who are around the age of forty and at a time when they are about to take up senior positions. The training is almost entirely devoid of formal instruction or academic study. It consists of an analysis of a number of problems calling for the full range of ability and practical experience of the trainee. The College draws members from all over Britain and from overseas. It was established by *private enterprise,* but the nominees of a large number of Public Corporations have availed of the facilities provided by the College.[20] The College aims at developing administrative skill at the highest level. Three times a year some sixty men and women (already experienced administrators holding responsible positions in varied walks of life) come and live together for about twelve weeks. The nominees of nationalized industries are thus associated with the nominees, *at their own level,* of private industry and commerce, banking, accountancy, finance, insurance, civil service, local government and fighting Services. Inspired by the British example, the Administrative Staff College has been established in India at Hyderabad with full residential facilities. The College is run by an independent Educational Society with its control vested in a Court of Governors. The College is meant for those who have already shown promise and commendable performance in responsible positions. The participants in each course constitute a cross-section of the executive group in the country, selected from private commercial and industrial organizations, Government and semi-Government undertakings, the Armed Forces, and social services.

At the Administrative Staff College, Hyderabad, members participating in a session are divided into syndicates, each of ten members, with a member of the Directing Staff associating with

[20] R. W. Bell (then Senior Member of the Directing Staff of the Administrative Staff College), 'The Relation of Promotion and Training in Higher Management in British Nationalised Industries', *Public Administration,* London, Vol. XXIX, Autumn 1951. In the case of the British Transport Commission, 'There appears to be no general programme for the development of senior managerial staff in non-technical grades, other than the very small numbers who are sent to the Administrative Staff College at Henley.' William A. Robson, *Nationalized Industry and Public Ownership,'* Allen & Unwin, London, 1960, p. 343.

each syndicate. Each syndicate drafts a report on the subject of its study by drawing upon the knowledge and experience of the members. The report is presented at a meeting of the College and is discussed at a common meeting of the syndicates. Syndicate discussions are supplemented by lectures by the Directors and distinguished visitors from time to time. When a presentation meeting is held, members of different syndicates sit in groups. During discussions, each group tries to defend its viewpoint. The activities of the Administrative Staff College have attracted the attention of several State Corporations in India. For example, the Life Insurance Corporation is a member of the College and deputes highly placed officers to participate in its sessions.[21]

We now come to the very important question of retaining competent men in the service of State Corporations. In the Union of Burma, 'the situation now seems to be that the Government industrial enterprises are the real training centres, producing promising young executives and technicians for the private industrial concerns'.[22] State scholars trained abroad by the Government are leaving the State industries after serving for the terms required in the bond (normally five years). The highest pay scales of executives working in public industrial enterprises, in line with civil service scales, do not rise above K 1,600 per month; whereas, in the case of large private enterprises, the second line top executives may draw a salary somewhere between K 2,000 and K 3,000 per month. A somewhat similar situation is to be found in Indonesia. Although the BIN enterprises (Development and Finance Corporations) have a higher pay scale than that in the civil service, this pay scale is lower than the regular rates of private enterprises, especially of foreign concerns. However, graduates who have studied on a State fellowship are obliged to serve the Government. A Government regulation proposes to make public service for a number of years compulsory for all graduates of State Universities. However, even this provision would mean that the State Corporations have to depend on inexperienced technicians. A more effective device could be to impose restrictions on the level of emoluments in the private sector. In India, however, there is a traditional preference for State service.[23]

[21] Mr K. R. Puri, Deputy Zonal Manager, Delhi, was the first officer to attend the September-December 1959 session and Mr R. B. Pradhan, Deputy Zonal Manager, Bombay, participated in the January-April 1960 session (S. S. Giri, 'Administrative Staff College', *Yogakshema*, Jéevan Kendra, Bombay, March 1960, p. 24).

[22] *Development of Public Industrial Enterprises in Burma*, December 1959, p. 14.

[23] In this connection, the decision of the Government to establish an Indian Economic Service needs particular attention. Moreover, the Industrial

A similar difficulty has manifested itself in Sweden. A study recently made by the Swedish State Power Administration showed that the average length of employment for engineers in high salary brackets, who had left the Administration before the retirement age, had fallen from between nine-ten years in 1945 to a little less than five years in 1950 (results published in 1957). In 1957, out of 870 vacant engineering posts in the Government service, only 170 or less than 20 per cent could be filled. 'Business Agencies' in Sweden are much more restrictive (rigid in adhering to qualifications required for Government service) in their recruitment than private firms or the Government-owned Joint Stock Companies, which are free from all regulations in this regard. The 'Business Agencies' are also at a disadvantage with respect to salaries and promotion.

The problem of offering suitable and quick opportunities of promotion, with a view to retaining competent men and ensuring their lasting co-operation, is quite a difficult one. Firstly, it would be bad for the State Corporations to make promotions or demotions merely on the basis of personal pleasure or displeasure. Secondly, in those public enterprises which are small-sized (even though their national importance is very great) the possibilities of promotion must necessarily be limited, unless we are able to evolve a satisfactory system of inter-unit transfers. In fact, for highly technical staff this system may not work at all. Hence, after working in a State Corporation for ten or fifteen years, many people may begin to feel frustrated. In this connection, the *Ladder Plan* of the National Coal Board in the United Kingdom is of particular interest. It aims at ensuring a flow of promising recruits to the medium levels of industry. For all new entrants there should be available a definite ladder of promotion to higher ranks. As a person moves upwards, the available ladders should increase in number as they diminish in width, so that the best use can be made of varying talents. The *Ladder Plan* visualized that about 20 per cent of each year's entrants should get on to the main ladder right away. The number of employees taking courses in the Board's *Ladder Plan* was 20,194 in 1958.[24]

In certain cases it may be feasible to correlate the prospects of promotion with actual performance of the employees from year to year. Thus on June 27, 1959, Mr P. A. Gopalkrishnan, Chairman of the LIC, issued orders granting wage increment to Corporation's field workers on the basis of their performance in 1958. The percentage increase of the division's own business in 1958 over the previous year

Management Pool has already a list of prospective managers of public enterprises divided into several categories (on the basis of salaries to be offered and the responsibilities to be entrusted).

[24] *National Coal Board,* Annual Report and Accounts for the year ended January 3, 1959, Volume I, p. 47.

forms the basis of this increase, a field worker being entitled to one increment if he satisfies any of the following conditions:

(1) The percentage of his increase in new business in 1958 over the previous year should be more than half of the division's percentage increase.

(2) The new premium income derived by the Corporation in the business of the field worker should, on the basis of percentage, be more than half of the percentage of increased business of the division.

(3) The new premium income should be more than six times the remuneration given to the field worker.

In addition, a field worker would be entitled to another increment if his percentage of new business or premium income was more than half of the division's percentage of increased business and also his own expense ratio to the business secured by him was less than 15 per cent. Field workers who had not fared well were not subjected to any cut; they were given another chance to 'come up'. Further, the Life Insurance Corporation is one of the exceptions to the general practice of State undertakings in India not to pay bonus to their employees. An important achievement of the Corporation during the year 1959 was the conclusion of a five-year agreement regarding bonus with the representatives of administrative employees. Long-term agreements could be considerably helpful in improving industrial relations.

C. WORKERS' WELFARE

The following table gives an indication of the percentage of annual income spent on welfare activities by some of the State Corporations:

	1953-54	1954-55	1955-56	1956-57	1957-58	1958-59
1. Air India	1.0	0.5	0.3	0.2	0.2	0.5
2. DVC*	1.3	2.3	1.9	1.9	(a)	(a)
3. Hindustan Antibiotics ...	1.5	0.6	0.6	0.6	0.4	0.4
4. Hindustan Shipyard ...	(a)	1.0	0.9	0.7	0.8	(a)
5. Indian Airlines	0.2	0.3	0.2	0.3	0.3	(a)
6. National Coal Board (UK)**	0.7	0.7	0.6	0.6	0.6	0.7

(a) Denotes Not Available
* Percentage of total expenditure (Revenue account)
** Figures for calendar years

Before drawing any conclusions from the above table, its limitations must be considered. The definition of welfare varies not only from Corporation to Corporation, but also from year to year in the same Corporation. For example, in case of Air India International the presentation of accounts (breakdown of items of expenditure) in the year 1958-59 was so changed as to greatly enlarge the definition of welfare as compared to earlier years. On the old basis, the proportion of welfare expenditure was still about 0.2 per cent. With regard to inter-Corporation differences in interpretation, an attempt has been made to arrive at a common basis in so far as it could be done on the basis of the Profit and Loss Accounts.

Now we can see our way to the following tendencies:

(1) In several of the Corporations, the percentage of expenditure on welfare activities has a tendency to decline. In the first year of its operation, Air India International spent 1.0 per cent on welfare items; this fell to 0.2 per cent in the fourth year of its working. In case of the Hindustan Antibiotics, the percentage fell from 1.5 per cent in the first year to 0.4 per cent in the fifth year. To some extent, the Hindustan Shipyard has also experienced this decline.

(2) In some of the Corporations, expenditure on welfare activities is fairly stable. The best example of this stability is the National Coal Board. However, in that organization, welfare grants form a very small part of the total welfare expenditure. Hence, although the welfare levies and grants rose from £349,146 in 1953 to £1,376,623 (nearly four times) in 1958 (welfare grants only), they did not upset the overall percentage. The Indian Airlines Corporation is another organization which has succeeded in maintaining stability in the matter of welfare expenditure, although at a very low level.

(3) Long-term benefits have generally an upper hand in all the Corporations. These benefits, in many cases, have to be compulsorily provided for either as part of service contracts or under statutory obligations. Provident Funds and Pension Benefits fall in this category. In the case of Damodar Valley Corporation, if the expenditure on Provident Funds is excluded, the percentage of expenditure on welfare activities would fall to a ridiculously low level. In the case of Hindustan Antibiotics, during the year ended March 31, 1959, a sum of Rs 67,403 was the Company's contribution to Provident Fund, Rs 5,940 was the Employers' State Insurance contribution, and the sum of Rs 62,351 represented other expenses on Workmen and Staff Welfare.

(4) On the whole, the expenditure on welfare activities has been quite low. During the year 1957-58 three of the six Corporations in the table spent less than half ($\frac{1}{2}$) per cent on such activities. The two exceptions were the Hindustan Shipyard and the National Coal Board. Five of the six Corporations spent less than 1 per cent of their income on workers' welfare. In absolute terms, the welfare expenditure was Rs 125 per employee in case of the Air India International and Rs 136 in the case of the Hindustan Antibiotics for the year 1958-59 as against £89 (Rs 1,187) in the case of the National Coal Board for the year 1958.

(5) Some of the Corporations have pooled their resources in pro-

viding welfare facilities to their respective employees. Thus the Air India International recovered a sum of Rs 98,996 out of a total expenditure of Rs 6,68,154 in this connection during the year 1958-59. There is considerable prospect for extending such co-operation among the various State Corporations, e.g. in the matter of providing holiday homes, excursions and visits to other organizations.

State Corporations have paid particular attention to the problem of housing. The view that a public enterprise should have ideal surroundings was first given a practical shape in this country in the case of the Chittaranjan Locomotive Works (which is not a corporate enterprise). Out of the total capital at charge amounting to Rs 14.70 crores as on December 31, 1956, a sum of Rs 6.71 crores had been spent on the township. Staff residences were provided for 5,078 employees, the chargeable rent being a maximum of 10 per cent of the salary or the ceiling rent whichever is less.[25] The three Steel Projects managed by the Hindustan Steel Ltd have carried out this experiment on an even bigger scale. At Rourkela, a modern township is being built in accordance with a master plan which provides for the construction of 20,000 houses for a population of 1,00,000. By December 31, 1959, as many as 5,381 houses had been completed.[26] The township plan includes the construction of auxiliary buildings like hospitals, schools, markets, parks, etc. At Bhilai, out of 7,500 houses to be built initially, 4,805 had been built and occupied. At Durgapur, the overall target is again 20,000 houses, with an initial plan of constructing 7,500 houses, out of which over 3,000 residential houses had already been constructed.

Other State enterprises have conducted this activity on a miniature scale because of their smaller requirements. In case of Sindri Fertilizers and Chemicals Ltd, 89 per cent of the monthly-rated employees had been provided with quarters by the end of the year 1955-56. The Hindustan Machine Tools Ltd had constructed 683 quarters by March 31, 1959. This covered only one-fourth of the total manpower employed by HMT (2,659). But the important fact is that greater attention was given to workers' quarters as against accommodation for administrative staff. About one-third of the workers could be provided with quarters. In the case of Hindustan Antibiotics Ltd, the total number of people in employment on

[25] The ceiling rent (per month) was fixed as follows: Rs 4.50 for 'A' type residences (also free to some categories of staff); Rs 10 for 'B' type residences; Rs 18 for 'C' type residences; and Rs 32 for 'D' type residences. Even the smallest house was provided with two living rooms and electric fittings. The annual rent varied from 1.3 per cent of the cost of construction in case of 'A' type residences to 2.1 per cent in case of 'D' type residences.

[26] Government of India, Ministry of Steel, Mines and Fuel (Department of Iron and Steel) Annual Report, 1956-60, p. 19.

March 31, 1959, was 980. As against this, 430 quarters had been completed. Commercial Corporations like the Air India International, Indian Airlines Corporation and the State Trading Corporation of India, too, have found it necessary to worry about the housing problem.

Most of the State Corporations have provided medical facilities. The Chittaranjan Locomotive Works (non-corporate enterprise) had shown the way by establishing a Hospital with seventy beds, four Dispensaries and four Maternity and Health Centres. Employees and their families, and even outsiders, have been given medical assistance. The new hospital of Hindustan Antibiotics Ltd has proved to be of great benefit to the residents of the colony. Similarly, the 100-bed hospital of Sindri Fertilizers and Chemicals Ltd, completed and occupied during the year 1956-57, has proved very popular. In certain cases Child Welfare and Family Planning Centres have also been established.

Among other amenities provided by the State Corporations we may mention the following:

(1) Establishment of schools with concession of free education for the children of staff drawing up to (say) Rs 100/- per month and the provision of free milk in the kindergarten and primary schools (often with the assistance of UNICEF);

(2) Provision of lunch rooms and canteens supplying food at low (subsidized) rates, e.g. full lunch for six annas (the New Air India Canteen adjacent to the Corporation's Technical Headquarters at Santa Cruz Airport, built at a cost of Rs 4 lakhs and commissioned on May 18, 1959, has been acclaimed as one of the finest industrial canteens in India; it has been equipped with the most modern electrical cooking equipment);

(3) Transport at subsidized rates (e.g. to all employees of the Hindustan Machine Tools living in Bangalore City) including transport, free or subsidized, to school-going children;

(4) Assistance to Co-operative Credit Societies and Consumers' Stores supplying foodgrains and other necessities of life at specially reduced rates, with particular emphasis on quality (the Railways in India during and after the Second World War thus saved their employees from the rigours of inflationary price spirals);

(5) Clubs and Welfare Centres (like Basanti, Srilata and Chittaranjan Club in the case of Chittaranjan Locomotive Works and Antibiotics Recreation Club in case of the Hindustan Antibiotics Ltd) subsidized by the employers and providing facilities for badminton, tennis, hockey, football, volleyball, other games and sports (including inter-unit matches), fancy dress shows and dramatic performances; and

(6) Publication of magazines like *Sindri News* and *Sindri Samachar*

in case of the Sindri Fertilizers and Chemicals Ltd, *DDT News* in case of the Hindustan Insecticides Ltd, the *House Magazine* of the Indian Telephone Industries Ltd, and *Yogakshema* in case of the Life Insurance Corporation of India.

In certain cases, welfare activities have been linked with monetary awards.[27] For example, the Hindustan Antibiotics Ltd sanctioned Six Annual Awards of Rs 100 each for the 'Distinguished Worker' in the different categories of employees during the year 1958-59. The 'distinguished worker' will be judged on the basis of regularity in attendance, diligence in work and amenability to discipline. The awards will be confined only to non-supervisory staff and made on August 15 (Independence Day) every year. There could have been separate awards for punctuality and other such attributes. The Hindustan Machine Tools introduced, with effect from January 1, 1958, an Incentive Bonus Scheme and an Attendance Bonus Scheme. In that organization, the minimum earnings of Rs 52 per month for unskilled workers were enhanced to Rs 64 per month from August 1, 1957, and Rs 70 per month from June 1, 1958. Enhanced dearness allowance was also paid to low-paid employees and the rate of provident fund contribution was raised from $6\frac{1}{4}$ per cent to $8\frac{1}{3}$ per cent. 'Suggestion schemes' were introduced in several Corporations like the Hindustan Shipyard Ltd and the Air India International. The former, in their Report for 1955-56, published the photographs of four prizewinners. The practice of making decent awards to workers who offer useful suggestions is now a fairly universal one. It has been taken advantage of by the Tennessee Valley Authority in the United States and extensively adopted by the public enterprises in People's China and the Soviet Union. While such awards are of great utility, we should not forget that it is one of the responsibilities of State Corporations to promote the patriotic spirit.

Finally, there is the moot question: Will the mere provision of welfare facilities satisfy the workers? Or, will they insist on the disbursement of the welfare fund through their own representative organizations? There are certain statutory obligations imposed on State Corporations (often like their counterparts in the private sector). Here there is not much scope for workers' management (e.g. in case of statutory Provident Funds). With regard to other items of expenditure, workers' preferences must be duly weighed and their representatives duly associated with the operation of welfare schemes.

---

[27] Paid holidays also are, indirectly, monetary awards. In the Soviet Union such holidays vary from two weeks to two months per year. Maternity leave in the Soviet Union is 112 days—56 days before giving birth and 56 days afterwards.

CHAPTER VIII

PRICE AND SALES POLICIES AND APPROACHES TO EFFICIENCY

A. PRICE AND SALES POLICIES

The price policy of public enterprises is of far-reaching importance. It has a fundamental rôle to play in allocating resources and in ensuring their optimum utilization. It also forms the basis of future development and expansion of public undertakings. As a matter of fact, in an economy which is being progressively socialized, the entire fiscal structure has to be built on the strong foundation of profitable public enterprises. On the other hand, the goodwill of the consuming population can be sustained only through the adoption of a well-reasoned price policy which clearly indicates that public monopolies are laying adequate stress on business efficiency. At the same time, the promotion of egalitarian objectives may necessitate detailed calculations of costs and benefits to the various sections of the society. Moreover, the requirements of foreign trade, inter-undertaking relationships (within the public sector) and competition from private enterprises, whether direct or indirect, all make it incumbent on public sector undertakings to cast their price policy in a suitable mould. A study of the price policy followed by the State Corporation in India reveals the following noteworthy features:

(1) Bias in favour of Government Departments and other public organizations including International Agencies;

(2) Bias in favour of bulk customers even though such customers may be private organizations;

(3) Bias in favour of long-term contracts;

(4) Bias in favour of the region or locality where the productive operations are carried on (including bias in favour of their own employees);

(5) Adherence to import parity prices;

(6) Adherence to no-profit basis;

(7) Incurring losses when dictated by development, humanitarian, social or political considerations;

(8) Reducing prices when so dictated by cost considerations and also with a view to winning the goodwill of the people when the Corporations are in their infancy;

(9) Increasing prices when so dictated by cost considerations and also with a view to effecting improvements and raising the standard of comforts for the consumers;

(10) Making profits for purposes of self-financing as also for contributing to the State exchequer.

Many of these features also hold good for the State Corporations working in other countries. We now proceed to examine the above characteristics in some detail.

(1) *Government Departments*

Public Corporations and Government Companies, as sons and daughters of the State, cannot be completely shorn of maternal affection. The incorporating charters generally ensure that the children do not become ungrateful to the parent.

The bias in favour of Government Departments has manifested itself in varying degrees. At its highest point it takes the shape of free services (and even goods) being supplied to the Government. For example, upon the requisition of the Secretary of War, the TVA 'shall allot and *deliver without charge* to the War Department so much power as shall be necessary in the judgment of the said Department for use in operation of all locks, lifts or other facilities in aid of navigation'. A similar provision is to be found in the case of the Snowy Mountains Hydro Electric Authority which was established in Australia in 1949. The British Broadcasting Corporation is duty bound to broadcast 'an impartial account day by day prepared by professional reporters of the proceedings in both Houses of the United Kingdom Parliament'. It is also under an obligation to make announcements, at its own expense, when so required by any Department of Her Majesty's Government.

Sometimes the State Corporations are prohibited from selling their products to non-Governmental organizations. Thus the TVA Act lays down that 'No products of the Corporation shall be sold for use outside of the United States, its territories and possessions, except to the United States Government for the use of its Army or Navy, or to its allies in case of war, or until six months after the termination of national emergency proclaimed by the President on December 16, 1950 . . .' The TVA Act further prescribes that 'The board shall give preference to States, counties, municipalities, and co-operative organizations of citizens or farmers, not organized or doing business for profit.' It has been clarified that the sale of power to industry shall be a secondary purpose to be utilized principally to secure a sufficiently high load factor and revenue returns *which will permit domestic and rural use at the lowest possible rates.*

Supplying the needs of Government Departments at low prices is a practice followed by several State Corporations in India. Thus the Indian Telephone Industries sold an auto-telephone to the Posts and Telegraphs Department for Rs 82 against the imported cost of

Rs 103 for such an equipment.[1] This price later on was reduced to Rs 79.[2] The Nahan Foundry has tried to procure business from Governmental organizations like the Railways, the Posts and Telegraphs Department and the Khadi and Village Industries Commission. It has followed a concessional price policy for this purpose. The Directors' Report dated April 29, 1959, points out: 'The price of the main product, Sultan cane crusher, was increased from Rs 360/- to Rs 380/- each. Government departments continued to enjoy a concessional price of Rs 355/- each which before the increase was Rs 335/-.'

The finished product of the Sindri Fertilizers and Chemicals (ammonium sulphate) has been sold, under the advice of the Government of India, through the Central Fertilizer Pool, by the Ministry of Food and Agriculture, New Delhi. Under these arrangements, all the State Governments and other consumers (like tea and coffee plantations) furnish their demands to the Pool. After screening these demands, the Pool issues quarterly allocations (followed by monthly releases). Within their allotments, the choice of consignees has been entirely within the discretion of the States. The Estimates Committee, in their 13th Report (1954-55), recommended that, as far as possible, distribution in rural areas should be done through the *Panchayats,* Co-operative Societies, Community Projects, National Extension Service Schemes and other development agencies. The idea was to eliminate extra cost to the farmers on account of distributors' commission.

(2) *Bulk Customers*

Government Departments are generally bulk customers. As such, a bias in favour of Governmental organizations automatically leads to a bias in favour of bulk customers. However, this principle has been extended to private organizations as well. It is, of course, true that even private enterprises often adhere to this practice while framing their price policy. But State Corporations, starting from scratch, and possessing no or inadequate marketing organization, find it more convenient to rely on bulk arrangements. The fact that many of the Corporations are supplying producer goods and basic services, rather than consumer goods, lends additional support to bulk dealings.

The Damodar Valley Corporation entered into an agreement for bulk sale of power with the Calcutta Electric Supply Corporation Ltd on April 15, 1954. The supply commenced on April 22, 1957, and up to March 31, 1958, the total power sold to this party aggregated 258 million kWh. This represents 32 per cent of the total sale

[1] *Department of Communications and Civil Aviation Report,* 1957-58, p. 53.
[2] *Ibid.,* 1958-59, p. 60.

of power during the year 1957-58 (807 million kWh). However, the Corporation realized Rs 75.35 lakhs from this customer, which represents only 22 per cent of the total electricity revenue realized during the year 1957-58 (Rs 349.15 lakhs). The rate at which power was sold to this customer works out to 2.9 Naye Paise per kWh, which is less than the cost of generation and transmission (3.8 nP) per kWh even on a provisional basis. The rate of surcharge is also lower in this case (.015 nP) than that for other customers (.018 nP) for each 25 nP variation in the price of coal per ton. Further, in this case, energy charge can be increased (under the fuel cost adjustment clause) only when the cost of coal exceeds Rs 15.87 per ton. In other cases the charge is increased if the cost of coal exceeds Rs 9 per ton. On a rough computation, the DVC would have realized Rs 14.32 lakhs more up to March 31, 1958, if the surcharge had been based on a factor of Rs 9 per ton.[3]

In respect of another bulk customer taking energy from the DVC with effect from October 1954, the basic cost of coal was fixed at Rs 10 instead of Rs 9 per ton. This resulted in an aggregate loss of Rs 2.32 lakhs up to March 1958.

In the past, the DVC relied a good deal on a two-part tapering system of electrical rates. Under the Tariff for H.T. (both hydel and thermal) supply at 66/33 KV (old), the monthly demand charge was to fall from Rs 5.87 per KVA for the first 2,000 KVA to Rs 3.87 per KVA beyond 20,000 KVA. The energy charge was to fall from 0.5 Anna (3.125 nP) for the first 200,000 kWh to 0.4 Anna (2.5 nP) for excess over 2,000,000 kWh. As against this, for supply at 33 KV (new), the energy charge is to remain constant at 2.7 nP per kWh for consumers with *no* generating station and 2.2 nP per kWh for customers *with* generating station. But the monthly demand charge would still fall from Rs 6.75 per KVA for the first 5,000 KVA to Rs 5.75 per KVA for excess over 25,000 KVA. It may be mentioned that at Bhakra Nangal Power Project (Hydro Electric) the demand charge is fixed at Rs 5/- per KVA whereas the energy charge (for 66/33 KV) varies from 0.45 Anna (2.8 nP) to 0.4 Anna (2.5 nP). At Hirakud (Hydro Electric) the demand charge as well as the energy charge are constant at Rs 5.50 per KVA and 1.25 Anna (7.8 nP) per kWh respectively. Thus DVC power is substantially cheaper than Hirakud power, but somewhat costlier than Bhakra Nangal power.

(3) *Long-term Contracts*
In the case of basic industries, output has often to be planned

---

[3] This was done with effect from January 1, 1959. Even then, on the whole, the revised rates given to this customer are more favourable than the new tariff applicable with effect from January 1959 to other customers having generation systems of their own.

several years in advance. As such, State Corporations find it convenient to enter into long-term contracts for the disposal of their products so that development work may proceed smoothly. Apart from providing an assured market, such contracts reduce the speculative element in the matter of prices. This, of course, is a double-edged weapon. On the one hand, there is a safeguard against a possible fall in the price level; on the other hand, the possibility of raising prices, when so warranted by circumstances, may be precluded. However, not all agreements are based on the rule-of-thumb doctrine; many of them stipulate variations in rates in specified situations, and also the termination of agreement on giving notice of a particular duration.

To start with, we take the example of an undertaking where the State holds only a minority interest (28 per cent). The Tata Engineering and Locomotive Company Ltd, promoted and registered in September 1945, is the case in point. The Government of India had entered into an agreement with Tata Sons Ltd for the promotion of a company to acquire and develop the Singhbhum Shops for the production of 100 locomotive boilers per year in the first instance, and for the manufacture of fifty complete locomotives and fifty spare boilers as soon as possible after the war. The agreement was for a period of 16 years from the date on which possession of the Singhbhum Shops was given to the Tatas, i.e. June 1, 1945, to May 31, 1961. In the Development Period (first two years) the price to be paid was the actual cost of production payable in two parts. The first part was the equivalent of the landed duty-paid cost of similar boilers and locomotives imported from the United Kingdom during the above period. The second part, being the difference between such landed cost and the Company's actual cost of production, was to be kept in a Development Account and paid to the Company in one or more instalments, at the option of the Government, after the Development Period. In the post-Development Period, the price was to be fixed before the commencement of each contract year on a basis estimated to give the Company its cost of production, *plus* a return of 7 per cent on the capital employed in the locomotive business.

It may be mentioned that the mere fact of a long-term agreement does not provide adequate stability to production programmes. In the above example, except for the first order which was for 100 SGS boilers, subsequent orders for boilers were of various types and of comparatively small numbers.[4] As against this, the Chittaranjan

---

[4] *Facts about TELCO*, published in 1957, p. 10. It may be mentioned that the first locomotive came out from the assembly line in 1952 (seven years after the agreement) and the development period was extended up to July 1954.

Locomotive Works (exclusively controlled by the Railway Board) has been able to obtain a long run of orders for only one type of locomotive without depending on any formal agreement. Although the planning of Chittaranjan was started two years after the promotion of TELCO, the former completed its Development Period two years earlier. As compared to the duty-paid cost of Rs 4.87 lakhs for an imported British locomotive (indicated in the official statement placed on *Lok Sabha*'s table in August, 1957), the prices charged by TELCO were as follows:

First Price Period	Rs 6.90	lakhs
Second „ „	Rs 6.38	„
Third „ „	Rs 5.41	„
Current Supplies (1957)	Rs 4.43	„

As against these prices, the cost at Chittaranjan was Rs 7.0 lakhs in 1950-51; Rs 7.65 lakhs in 1951-52; Rs 7.46 lakhs in 1952-53; Rs 6.41 lakhs in 1953-54; Rs 5.50 lakhs in 1954-55 and 4.34 lakhs in 1955-56. Thus, although Chittaranjan started with higher costs, it was able to supply locomotives in 1956 at a much lower cost than TELCO. As such, in 1957, the long-term agreement with TELCO was severely criticized in Parliament. It is in the very nature of long-term contracts that they easily get out of tune with prevailing circumstances. When the Government had negotiated the deal with TELCO, Chittaranjan was not in the picture. If TELCO had started production at an early stage, much of the bitter controversy could have been avoided.

Reference has already been made to some of the agreements entered into by the Damodar Valley Corporation.[5] While such agreements often permit the revision of tariff on twelve months' notice after the expiration of the third year, the agreement with the Calcutta Electric Supply Corporation Ltd did not provide for any revision of tariff for the duration of the agreement which is for a minimum period of ten years.

The TVA Act provides that the Board shall not enter into contracts (for sale of power) exceeding twenty years. But in the case of contracts covered by Rule 1 (preferential category of customers like the States, municipalities and co-operative organizations) this limit shall be thirty years. Further, all contracts made with privately-owned companies or private individuals shall contain a provision authorizing the Board to cancel the said contract upon five years' notice in writing. All contracts entered into between the Corporation and any municipality or other political sub-division or co-

[5] A number of agreements were entered into with the Governments of Bihar and West Bengal, the West Bengal State Electricity Board, the Eastern Railway, the Chittaranjan Locomotive Works, the Associated Cement Co Ltd, and the Indian Iron and Steel Co Ltd.

operative organization shall provide that the electric power shall be sold and distributed to the ultimate consumer without discrimination as between consumers of the same class. The Corporation may extend credit for a period not exceeding five years to States, countries, municipalities and non-profit organizations.

(4) *Region or Locality*

Regional development authorities like the TVA and the DVC have necessarily to confine their activities to particular areas. Their main commercial activity (sale of power) is circumscribed by physical limitations of transmission distance. As regards non-commercial activities, there are statutory limitations depending on regional bias. What is of special significance is the fact that some of the non-commercial activities are necessarily associated with commercial activities. Thus when the dams and power houses are constructed, many people are displaced and their rehabilitation becomes an important problem. Further, the DVC was expected to perform such functions of regional benefit as 'to prevent pollution of any water under its control' and 'to undertake measures for the prevention of malaria'.

Users of the TVA power save more than $100 million a year compared with what they would have to pay for the same amount of electricity priced at the average of the rate schedules throughout the United States. Taking the example of cheap hydro-electric power in the Tennessee Valley, Harold Hotelling advised the United States Government to raise the whole level of economic existence, and so of culture and intelligence.[6] Supporting this as a 'good public policy', he emphasized that cheap power would cut down the costs of other industries, promote industrial development in general, and eradicate poverty (with its accompaniments of contagious diseases, crime and political corruption). Hotelling suggests that the only precaution which is necessary in this regard is that new electric power and other developments should be 'widely undertaken' to ensure adequate geographical distribution of benefits. While Hotelling's view that public projects need not be 'self-liquidating' is open to severe criticism, the idea of generating people's enthusiasm through the activities of Regional Development Authorities has much to commend itself.

Corporations in the manufacturing field, too, can earn the goodwill of the local population by following a concessional price policy (the extent of concession being such as not to encourage the resale of products to consumers of other localities) or by providing special

[6] Harold Hotelling, *The General Welfare in Relation to Problems of Taxation and of Railway and Utility Rates,* paper presented at a meeting of the Econometric Society at Atlantic City on December 27, 1937.

facilities for local customers. Thus the Estimates Committee in their 13th Report (1954-55) suggested that, as a measure of direct marketing, a small retail store should be opened by the Sindri Fertilizers and Chemicals for the benefit of the people living near the Sindri factory.

As regards their own employees, many Corporations, both in the public and private sectors of the economy, follow a concessional price policy. The best example is that of the Railways which have a long tradition of providing free as well as concessional travel to their employees both in the operating and non-operating sections. While in the case of railways such concessions have been misused to a considerable degree, the chances of such misuse are probably less in the case of many State Corporations. Thus the Air Corporations in India have granted similar facilities to their employees; and in view of the strict regulation of air traffic, the possibility of misuse is much less than in the case of Railways. However, a concessional price policy for the employees may not always be feasible. For example, the State Bank of India would not grant loans to its employees at lower rates of interest.

(5) *Import Parity Policy*

This criterion is relevant for those State Corporations whose products are in direct competition with imported goods. As such, Corporations enjoying statutory or practical monopoly would not be concerned with this basis. For example, the Damodar Valley Corporation or the Life Insurance Corporation of India have nothing to do with import parity prices.

By and large, the doctrine of import parity prices is applicable to those commodities which used to be imported from foreign countries but are now being produced within the country (but perhaps the country is still *not* self-sufficient and hence comparison with landed cost of foreign goods is of practical relevance).

The most important example[7] among State Corporations in India is that of Hindustan Shipyard, Visakhapatnam. To ensure that Indian shipowners do not have to pay a non-competitive price, the Government of India have accepted the principle of selling the ships built in the Visakhapatnam Shipyard at the United Kingdom Parity Price, i.e. the price approximately equal to the cost of building a similar ship in the United Kingdom. The difference is borne by the Government of India as a subsidy. Similar subsidies are in vogue in the USA, France, Italy and Australia.[8] However, apart from the fact that the UK Parity Price formula has proved to be unworkable in some cases, 'it is being urged by the shipowners that the UK prices are no longer

[7] In case of TELCO (already discussed), too, this formula was applied.
[8] 'A Note on the Principles underlying price fixation in our Shipyard', June 1960 (by courtesy of Hindustan Shipyard Ltd).

the lowest prices quoted in shipbuilding. Japan and some of the Continental countries have been quoting prices which are lower than those quoted by shipyards in the UK'.[9]

Apart from the difficulty of choosing a particular country which, over a reasonably long period, may continue to represent the most reasonable standard prices, there may be differences in construction and design. Since ships are usually built on the basis of particular orders and specifications, one ship may not be quite comparable with another. Moreover, since the *entire* difference between the actual cost of production and the Parity Price is made good by way of subsidy, there may be no incentive at all to improve the level of efficiency.

(6) No-profit Basis

Some of the Corporations are required, by virtue of promoters' agreements or the Memorandum and Articles of Association (or the incorporating legislation), that the products will be sold on no-profit (no-loss) basis. This feature has been found to exist largely in case of those Corporations whose products are essential for promoting health measures.

The Hindustan Insecticides was floated in 1954 with a view to providing large quantities of DDT required for combating malaria. In view of foreign exchange shortage, there was difficulty in importing adequate amount of DDT. Under Article V(7) of the Joint Plan of Operations dated July 19, 1952, drawn by the Government of India, the World Health Organization and the United Nations Children's Emergency Fund, the Company was required to operate on a no-profit basis. A tentative price of Rs 2.50 for technical DDT and Rs 2/- per lb. for formulated DDT was fixed in consultation with the Ministry of Health, Ministry of Finance and the Director-General of Supplies and Disposals. At the Board of Directors meeting held on February 26, 1956, these rates were brought down to Rs 2.25 and Rs 1.75 respectively. The cost of production on the basis of the working during 1956-57 came to Rs 1.52 for Technical DDT and Rs 1.37 for formulated DDT. Accordingly, a sum of Rs 8.70 lakhs was to be refunded to the Malaria Institute. During 1957-58 the actual cost worked out to Rs 1.99 and Rs 1.52 respectively. The excess of income over expenditure amounting to Rs 7.52 lakhs was to be returned to the Ministry of Health.

Similarly, for Hindustan Antibiotics, a Joint Plan of Operations was signed on July 24, 1951, by the Government of India, the WHO and the UNICEF. The objectives, as contained in Part I of the Agreement (*inter alia*), were:

(a) to produce penicillin most economically as a national enter-

[9] Hindustan Shipyard, *Seventh Annual Report*, 1958-59, p. 6.

prise on a sound basis but entirely on a non-profit making basis;

(b) to maintain a supply of penicillin and other antibiotics for purchase by State and municipal hospitals for free treatment of patients, particularly women and children; and

(c) to provide for free distribution to children in India under arrangements mutually satisfactory to the Government and the UNICEF.

In practice, the Hindustan Antibiotics has not adhered so strictly to the 'no-profit' rule as the Hindustan Insecticides. The Hindustan Antibiotics suffered losses initially, but now it is making substantial profits. The net profit for the year ending March 31, 1959, stood at Rs. 87.10 lakhs on a capital investment of Rs 3.85 crores (paid-up capital Rs 2.47 crores; Reserves and Surplus Rs 1.08 crores; and Government loan Rs 0.30 crores), i.e. a return of about 23 per cent. However, a sum of Rs 81 lakhs was transferred to General Reserve and no dividend was declared. Thus the no-profit clause has been interpreted liberally and possibly on a long-term basis (including provision for expansion and the development of new lines of production).

(7) *Incurring Losses*

Many of the State Corporations have suffered losses in the initial stages of their working. However, some of them are *expected* to incur losses in certain areas and in certain activities to be made good by profits in other areas or other activities or by subsidies from certain Development Funds or finally from the State exchequer as such.

A notable example is that of the State Bank of India which, in terms of the incorporating legislation, was required to open 400 new branches within a period of five years (and in areas which were not well served with banking facilities). This work was completed by June 1, 1960; but no less than 337 of these branches (out of a total of 384 which had worked for some time) were reported to be running at a loss. The losses were to be set against the Development Fund to which the Reserve Bank (as the holding corporation) credited the dividends received from the State Bank of India. In effect, the unprofitable branches were being fed by the profitable branches; and the apparent profit of the State Bank of India did not reveal the correct position because of concealed losses. However, it was a part of the State policy that banking facilities should be developed in rural and semi-urban areas because on that would depend marketing finance and the prosperity of some three-fourths of the Indian population.

The *Janta* policies initiated by the Life Insurance Corporation of India in 1958 provide another example. The full impact of such policies may not be revealed for a number of years (i.e. there may be heavier claims because of the fact that proposals for life insurance are accepted indiscriminately). Considering the small volume of business secured through these policies during the first two years, the overall burden may be negligible. But it may still be said that the whole experiment is based, less on commercial considerations, and more on social objectives, i.e. popularizing life insurance among people who have low incomes (and who suffer too much from conservatism).

The Rehabilitation Finance Administration in India and the Pakistan Refugee Rehabilitation Finance Corporation are instances of political necessity. The partition of the country which came into effect on August 15, 1947, resulted in a colossal movement of population between India and Pakistan. The rehabilitation of the displaced persons was, no doubt, a social question; but since political parties waxed eloquent on this matter, the main problem was of pacifying political passions by administering financial assistance and by providing employment on a preferential basis. The birth of the two Corporations almost coincided—the PRRFC was constituted in May 1948 and the RFA with effect from June 1, 1948. During the first ten years of their existence both the Corporations never earned any profit. The accumulated loss in case of PRRFC up to the year 1957-58 stood at Rs 37.60 lakhs. The RFA's aggregate loss up to December 31, 1957, was Rs 16.8 lakhs. The PRRFC had to pay 2 per cent interest on the capital advanced by the Government and it was allowed to charge only $4\frac{1}{2}$ per cent interest on its advances to meet its operating expenses. For RFA, these rates were initially 3 per cent and 6 per cent respectively. But, later on, this margin of 3 per cent was reduced to between $\frac{1}{2}$ and $1\frac{1}{2}$ per cent. Thus the RFA, too, could not charge more than $4\frac{1}{2}$ per cent interest. For medium-to-long-term finance with an inflated risk of bad debts, this rate proved to be too uneconomical—more so in the face of a top-heavy administrative organization set up for the facility of displaced persons.[10]

Many economists have argued that, in case of public enterprises, the general rule 'that every tub must stand on its water' is excessively conservative. We have already referred to Hotelling's demand for cheap electric power 'to raise the whole level of economic existence'. But he ignores the fact that cheap power alone cannot make for rapid economic development.[11] The major hurdle is that of finance. Profits of public enterprises are the propellers of socialist industrialization.

[10] It was realized from the very beginning that the working of these Corporations would be uneconomic. Hence, in case of the PRRFC (as also in the case of the RFA) 'it was not considered advisable to float its shares in the Capital market'—Government Sponsored Corporation, Karachi, 1959, p. 1.

[11] Moreover, power can be supplied at reasonably low rates without incurring losses. The DVC bulk rates (energy charge) are 2.7 and 2.2. nP per kWh for two categories of customers.

Hotelling suggests that it will be better to operate the railroads for the benefit of living human beings, while 'letting dead men and dead investments rest quietly in their graves, and to establish a system of rates and services calculated to assure the most efficient operation'.[12] But how can there be 'most efficient operation' if the fixed capital is allowed to decay and there is no provision for renewals and extensions? Although Hotelling suggests a widespread geographical distribution of public projects, the picture in his mind is essentially that of an isolated State enterprise. As Mr Little points out, 'The larger the nationalized sector the more important it becomes that this sector taken as a whole should make profits.'[13]

We do not agree with Meade when he says that 'the principle to socialize just those industries in which considerable economies of large scale production may be enjoyed'[14]—precisely, where marginal cost is below average cost, and loss is incurred by equating price with marginal cost. If we accept Meade's contention, then no socialized industry can run at a profit.[15] Moreover, where is the guarantee that only those industries which are working under increasing returns would generate the greatest social welfare? For example, the need to sell subsidized (cheap) food may be much greater than to subsidize electricity supply. Moreover, certain public projects, which are in the nature of social and economic overheads like health services, education and research, may have to be supported either absolutely free of cost, or at substantially below the marginal cost level.[16] It is therefore imperative that other public projects must earn substantial profits. Meade appears to be conscious of the 'announcement' and 'disincentive' effects of large-scale taxation (required to offset the losses of State enterprises). But he sticks to his guns and suggests that public ownership of income-yielding property should accompany the socialization of 'increasing returns' industries. However, when the socialized sector covers a substantial part of the economy, Meade's closed door analysis becomes completely unrealistic.

[12] *Econometrica,* January 1938, p. 269.
[13] I. M. D. Little, *A Critique of Welfare Economics,* Second Edition, Oxford, 1957, p. 184.
[14] Symposium on 'Price and Output Policy of State Enterprise', *The Economic Journal,* December 1944, pp. 322-3.
[15] In fact, Meade contradicts his own proposition when he says that the actual losses in the socialized 'increasing returns' industries would just be covered by what profits were still made in socialized industries where increasing returns were less marked.
[16] *The National Council of Applied Economic Research* in a recent study entitled 'Criteria for Fixation of Water Rates and Selection of Irrigation Projects' (1959) points out that 'these structural changes' cannot be made on the basis of marginal analysis alone. Without these changes, the underdeveloped countries cannot reach a stage of economic development from which a process of cumulation can start.

Meade, however, is on surer grounds when he says that a public monopoly is preferable to a private monopoly, and that where 'trust-busting' proves to be ineffective or leads to inefficiency, socialization in one form or another is the only radical cure of that particular situation. But it is surprising that Meade intends to do away with the principle of 'charging what the traffic will bear'. Thus he is actually throwing away the baby along with the bath water.[17]

Finally, Meade concedes that in his scheme only 'extreme' degrees of efficiency or inefficiency can be detected. But he ignores the fact that the rule for incurring losses may serve as a cloak for inefficiency and complacency in a large number of 'medium' cases. Moreover, if socialized industries are always to show red ink entries, the possibilities of ameliorating the workers' lot, in spite of best intentions, would be strictly circumscribed.

While it is desirable that State Corporations should adopt a simplified rate structure (as favoured by Hotelling), we must not overlook the fact that the marginal cost principle would make the rate structure extremely sensitive and instable. The fixed costs are known in advance, but the marginal cost rests in the realm of uncertainty. In many cases, the marginal cost may be indeterminate or nil, especially if the units of calculation are small, e.g. the cost of carrying one more passenger in a railway train. Hotelling himself admits that the cost of running an additional train should be taken into account. He also suggests a departure from the marginal cost in case of holiday travels.[18] In fact the marginal cost principle becomes very unreliable[19] because of the existence of imperfect competition, the indivisibility of the factors of production and the desirability of introducing collective bargaining, maintaining price stability and improving the pattern of income distribution (by utilizing to a

---

[17] While Meade favours 'a more equal distribution as between persons', perhaps it did not occur to him that a price policy based on 'what the traffic will bear' would be a potent weapon in the hands of the State for promoting egalitarian objectives.

[18] Hotelling says: 'Instead of selling tickets to the first in a queue, or selling as many as to bring about an excessive crowding that would neutralize the pleasure of the holiday, the economic way to handle this situation would be to charge a sufficiently high price to limit the demand. The revenue thus obtained, like the site value of land, may properly be taken by the State.'

[19] Dr J. de V. Graaff (*Theoretical Welfare Economics*, Cambridge, 1957, p. 154) says that 'the survival of the marginal cost principle is probably no more than an indication of the extent to which professional economists are ignorant of the assumptions required for its validity'. Mr M. J. Farrell ('In Defence of Public-Utility Price', *Oxford Economic Papers*, February 1958, p. 121), in his attack on Dr Graaff, says that if clocks and watches are subject to error shall we take 'astronomical observation' whenever we want to know the time? But if a watch is so unreliable that it moves and stops at its own discretion, it is better not to use it.

greater extent factors of production supplied by the poor, and by expanding the output of goods or services predominantly consumed by such people).

(8) *Reducing Prices*
Price reductions may have great psychological value specially when a State Corporation is running an industry formerly controlled by private entrepreneurs. Further, those Corporations which started with a high cost structure may find it necessary to embark on a programme of price reductions.

The first situation is illustrated by the nationalization of life insurance in India. The LIC premium rates were kept somewhat lower than those charged by top companies. After the announcement of the first valuation results of LIC we can appreciate that these lower rates did not mean any net benefit to the (with profit) policyholders who received a substantially lower bonus than the erstwhile policyholders of the 'special group' companies. Moreover, there was already a downward trend in premium rates because of better mortality experience and competitive reductions.

The second situation is typified by the Hindustan Antibiotics which started with a high cost structure but which has effected successive reductions in prices. However, all these reductions are not necessarily because of internal economies. There has been a world-wide reduction in the price of penicillin and other allied drugs. New products, which are highly efficacious, often sell very dear in initial years. The production costs may be high because of limited production and other physical limitations. As the products become popular, new techniques of production are employed and it is worthwhile to effect price reductions. It may be mentioned that the Hindustan Antibiotics does not enjoy monopoly rights in the production of penicillin and other antibiotics. Although the competition from (dumped) foreign drugs has ceased because of import restrictions, there is keen competition offered by the private sector within the country. The Hindustan Antibiotics, therefore, cannot sell its products above the rates offered by the private sector. It may be mentioned that between October 1958 and August 1959, there were three price reductions.[20] Further, during 1958-59, the rate of discount was raised from 5 per cent to 10 per cent for Government and semi-

---

[20] Mr S. T. Raja, the Managing Director of Hindustan Antibiotics, in his paper on Price Policy (December 1959), states that 'After having carefully fixed the price . . . the announcement of price reduction should not be made at frequent intervals or too much before the effective date. . . . Too many and too frequent changes, even if the prices are to be reduced, instead of being appreciated by the public are likely to shake their confidence in the price structure and might adversely affect sales' (p. 4).

Government hospitals and other institutions on all the products of the Company.[21]

(9) *Increasing Prices*

These have particularly occurred in the field of transport and communications. These services are often being performed by the State (either through Corporations or departmentally) on a monopolistic basis. When the railways, the airways and the roadways are all publicly operated, the monopoly becomes all-pervading. Further, as people get accustomed to modern amenities, the pattern of demand becomes highly inelastic. As such, transport undertakings generally do not think of making travel cheap (and reducing certain amenities). On the other hand, the usual procedure is to push the rates upwards and to announce an increase in amenities (not necessarily commensurate with the increase in the charges) on every such occasion. This is necessary to keep the consumers in good humour.

After the nationalization of air transport in India, the Air Corporations (unlike LIC) did not effect any reduction in rates. On the other hand, the consumers were asked to pay more in exchange for an implicit assurance that they would receive better service—greater hospitality, courtesy, personal attention, the increased number of services and their regularity, and the use of modern aircraft. However, in the beginning the fleet of the Corporations was not only too small but also very much out of date. In course of time progress has been made in both the directions. Hence the excess fares paid by the consumers in the earlier stages are now bearing fruit.

However, since air transport is still not on quite a firm footing, and there has been unutilized capacity in many cases, certain incentives (apart from better service) have been employed to popularize air travel. The Air India International has resorted to extensive advertising both in India and abroad.[22] Keen competition with foreign lines has probably necessitated this. Of late, several international airlines like the British Overseas Airways Corporation, the Air India International and Australia's Qantas have entered into pooling arrangements. Thus, common advertising has been carried on recently. Further, in 1959, Air India International adopted the practice (in vogue for a number of years with BOAC) of 'fly now and pay later', only 20 per cent being required to be paid in advance.

[21] In case of Pen. *v.* Tablets, five free sample packets were issued with every 100 packets with effect from March 1, 1959.

[22] The Life Insurance Corporation of India (although a virtual monopoly) has probably paid the greatest attention to advertising. The Indian Airlines Corporation, the State Bank of India and several other Corporations have practised advertising. But many of the Corporations like the IFC (with a restricted clientele) have not found it necessary.

181

(10) *Making Profits*

We have already stated that socialist industrialization rests on the profitability of public enterprises. They provide a less cumbersome source of public finance; at the same time, they are helpful in making the process of economic development self-financing. As a general rule, each Corporation should be left with sufficient resources for its expansion and further development. There may, however, be exceptions where it is desired to put a ceiling on the production capacity of a particular Corporation or of an industry as a whole.

According to the *Statement of Financial Working of Major Industrial and Commercial Public Enterprises* (New Delhi, 1959), 16 of the 21 Corporations in that list had shown profit during 1957-58. Out of the 16 profitable Corporations, 9 had consistently shown profit during the past three years (1955-58); 5 had functioned for less than this period but had shown profit up to 1958; in respect of one, figures had been given for two years only and these showed profits; and one had suffered loss during 1955-56, but profits during 1956-57 and 1957-58 (Hindustan Antibiotics). Out of the five unprofitable Corporations four had shown loss during all the three years, and one had worked for two years only and had shown losses in both these years (Ashoka Hotels). The first four Corporations were Hindustan Shipyard, Indian Airlines, Bharat Electronics and Indian Rare Earths. Two of these belong to the Ministry of Transport and Communications, the third to the Ministry of Defence and the fourth to the Department of Atomic Energy. The red ink entries were led by Indian Airlines which suffered an aggregate loss of Rs 3.31 crores during the three years (1955-58), whereas the list of profitable Corporations was led by Sindri Fertilizers and Chemicals with three-year total of Rs 5.11 crores.[23]

According to *Principal Public Sector Undertakings in India* (March 1960), 44 Corporations (excluding 2 non-corporate enterprises) were taken into account. During the year 1958-59, 27 Corporations had shown profits; 6 had suffered losses; 8 were reported to be in the 'Nil' category (7 of these being incomplete and not in full operation); and in respect of the remaining 3, figures were not available. The profits of the 27 profitable Corporations aggregated Rs 53.57 crores, whereas the aggregate losses of 6 Corporations amounted to Rs 1.43 crores only. After allowing for Government subsidies amounting to Rs 0.90 crores, the net positive figure amounted to Rs 51.24 crores. However, the major part of this surplus

---

[23] The list of twenty-one is not exhaustive. Moreover, the selection has been rather haphazard. While major Corporations like the DVC, LIC and Reserve Bank were excluded, small entities like the Hindustan Housing Factory were included.

came from the Reserve Bank of India as will be evident from the following list of most profitable Corporations:[24]

(1) Reserve Bank of India	...	...	...	Rs 40.00 crores
(2) State Trading Corporation	...	...	...	Rs 2.82 ,,
(3) Employees State Insurance Corporation	...			Rs 2.35 ,,
(4) State Bank of India	...	...	...	Rs 1.87 ,,
(5) Sindi Fertilizers and Chemicals		...	...	Rs 1.59 ,,
(6) Hindustan Antibiotics	...	...	...	Rs 1.47 ,,
			Total[25]	Rs 50.10 ,,

The annual surplus payable by the Reserve Bank of India to the Central Government stood at Rs 30 crores during 1956-57 and 1957-58. Thus, during the three years ended June 30, 1959, the Reserve Bank of India had contributed Rs 100 crores to the Central exchequer.[26] On the basis of a tentative estimate, the Railways were expected to contribute Rs 150 crores during the Third Five-Year Plan and other State enterprises Rs 440 crores. This means that the State Corporations should yield Rs 88 crores per year. In the initial year this figure may not be reached, but the profits may grow progressively as the Plan advances.

B. APPROACHES TO EFFICIENCY

The problems of judging the efficiency of State Corporations has proved to be a most baffling one. While it is easy to lay down a vague stipulation that such Corporations should operate to the best advantage of the community, it is difficult to formulate a simplified objective test for this purpose. In order to obtain an overall picture, which may be sufficiently illustrative, we may approach the problem from several standpoints:

(1) 'Profit and Loss Account' Approach

This is the conventional approach which the shareholders in Privately-owned Corporations generally employ (and which the State

[24] In these calculations, provision for taxation has not been deducted from net profit. Where it was already deducted, the same has been added back, e.g. the net profit of Hindustan Antibiotics was shown as Rs 87 lakhs.

[25] The annual surplus in case of Life Insurance Corporation, on the basis of the valuation as at December 31, 1957, may be estimated (without deducting taxation) at Rs 16.50 crores and after taxation at 14.50 crores. But 95 per cent of this goes to the policyholders. In case of Damodar Valley Corporations (shown as incomplete) the surplus in the power account for 1957-58 was Rs 0.45 crores.

[26] Reserve Bank of India, Report of the Central Board of Directors for the year ended June 30, 1959, p. 37. This is comparable to the contribution made by the Indian Government Railways.

Corporations must also respect, i.e. as a general rule they should work as commercially profitable enterprises). However, most of the shareholders are concerned with immediate profits and dividends rather than with long-run prosperity. But in case of State Corporations where, at least in theory, the equity is owned by the nation, the 'Profit and Loss Account' approach may prove to be too narrow and somewhat superficial. It is narrow in the sense that it ignores the host of objectives with which State Corporations are promoted; and it is superficial because profitability and inefficiency may co-exist on many occasions.[27] For example, State Corporations may utilize the administrative power of the State to earn profits. Foreign competition may be shut out by imposing import restrictions and domestic competition may be outlawed by creating Statutory Monopolies. Alternatively, Government Departments may orient their stores purchase policy in such a manner that the products of State Corporations get a price advantage, either on the basis of supposed superiority in quality or through an open preferential system.[28] When the Government is the principal customer of the products of a Corporation, as in the case of Hindustan Insecticides, the amount of profit may very much depend on administrative convenience.

Apart from provision for taxation, which has been made most irregularly by many of the Corporations,[29] the payment of interest on Government investment has created accounting complications. The rate of interest has varied from Corporation to Corporation. In some cases (e.g. Air India and Indian Airlines) a rate of interest is laid down but a moratorium is granted for the first few years. In many cases Government loans have been converted into share capital either partly or wholly. In a few cases, subsidies have enabled the Corporations (e.g. the Hindustan Shipyard) to conceal a part of their loss. It will be better if some uniform standards are laid down for the presentation of Profit and Loss Accounts so that the per-

[27] Profits may be due to a sudden rise in the price of that particular commodity or due to specially favourable opportunities. In other words, if the management were competent, the profits could have increased still further. Conversely, if the management were incompetent, losses could have been much greater.

[28] The purchases made by the Government of the Philippines from the National Development Company's textile mills are a case in point. In India the products of small industries (through the National Small Industries Corporation) have enjoyed an open price preference.

[29] The Air India International did not make any provision for taxation during 1958-59. The State Trading Corporation treats taxation as an expenditure; many other Corporations consider it as an appropriation. Air India, up to 1956-57, made provision for deferred taxation and showed only the net profit by way of balance. The profit for 1957-58 was inflated to Rs 1.26 crores by showing a capital receipt (surplus on assets sold) of Rs 1.16 crores.

formance of several Corporations can be mutually compared (as also the performance of the same Corporation from year to year).

(2) 'Balance Sheet' Approach

If the Balance Sheets of a Corporation, at two different dates, are compared, we may be able to form some idea of the progress of that Corporation during the intervening period. That is, we can find out whether the net worth of that Corporation has gone up or declined. In case adequate provision has not been made for depreciation of fixed assets and for bad and doubtful debts (the debtors being very important for Finance Corporations), either because of losses or because the profits were all dissipated, the net worth would show a decline. In other words, what we are looking for is the fact whether the capital originally invested has undergone a decay, has been properly maintained, or has been enhanced. Thus the shortcomings of the 'Profit and Loss Account' approach are partly overcome. However, the Balance Sheet approach is much less significant for State Corporations because they are not to be sold or liquidated (and generally, their shares are not the subject of Stock Exchange speculation). Moreover, a Corporation which contributes all its profits to the State Treasury every year will show no rise in its net worth. Thus the Reserve Bank of India is the most profitable State Corporation in India, but after contributing over Rs 100 crores between July 1, 1956, and June 30, 1959, it did not retain anything within the organization. As against this, Reserve Fund and Other Reserves of the State Bank of India went up from Rs 6.38 crores on December 31, 1956, to Rs 7.20 crores on December 31, 1959.

(3) Fiscal Approach

For each Corporation we can calculate the aggregate contribution made to the State Treasury, consisting of:

(a) dividend on the shares held by the Government of other State Corporations;

(b) interest on the loans advanced by the Government;

(c) taxes realized from the Corporation by Governmental authorities;

(d) excess profits paid to the Government; and

(e) benefits of lower prices enjoyed by Governmental organizations.

If we want to consider the activities of State Corporations in a broader perspective, and on a collective basis, we can calculate their total contribution to national income. Such ratios worked out from year to year would give an indication of the progress of the public sector vis-a-vis the development in the economy as a whole.

The saving in foreign exchange resources effected by the State

Corporations would be another important criterion for India and most of the other underdeveloped countries whose programmes of economic development have often suffered because of imbalance in foreign trade relations. For example, if the three Steel Plants had been established in India five years earlier (when certain proposals were considered and then dropped), the saving in foreign exchange resources during this period would have exceeded the cost of establishing the three Plants. Not only have we to consider the economy in imports, but also the expansion in exports through the activities of State Corporations.

(4) *Employment Approach*

This approach is of particular significance for most of the under-developed countries where unemployment and underemployment are serious problems. Public enterprises are expected not only to provide more jobs but also to improve the lot of those who are already at work. Hence the performance of State Corporations will be judged by their ability in providing employment on the basis of merit (i.e. without personal or political bias), enforcing reasonable standards of wages (correlated to the amount and the quality of work), providing better conditions of work and living, and arranging for a high standard of welfare facilities. In fine, a State Corporation is expected to be a model employer. It has to treat the workers nicely and it has to make them feel that they are being treated nicely. The latter task is most difficult and State Corporations in India have generally failed in that respect. In other words, the employees of such Corporations have not developed that patriotic sense which can be the largest single factor in improving the level of efficiency.[30]

For an objective analysis in this regard we may consider:

(a) the percentage of absenteeism;

(b) the amount of lost time due to late coming, loitering, go-slow tactics and labour troubles;

(c) the amount of defective work, spoiled materials and other forms of wastage; and

(d) the results of psychological tests giving an idea of the workers' liking or disliking for work, aptitudes, agility and the extent of training (including understanding about the Corporation's social and economic objectives, its difficulties and its policies with regard to labour matters).

[30] Professor Robson has almost the same thing to say about the Public Corporations in Great Britain: 'It was quite unrealistic and naïve to expect that there would be a change of heart the moment the NCB's pennant fluttered from the pithead masts in 1947. It is equally unrealistic to deny that the progress so far made in inducing a more receptive, co-operative and flexible frame of mind among the miners has been disappointing to say the least . . .' (*Nationalized Industry and Public Ownership*, 1960, pp. 324-5.)

The total employment provided by thirty-five State Corporations (in respect of whom figures were available) stood at 4,25,575 during 1958-59. This figure includes construction staff also. Most of the employment was concentrated in a few Corporations:

(1) Hindustan Steel	... ...	1,72,068
(2) DVC (Regular) ...	... ...	4,696
(Daily Wage Basis)	... ...	94,696
(3) Life Insurance Corporation	... ...	34,800
(4) State Bank of India	... ...	23,757
(5) Neyveli Lignite Corporation		
(Regular)	... ...	2,807
(Daily Wage Basis) ...	... ...	11,000
(6) Indian Airlines Corporation ...	...	9,463
	Total	3,53,287

The Hindustan Steel, the DVC and the Neyveli Lignite Corporation provided new employment, but the LIC, the State Bank of India and the Indian Airlines only extended the scope of employment already existing in the private sector. The total wages bill for thirty-three Corporations amounted to Rs 14.50 crores.

(5) *Productivity Approach*

State Corporations may be expected to economize the relatively scarce factor of production. Alternatively, attempts may be made to raise the productivity of that factor. As such, public enterprises should make every effort to increase the productivity of capital, which is the scarce factor in India.[31] However, in actual practice, it has become fashionable to establish relationships between labour input and total output. While it is true that unskilled labour is, in most cases, plentiful, highly skilled labour has a scarcity element which is greater than that for capital. The productivity per worker may be compared from year to year.[32] It may also be compared as between several Corporations where the work is more or less identical.

(6) *Cost Accounting Approach*

This is a very powerful instrument for checking the efficiency of State Corporations, particularly those which are large-sized. We pointed out earlier that profitability and inefficiency may go together. A detailed analysis of costs per unit[33] in various departments

[31] Mr S. B. Prasad defines productivity as 'ratio of physical output per machine value' (instead of output per man hour). See his very interesting article, 'Productivity Measurement in Manufacturing Industries in India's Public Sector', *The Indian Journal of Economics,* Special Number on Problems of Socialist Economy, July 1958, pp. 135-40.

[32] For example, the available ton miles per employee in case of Air India International rose from 11,292 in 1955-56 to 12,608 in 1958-59.

[33] Other useful information is often published, e.g. the Air India International publishes figures of load factors, aircraft utilization (per annum

and processes and at various stages of manufacturing and marketing will enable the Corporations to discover their weak points which may otherwise remain hidden behind an attitude of complacency. To take a very simple example, certain unprofitable activities may be lumped together with profitable ones and, because there is over-all surplus, there may be no attempt to improve efficiency. It does *not* mean that State Corporations will conduct only those activities which yield profit. But it does mean that the Corporations will not be in the dark when they conduct *any* activity. Social considerations (and not ignorance) will dictate the desirability of conducting loss-incurring functions.

(7) *Development and Stability Approach*

This is the most crucial criterion. It may often be a matter of subjective assessment as to whether a particular Corporation has succeeded in fulfilling its statutory obligation of developing a particular industry or service (e.g. air transport and life insurance in India) to the best advantage of the society. However, certain objective tests can be employed here as well.

The first test may be the achievement of planned output and improvement in its quality (including safety of operation, i.e. reduced number of accidents, in case of Transport Undertakings). Long-term targets may be laid down either under the Development Plans of the country or under a separate Plan for each Corporation. Thus the Life Insurance Corporation has embarked on a five-year plan of its own (1959-63). The target for 1963 is a business of Rs 1,000 crores. The annual target for 1959 was Rs 415 crores and the same has been overfulfilled. For the newly-established enterprises, the carrying out of promotional work according to schedule and the starting of production on or before the appointed date may be considered as an important achievement. To repeat an old saying, well begun is half done. However, these schedules of preliminary work could not be adhered to in most of the cases in India. The entire blame cannot be left at the doors of State Corporations, because these Corporations were often created when some of the miscalculations were already on the way. Further, some of the schedules were unrealistic in themselves, and they were drawn either because of ignorance and inexperience or because there was an element of ostentation.[34] Likewise, production schedules drawn up

and per day), revenue hours flown available ton miles, available seat miles, operating revenue per A.T.M. and operating cost per A.T.M.

[34] For example, in case of the Hindustan Shipyard, the French Technical Director had observed in his report dated December 9, 1954: 'Our first schedule was accordingly drawn at four ships a year, but it was pointed out to Mr Gupta, and he agreed, that this figure was only a theoretical one.'

from time to time may be either overambitious or too low. In the first case, the managers may lose all hope of achieving the target; and, in the second case, there may be unwarranted boasting about overfulfilment.

The second test may relate to the trend in operating revenues. The amount of increase from year to year may be compared either on the basis of natural scale or logarithmic scale. However, due allowance will have to be made for inflationary and deflationary elements and the social objectives of the price policy.

The third test, applicable mostly to Development Corporations, is the extent to which they have been successful in securing the participation of private entrepreneurs and the rapidity with which new units are being promoted. Whether these 'daughter' companies are firmly established is, again, of cardinal importance. Development Corporations in India have been, on the whole, a failure. The NIDC has been roosting in comfortable nests, giving its major attention to the granting of loans for the rationalization of cotton and jute industries. The National Small Industries Corporation has involved itself in uneconomic and impracticable pursuits.[35] However, the Pakistan Industrial Development Corporation has brought about tremendous industrial development, though even that institution is now finding it difficult to secure the participation of private capital.

The fourth test, largely applicable to Marketing Boards, is that of bringing about relative stability in the prices of (agricultural) commodities. The pattern of income distribution and the prosperity of nearly three-fourths of India's population depends on the maintenance of agricultural prices at a fair level. The Marketing Boards may attempt to bridge the gulf between in-season and out-of-season prices as also between the bad-harvest-year and good-harvest-year prices. The ceiling and floor prices may have to be fixed in consonance with international commodity agreements. Hence the effectiveness of Marketing Boards would depend to a considerable degree on the successful working of international agreements. However, the Boards must be equipped with a sizeable working capital, large and dependable warehouses, an extensive network of branches (so that middlemen are not able to thrive), and an expert and agile staff capable of acting quickly yet correctly. Apart from Marketing Boards, other Corporations may also play some rôle in the stabilization of the general price level. They may adjust their price policies in such a way as to combat inflationary or deflationary tendencies. Even the Life Insurance Corporation tried to stabilize the stock

[35] The Estimate Committee were surprised that it was necessary for the Corporation to operate the marketing scheme for four years to realize its ineffectiveness when it was incurring heavy losses since its inception—*Commerce,* May 7, 1960, p. 822.

market in the wake of the Mundhra deal. However, that was a most unwarranted and unfortunate experiment.

Finally, there is the (largely subjective) test of developing suitable public relations. Some of the State Corporations in India like the Sindri Fertilizers and Chemicals have established Public Relation Departments. The success of such Departments can be judged by the number of inquiries received from time to time, the speed and fullness with which they are disposed of, and the qualitative improvement in the nature of inquiries (resulting from increased knowledge about the working of Corporations). Likewise, the efficiency and goodwill of State Corporations would be judged by the attention which they are able to pay to consumers' inquiries, complaints, grievances, misconceptions and even idiosyncrasies.

CHAPTER IX

PUBLIC ACCOUNTABILITY

Public accountability is the essence of a socialized enterprise. The criterion to be fulfilled is the responsiveness of public undertakings to the wishes of the people. There is no doubt that efficiency, in its technical connotation, and as measured by economic indicators, is of prime importance in the case of all business enterprises, whether public or private. But, over and above this basic minimum, public enterprises are expected to serve the deeper social objectives. In other words, State Corporations have to perform the uphill task of convincing the people that public undertakings are being run in the best interests of the society. From a practical point of view, 'this principle means that the public must have the final word in the control of the industries it owns'.[1] The nation, as equity shareholder, should be able to pull the strings of State Corporations through a network of organizational techniques and procedural devices. The problem may be examined under the following headings:

(1) PARLIAMENTARY CONTROL

The central feature of public accountability is often described as parliamentary control. This is based on the assumptions that Parliament is the true representative of public opinion, that it is sovereign and has the final say in all matters. In actual practice these assumptions may prove to be too theoretical. Hence it becomes necessary to tap other channels of public accountability.

The starting point of parliamentary control is the introduction of the Bill seeking to establish a particular Public Corporation. At this stage, Parliament establishes the basic framework of public accountability. While retaining the right to make amendments in the light of future experience, Parliament tries to effect a judicious allocation of responsibilities. While in many cases it may grant monopoly rights to particular Corporations, it also imposes limits on the powers of management so that public monopoly is not abused and public funds are not misapplied for personal benefit.

Up to the end of 1953 it was strongly urged by the spokesmen of

[1] *Some Problems in the Organization and Administration of Public Enterprises in the Industrial Field,* United Nations, 1954, p. 55.

the Government of India that while ordinary Departments were fully accountable to Parliament, and Public Corporations were accountable within the limits of incorporating legislations, Government Companies (for the most part) fell outside the periphery of public accountability. Certain information relating to the Sindri Fertilizers and Chemicals Ltd was not divulged to Parliament on the ground that the concern was a Private Limited Company (within the terms of the Companies Act) and that its affairs were supposed to be secret (September 1953). On November 16, 1953, in the question hour, Dr Choitram Gidwani wanted to know why Sindri's agreements were not being disclosed to Parliament. The Speaker, Mr G. V. Mavlankar, remarked that while the House was entitled to have all information which was reasonably necessary just to judge whether the administration of a particular Corporation (which was autonomous) was being properly carried on or not, it ought not to enter into discussion of day-to-day administration. On December 10, 1953, Dr Lanka Sundaram, while initiating a debate on 'Parliamentary Control over Public Corporations', again raised the Sindri issue. He said that once the Companies were brought into existence, they became impervious to public or parliamentary control. He wanted a Parliamentary Committee to sit all round the year 'specifically charged with the task of looking into the affairs of the various corporations, companies and institutions'. The Finance Minister, Mr C. D. Deshmukh pleaded for 'self-abnegation' on the part of Members of Parliament. On December 11, 1953, Mr Deshmukh argued that the setting up of a new Committee was inadvisable at that stage and 'in the fullness of time there is nothing to stop us from setting up any body for the special purposes of going through the accounts and the affairs of these Corporations'.

The theory that Government Companies can maintain secrecy about their working was finally exploded in 1956 when the new Companies Act made special provisions regarding the preparation of accounts, audit and presentation of annual reports to Parliament in respect of the Government Companies. It may be mentioned that during the four years 1953-56, Government Companies were the object of great curiosity (Sindri, of course, leading the way). The following table illustrates the position about some of the Government Companies:[2]

[2] Questions relating to plants subsequently taken over by the Government Companies have also been included. In all 343 questions were asked on Government Companies (including general questions). The questions ranged from the number of copies of *Sindri News* (magazine) supplied to subscribers and complimentaries distributed in the case of Sindri Fertilizers and Chemicals Ltd to the names of persons to whom lathes have been sold (rates, annual sale, foreign parts used) in case of Hindustan Machine Tools Ltd.

Number of Parliamentary Questions (Lok Sabha)

	1953	1954	1955	1956	*Total*
1. Sindri Fertilizers	22	14	15	8	59
2. Hindustan Steel	5	9	19	20	53
3. Hindustan Aircraft	1	16	4	5	26
4. Hindustan Shipyard	12	3	6	4	25
5. Hindustan Insecticides	5	3	5	6	19
Total	45	45	49	43	182

Since 1956, as far as parliamentary control is concerned, no distinction is made between Public Corporations and Government Companies. However, Government Companies can be registered without prior approval of Parliament, whereas Public Corporations are established after parliamentary legislation.[3] Moreover, when incorporating legislations are sought to be amended, Parliament gets an additional opportunity of assessing the progress of Public Corporations.

Under the Canadian Financial Administration Act there is a fourfold classification—Government Departments, Departmental Corporations, Agency Corporations and Proprietary Corporations. Departmental Corporations are treated on the same footing as Government Departments. Sections 79-88 apply to Agency and Proprietary Corporations. Section 79 lays down that the financial year of a Corporation is the calendar year unless the Governor-in-Council otherwise directs.[4] Section 80 provides that each Agency Corporation shall annually submit to the appropriate Minister an operating budget for the next following financial year of the Corporation for the approval of the appropriate Minister and the Minister of Finance. Further, for each Agency and Proprietary Corporation, the appropriate Minister shall annually lay before Parliament the capital budget for its financial year approved by the Governor-in-Council on the recommendation of the appropriate Minister and the Minister of Finance. Thus Proprietary Corporations are not required to get their operating budgets scrutinized. Under Section 82, the Minister of Finance may, from time to time, lend money to a Corporation for working capital, but the aggregate amount of loans outstanding

[3] In certain cases (not in India) Public Corporations have been established by an Ordinance issued by the President or the Governor-General, e.g. the Pakistan International Airlines Corporation. As far as Royal Charters are concerned (as in case of BBC) they are generally issued after parliamentary discussion.

[4] There is need for such uniformity in India. Although a large number of Corporations close their accounts on March 31 (to coincide with Government's financial year), there are a good many Corporations having diverse accounting periods, e.g. Reserve Bank, IFC and State Trading Corporation (June 30); Ashoka Hotels (September 30); RFA, State Bank and LIC (December 31).

193

against any Corporation shall not at any time exceed $500,000. A report of every loan shall be laid before Parliament within fifteen days after it is made (or within fifteen days after the commencement of the next ensuing session). Under Section 85, every Corporation is required to submit an annual report to the appropriate Minister within three months after the termination of each financial year.[5]

The State Industrial Corporations Act (No. 49 of 1957) in Ceylon provides that the Corporations shall start with capital as approved by Parliament. This capital is generally sufficient to meet the initial capital outlay and to provide working capital. The capital of the State Corporations can only be increased through money voted by Parliament. In this sense, the approval of investment decisions rests with Parliament.[6]

The activities of State Corporations in India have been examined with great thoroughness by the Estimates Committee and the Public Accounts Committee of Parliament, the rôle of the former being all the more praiseworthy. An interesting example is provided by the 27th Report of the Estimates Committee (April 1956). The Committee wanted to refer to certain details in the six-year agreement between the Government (concluded in 1953, and later on assigned to the Hindustan Insecticides Ltd) and the DCM Chemical Works regarding the supply of raw materials, water and steam. But it was represented to them by the Ministry 'that it is not usual for business concerns to make public such details including the prices at which the raw materials are purchased by them and the waste products are disposed of'.[7] Though the Committee did not, accordingly, give the details of that agreement in their Report, they felt 'that such an argument should not be held to apply to nationalized industries'. They were of the view that the publication of such details would

---

[5] In India there is a similar provision in case of IFC and Central Warehousing Corporation. The former has always adhered to the rule, but the latter has failed to do so on the first two occasions. The Reserve Bank and the State Bank publish their annual reports in about two months' time. But many other Corporations take much longer. The first LIC Report for the period ending December 31, 1957, was released in 1959. The DVC Report for the year ending March 31, 1959, could not be placed before Parliament even up to May 1960.

[6] *Some Problems of Organization and Management of Public Industrial Enterprises,* a case-study on Ceylon by the ECAFE Secretariat, December 1959, p. 13. In India, although Parliament lays down the authorized capital in certain cases, the Government is permitted to raise it beyond that figure if necessary (e.g. in the case of the State Bank). In case of Government Companies, Government has absolute discretion in the matter.

[7] As pointed out earlier, the exact location of the site of the DDT Factory was included as an item in the agreement between the Government and the International Organizations even before the negotiations with the DCM Chemical Works had been concluded. This put the Chemical Works (private sector undertaking) in a favourable bargaining position.

194

have a 'salutary effect leading to the correction of such unfortunate features'. The Committee recommended that 'Government should, as soon as practicable, place a copy of the agreement . . . on the Table of Lok Sabha and should also take steps to make public such agreements as far as possible'.

During the last few years the question has loomed large whether the establishment of a Special Committee of Parliament on Nationalized Industries is desirable. The Select Committee on Nationalized Industries appointed in England on November 6, 1952, suggested[8] the appointment of a Committee of the House of Commons by Standing Order, to examine the Nationalized Industries, with power to send for persons, papers and records, power to set up sub-Committees, and to report from time to time. They recommended that the Committee should direct their attention to the published Reports and Accounts, and to obtaining further information as to the general policy and practice of the Nationalized Industries 'established by Statutes whose controlling Boards are wholly nominated by the Ministers of the Crown, and whose annual receipts are not wholly derived from moneys provided by Parliament or advanced from the Exchequer'. In their view, the object of the Committee should be that of informing Parliament about the aims, activities and problems of the Corporations and not of controlling their work. It was proposed that the staff of the Committee should include an officer of the status of the Comptroller and Auditor General who should be an officer of the House of Commons, with high administrative experience; at least one professional accountant, and such other staff as required. Further, it was stipulated that the statutory auditors of the corporations should, in preparing their annual reports, give such information in addition to that provided by them as may be of use to the Committee and of interest to Parliament.[9]

[8] *Report from the Select Committee on Nationalized Industries* together with the proceedings of the Committee, Minutes of Evidence and an Appendix ordered by the House of Commons to be printed, July 23, 1953, London, p. xii.

[9] Mr Hugh Molson, M.P., in his evidence on February 19, 1953, put the case for such a committee as follows: 'First, in order that a few Members of Parliament may give intensive study to the problem; secondly, that there may be interrogation of witnesses and investigation of papers and maps; thirdly, in order that in the seclusion of a committee room there may be comparative freedom from political prejudices. . . .' Lord Hurcomb, Chairman of BTC, on March 5, 1953, felt that it would satisfy 'the very legitimate demand of Parliament for a greater knowledge' but he rejected the idea of efficiency audit or 'expertise'. Mr (Lord) Morrison, on February 26, 1953, expressed fears that it might develop 'a rather red-tapeish, unadventurous and conventionally civil service frame of mind'. He favoured a seven-yearly Committee of Inquiry with a few M.P.s and many outsiders.

On March 16, 1955, a Select Committee was appointed to examine the Reports and Accounts of Nationalized Industries established by Statute whose controlling Boards are wholly appointed by Ministers of the Crown and whose annual receipts are not wholly or mainly derived from moneys provided by Parliament or advanced from the Exchequer, and to obtain further information as to so much of the current policy and practices of those industries as are not matters which:

(a) have been decided or clearly engage the responsibility of any Ministers;

(b) concern wages and conditions of employment and other questions normally decided by collective bargaining arrangements;

(c) fall to be considered through formal machinery established by the relevant statutes, or

(d) are matters of day-to-day administration.

The Attorney-General appeared before this Committee on April 20, 1955, and he felt that it would be difficult to conclude in advance where the limits of the exclusion lay. According to Mr George Strauss, the Committee were in 'an impossible dilemma'. The Minister could say, 'I do not think it is really my responsibility. That is the responsibility of the Coal Board'; and the House could say: 'But you have power to give general directions on all matters affecting the national interest.'[10] Colonel Lancaster felt: '. . . we may find ourselves inquiring 60 per cent of one Nationalized Industry and 10 per cent of another. That cannot be satisfactory. Either we broadly approach each industry along more or less the same lines, or we shall be not only restricted but our work will be conditioned by the approach of the Ministry to what they consider to be their own purview.'[11] He felt that this would also depend on whether a Minister was industrious or indolent.[12]

On November 29, 1956, the House of Commons decided that a Select Committee should be appointed to examine 'the Reports and Accounts of the Nationalized Industries established by Statute whose controlling Boards are appointed by Ministers of the Crown and whose annual receipts are not wholly or mainly derived from moneys provided by Parliament or advanced from the Exchequer'. The

[10] *Special Report from the Select Committee on Nationalized Industries* together with the proceedings of the Committee, Minutes of Evidence and Appendices, ordered by the House of Commons to be printed, November 14, 1955, London, p. 34.

[11] *Ibid.*, p. 39.

[12] The March 1955 Committee adjourned *sine die* after only one sitting. On July 7, 1955, a Select Committee was appointed with exactly similar terms of reference. After considering Ministers' replies (regarding their powers and responsibilities) the Committee reported to the House that there was 'insufficient scope to make enquiries or to obtain further information'.

Committee started their consideration of the National Coal Board's Report and Accounts for 1956 in July 1957, and after taking written and oral evidence from the Board, Government Departments and other organizations, presented their Report on April 29, 1958.

The Select Committee feel that they have received more information about the NCB than the House of Commons had ever previously had on the working of a nationalized industry. Although the Committee were primarily concerned with the Report and Accounts for 1956, the discussions covered current policies and trends, particularly in the fields of capital expenditure, production and marketing:

(1) The Committee examined the Board's investment plan, 'Investing in Coal', published in 1956. They suggested that the plan should be continually examined, and when necessary amended, since it was based on a number of uncertain factors. The Minister of Power should be able to make a greater financial check on the Board's investment schemes. The Board should present the Ministry each year with full details of those major schemes *which they expected would be least profitable*. The Board, however, feel that 'the responsibility for deciding whether or not to proceed with a particular scheme must remain with them, the Minister's function, as prescribed in Section 3(2) of the Coal Industry Nationalization Act, being limited to general control over programmes of reorganization or of development'.[13] However, at the Minister's request, arrangements were made to submit brief details of all schemes expected to cost more than £2½ million, which are estimated to yield, before charging interest on capital, less than 7½ per cent calculated either on total investments or on new investment. The Committee suggested that the Board should consider an upward revision in the authority of Divisional Boards to approve capital schemes in respect of collieries. The Board, however, felt that it would be a mistake to enlarge the delegated authority (beyond £250,000).

(2) The Committee were alarmed at the rise in coal prices since the Day of Vesting. They also remarked that there had been no sign of increased output per man-year (the abandonment of Saturday working after April 1958 being a later event). The Board's policy of providing depreciation on the basis of historical cost was rightly criticized by the Committee. They suggested that full cost of replacement of assets should be provided for.

(3) The working of the 'Gentleman's Agreement' between the Board and the Minister of Power on coal prices was examined by the Committee. The original agreement made between the colliery owners and the Minister in 1939 was continued by the Board in 1946, and revised in 1954. In a letter from the then Minister to the

[13] *National Coal Board,* Annual Report and Accounts for the year ended January 3, 1959, p. 49.

Board, the former had suggested that the Board should let the Minister know of any proposal to change the price of coal and should pay regard to his judgment of where the national interest should be deemed to lie; the Board were free to give publicity to any letter from the Minister in this connection. The Committee proposed that the Board should consult the Minister as to the public interest when proposing changes in coal prices, but, having done so, should take full responsibility for the decision. The Minister should have power to give the Board specific directions on prices, but this power should be statutory and the directions should be laid before Parliament and published, so that Parliament and the public would be fully informed about the respective responsibilities of the Minister and the Board in a particular case. As revealed by the Parliamentary Secretary to the Ministry for Power on July 14, 1958, the Government did not accept this recommendation and reaffirmed their faith in the Gentleman's Agreement as it stood.

The Krishna Menon Committee, in their report dated November 14, 1959, definitely recommended that a Special Committee of Parliament should be established in India.[14] It would be a 'well-informed' Committee, but by no means an 'expert' Committee. It is not to be 'imbued with the feeling that it is a fault-finding body or that it is a Super Board of Management. At the same time, there cannot be any fettering of its judgment and the expression of its views in good parliamentary tradition'.[15] The idea was that any public expression of views which are intended to correct errors or to provide greater incentives should not be of such a character as would have the opposite result of lowering the concern in public estimation or 'affect our credit or capacity to be well regarded abroad'. Although it is difficult to avoid all fuss about such shortcomings and although some lowering in public estimation may be inevitable for the time being, the idea of a Special Committee on Nationalized Industries is quite sound. We favour this recommendation for several reasons.

First, the Estimates Committee and the Public Accounts Committee have created rich traditions of non-political, non-partisan and impartial scrutiny. As the third Committee would be similarly constituted, we hope that it will imbibe those very traditions. Secondly, the two Committees are already overworked, and as time passes, more Corporations will come into existence and the volume of work

[14] Dr Lanka Sundaram advocated this in 1953. The late Mr G. V. Mavlankar (Speaker) had also favoured the idea in a letter to the Prime Minister, Pandit Jawaharlal Nehru.

[15] Report of the Sub-Committee of the Congress Party in Parliament— *Parliamentary Supervision over State Undertakings*, 1959, p. 38. The Committee was appointed in April 1958 with Mr Feroze Gandhi (who 'discovered' the Mundhra Deal in December 1957 through parliamentary questioning) as convenor and Mr V. K. Krishna Menon as Chairman.

will increase. Thirdly, Parliament itself is overburdened with work. It has no time to go into the working of so many Corporations. But if Parliament loosens the strings, it would open the floodgates of corruption and inefficiency. Fourthly, the difficulties and shortcomings of State Corporations are such that they can be better appreciated in a Committee of manageable size rather than in a big assembly. Fifthly, a Committee of outside experts may have its own value, but it will not inspire as much confidence among Members of Parliament as a Committee constituted from within Parliament. Finally, we may expect that a well-informed Parliament will interfere less in the working of State Corporations because many damaging questions spring from ignorance and hearsay.

The American economist (now Ambassador to India), Professor Galbraith, who submitted a comprehensive paper to the Krishna Menon Committee, feels that Parliamentarians must be clear in their minds that when they question individual decisions of Companies they force Ministers to protect themselves by asking for advance information and approval of all decisions; this destroys the autonomy and hence the effectiveness of public enterprise. Our analysis, however, is just the other way. Since Ministers withhold important information and do not take Parliament into confidence, Members of Parliament are forced to seek information by pressing questions about individual decisions of Companies. But for Parliamentary questioning, the entire LIC-Mundhra Deal would have remained undiscovered. Professor Galbraith seems to have ignored the manner in which State Corporations in India, often managed by Departmental Secretaries, are very much under the thumb of Ministers.

Mr Paul H. Appleby, the American expert on public administration, had taken up an attitude almost similar to that adopted by Professor Galbraith. Mr Appleby's plea for good budgeting is commendable.[16] That is, pre-auditing can be much more effective than a post-mortem examination. However, the Comptroller and Auditor-General is not such a useless functionary as Mr Appleby would make us believe. His attack on the rôle of Parliament (second and sixth criticisms)[17] is based on an inadequate understanding of the

[16] The Public Accounts Committee of Parliament, after examining the civil accounts for 1953-54 and 1954-55, came to the conclusion that the 'estimates of the Union Government are just "guesstimates"'. (*Lok Sabha*, May 5, 1958.) The Comptroller and Auditor-General in an appendix to the Audit Report (Civil), 1955, mentioned political considerations and considerations of administrative prestige (superficial efficiency and energy) among the reasons for Government calling upon Parliament to vote funds which they cannot spend.

[17] The salient points stressed by Mr Appleby are as follows: (i) Parliament should give more attention to good budgeting, and should *not* exaggerate the importance of the Comptroller and Auditor-General because audit reports focus attention on little things which demean Parliament; (ii) there is

199

problems of underdeveloped countries. If the Estimates Committee point out that the nation has lost Rs 5 crores because of wrong judgment on the part of executive officials in locating the site of a particular State enterprise, we do not see how the Committee can be condemned for indulging in trivialities. Waste of national funds to the tune of Rs 5 crores (roughly $10 million) in a single enterprise would create a flutter even in Mr Appleby's country where the annual budget of the nation can cover seven 'Second Five-Year Plans' of India. In a poor and underdeveloped country like India, where onerous taxation causes heavy sacrifice, the proper utilization of public moneys is of cardinal importance. It has often been argued that the level of taxation in India is still low, and that there is considerable scope for raising public revenues for investment in various State enterprises, *provided the people are prepared to tighten their belts*. But it is conveniently forgotten that the prime requisite for the tightening of belts is a confidence regarding adequate control on waste and misapplication of funds. The higher the degree of confidence, the greater would be the willingness to tighten the belts.

Mr Appleby's efforts to build up a paradise for civil servants,[18] independent of the Comptroller and Auditor-General, independent of the scrutiny of Parliamentary Committees, immune from Parliamentary discussion and immune from all public criticism, would create a most dangerous situation for this country. At any rate, dictatorship by a group of civil servants would not be acceptable to the Indian people who have been imbibed with democratic fervour by national leaders. Mr Appleby has been wrongly advised that the stock of the civil service in India 'stands high with the public, but Parliament tends to be carping, unappreciative and miserly'. In fact, civil servants have yet to win the sympathy of the common man in India. In this regard, few persons can speak with greater authority

among Members of Parliament too much general and vague fear that its responsibilities are not being preserved; (iii) some of the worst failures in Government have been business and industrial leaders and, therefore, people from the private sector should be put in third levels of corporate hierarchies; (iv) Parliament yields too easily to the self-interest demands of small but influential business interests; (v) by endorsing the 'small and narrow' approach of the Public Service Commission, Parliament undermines its own responsibility; (vi) Parliament is a chief citadel of opposition to delegation of powers, its rôle being a negative one.

[18] There is substance in Mr Appleby's fourth criticism. But that does not necessarily establish his third point. His fifth criticism is totally misplaced. On the one hand he criticizes Parliament for encouraging the narrow approach of the Public Service Commission. On the other hand he says that Government have disrespected the Commission's recommendations in certain cases. Hence it is the Government which is at fault and not Parliament. The latter has only vindicated the prestige of the Commission. Mr Appleby has been shy of criticizing the Government and the party in power and has thrust all blame on Parliament.

than a seasoned civil servant like Mr A. D. Gorwala. He says that there is no more important weapon in the hands of opponents of democracy than the ability to show that under the democratic system power passes into the hands of the corrupt and the self-seeker. Mr Gorwala is most realistic in his approach when he suggests that it is not enough to act with integrity; moral standards must be so observed as to eliminate the possibility of suspicion and to secure the general recognition of the observers.[19]

(2) PRESIDENTIAL AND MINISTERIAL CONTROL

The following devices have been employed for ensuring Governmental control over the working of State Corporations:

(i) Maximum limits for incurring capital expenditure (beyond these limits, Presidential or Ministerial approval being required);

(ii) Maximum limits on borrowing powers (including limits on the rate of interest, maturity, etc.);

(iii) Governmental approval for the issue and increase of capital and the declaration of dividends.

(iv) Governmental approval for the appointment of high salaried staff;

(v) Governmental approval for the changes in prices or rates;

(vi) Prior approval of operating budgets and the submission of annual reports;

(vii) Power of the Government, the President or the Minister, to dictate policy matters *either* by issuing directives 'in the national interest', *or* requiring the Board of Directors to leave such matters for Governmental decision;

(viii) Power of Government (President or Minister) to appoint and recall or dismiss members of the Governing Boards (and certain other officers);

(ix) Power of the Government to revoke the charter and to take over the undertaking; and

(x) Informal contacts between the Minister and the Board, and wire-pullings through Departmental Secretaries and Government Commissioners.

As regards most of the above matters, Governmental power is infinitely greater in case of the Government Companies. Article 141 of the Articles of Association of the Eastern Shipping Corporation is illustrative of the wide range of such power. The Chairman of the Board of Directors of the Company may, and when required by the Special Director (Central Government's special nominee) shall, reserve for the consideration of the Central Government the following matters relating to the working of the Company:

[19] Government of India, Planning Commission, *Report on Public Administration*, by A. D. Gorwala, First Reprint, December 1953, pp. 12-13.

(a) Calling up the unpaid capital or increasing the authorized capital of the Company or issuing of any unissued shares.

(b) (i) Any proposal to borrow at a time exceeding Rs 15 lakhs.

(ii) Any proposal to borrow which will increase the aggregate of such individual borrowings to an amount in excess of 25 per cent of the then paid-up capital of the Company, or Rs 1 crore, whichever is less.

(iii) Any proposal to borrow at a rate of interest exceeding the Reserve Bank rate by more than 1 per cent per annum, if the Special Director considers that such a rate of interest is unduly high.

(iv) Any proposal for action relating to the reduction of capital.

(v) Any proposal for investment in a particular type of security or shares, if such investment exceeds Rs 10 lakhs.

(c) Issue of Debentures.

(d) Acquisition, construction or sale of vessels involving an amount exceeding Rs 10 lakhs.[20]

(e) Any other single item of expenditure exceeding Rs 10 lakhs.

(f) Winding up of the Company.

(g) Any important matter relating to the Company's establishment.

(h) Any other matter which in his opinion involves an important issue of general policy.

In the case of National Industrial Development Corporation, under Article 86, the main restriction is on 'granting by the company of a loan or the giving of a guarantee or any other financial assistance to any one particular concern of an amount exceeding Rs 1 crore'. There is no reference to borrowing powers and capital expenditure in this Article. Further, under Article 39, 'The Directors may from time to time at their discretion raise or borrow or secure the payment of any sum or sums of money for the purposes of the Company.' Article 86 of the National Small Industries Corporation is drafted on the same lines as Article 86 of NIDC, the only difference being that Presidential approval is required for loans exceeding Rs 2.5 lakhs. Thus both the Development Corporations have a common pattern of control, the difference in the amount signifying the difference between big and small industries.

Although Public Corporations often escape petty restrictions, they are, nevertheless, subjected to a good deal of financial control. Thus the DVC can borrow money in the open market or otherwise 'with the approval of the Central Government'. The Corporation is required

[20] The limit regarding capital expenditure was fixed at Rs 50,000 in the case of Nahan Foundry (a small organization), Rs 5 lakhs in the case of Hindustan Insecticides, Rs 10 lakhs in the case of Hindustan Antibiotics, Rs 20 lakhs in the case of Hindustan Shipyard and Rs 40 lakhs in the case of Hindustan Steel.

to prepare, in consultation with the financial adviser and in the prescribed form, a budget in October each year for the next financial year. Printed copies of the budget shall be made available to each of the three participating Governments by November 15 and the budget shall be laid before the Central and Provincial legislatures after that date. Further, under Section 45, the Corporation shall prepare in the prescribed form (with particular reference to eleven items—irrigation, water supply, electrical energy, flood control, navigation, afforestation, soil erosion, use of lands, resettlement of displaced population, sanitation and public health measures, and economic and social welfare of people) an annual report within six months after the end of each financial year giving a 'true and faithful account' of its activities. Printed copies of the annual report shall be made available to each of the three participating Governments by October 15. The annual report shall be laid before the Central and Provincial Legislatures as soon as may be after it is prepared.[21] The Corporation shall also prepare such other annual financial statements, in such form and by such dates as may be prescribed.

The Air Corporations in India are required to submit to the Central Government, not less than three months before the commencement of each financial year, a statement showing the programme of operation and development of air transport services during the forthcoming financial year and its other activities as well as financial estimates in respect thereof, including any proposed investment of capital and increase in the strength of its total staff. Mid-year alterations would necessitate a supplementary programme, though the Corporation may undertake any additional service or ancillary activity to meet unexpected traffic demands and subsequently submit a report to the Central Government. Further, the Air Corporations cannot, without the previous approval of the Central Government:

(a) undertake any capital expenditure for the purchase or acquisition of any immovable property or aircraft or any other thing at a cost exceeding Rs 15 lakhs;

(b) enter into a lease of any immovable property for a period exceeding five years; or

[21] All the State Corporations in India are required to submit annual reports. While the DVC Reports are sufficiently informative, they are issued very late (the statutory time limit is violated). Apart from delay, which is quite a common feature, there is no consistency in the presentation of various items of information from year to year. There is no 'follow-up' in many of the cases. This may be because of certain weak points which are desired to be concealed. Some of the Reports (e.g. Sindri's Report for 1958-59) are much too inadequate, feeling satisfied with a few pictures meant for the layman.

(c) in any manner dispose of any property, right or privilege having an original or book value exceeding Rs 10 lakhs.

In the case of Tennessee Valley Authority an elaborate financial discipline was imposed. With the approval of the Secretary of the Treasury, the Corporation was allowed to issue bonds not exceeding $61,500,000 for the purchase of electric utility properties. Further, the Corporation could issue bonds not exceeding $50 million, having a maturity not more than fifty years and bearing interest not exceeding 3½ per cent, for the construction of future dams, steam plants or other facilities. The amounts and prices were to be approved by the Secretary of the Treasury. A further sum of $50 million could be obtained through the sale of bonds for extending credit to municipalities, etc., for the development of power. Under Section 9(a) of the TVA Act, the Board shall file with the President and with the Congress, in December each year, a complete report as to the business of the Corporation covering the preceding Governmental fiscal year. The report shall include an itemized statement of the cost of power at each power station, the total number of employees and the names, salaries and duties of those receiving compensation at the rate of more than $1,500 a year.[22] Along with each annual report, the Board shall file a statement of the total cost of all power generated by it at all power stations during each year, the average cost of such power per kilowatt hour, the rates at which sold, and to whom sold, and copies of all contracts for the sale of power. In order to make power projects self-supporting and self-liquidating, the surplus power shall be sold at rates which, in the opinion of the Board, when applied to the normal capacity of the Authority's power facilities, will produce gross revenues in excess of the cost of production. Finally, all purchases and contracts for supplies or services (except for personal services) made by the Corporation shall be made after advertising 'to be adequate to insure notice and opportunity for competition'. Advertisements will not be required when (a) an emergency requires immediate delivery; (b) repair parts and accessories are required for supplies or services previously furnished, or (c) the aggregate amount involved does not exceed $500. In comparing bids, the Board may consider relative quality and adaptability of supplies or services, the bidder's financial responsibility, skill, experience, record of integrity in dealing, ability to furnish repairs and maintenance services and the time of delivery or performance offered.

---

[22] This is a rather low limit (about Rs 600 per month). In India, Presidential approval is required for making any appointment the maximum pay of which is Rs 2,000 or more per mensem in case of Hindustan Antibiotics, Rs 1,000 in case of Hindustan Insecticides and Rs 500 in case of Nahan Foundry and Employees' State Insurance Corporation (Central Government's approval).

In case of Government Companies in India, 'The President may from time to time issue such directives as he may consider necessary in regard to the conduct of the business of the Company or Directors thereof, and in like manner may vary and annul any such directive. The Directors shall give immediate effect to directives so issued.'[23] Another common provision entitles the President of India to remove any Director (including the Chairman and Managing Director) from office at any time *in his absolute discretion*. Ashoka Hotels Ltd is an important exception.

In case of Public Corporations, the power of the Government to issue policy directives is fairly universal. Some verbal differences, no doubt, are to be found in the various legislations. Thus the DVC Act provided that (1) in discharge of its functions the Corporation shall be guided by such instructions on question of policy as may be given to it by the Central Government; and (2) if any dispute arises between the Central Government and the Corporation as to whether a question is or is not a question of policy, the decision of the Central Government shall be final. The LIC Act added the words 'involving public interest' after 'matters of policy'. The State Bank of India Act had used wordings similar to the LIC Act, but the directions shall be given 'in consultation with the Governor of the Reserve Bank and the Chairman of the State Bank' and 'through the Reserve Bank'. The Air Corporations Act used strong language for this purpose: 'The Central Government may give to either of the Corporations directions as to the exercise and performance by the Corporation of its functions, and the Corporation shall be bound to give effect to any such directions.'

The Reserve Bank of India Act authorizes the Central Government to 'declare the Central Board superseded' if in the Government's opinion the Bank had failed to carry out any of the obligations imposed on it by the Act. In case of the Employees' State Insurance Corporation, the Government enjoy similar power of supersession, but the same can be exercised only after giving an opportunity to the Corporation (or the Standing Committee as the case may be) to explain its position.

The British Broadcasting Corporation, under the Licence and Agreement dated June 12, 1952, 'shall comply with all reasonable directions which shall be given to the Corporation by the Postmaster-General'. The word 'reasonable' signifies that the 'Postmaster shall give consideration to any objections raised by the Corporation'. But if the Postmaster-General still maintains such directions, rules or regulations, his decision shall be final. Further, if the Corporation

[23] This provision is contained in the Articles of Hindustan Insecticides Ltd, but (with minor changes) is to be found in the Articles of most of the Government Companies.

fails to give effect to or comply with the requirements within a specified time, the Postmaster-General may certify the same under his
hand to the Crown; and upon such Certificate it shall be lawful for
the Crown 'absolutely to revoke and make void this Our Charter'.
However, the usual framework of Government directives in the
United Kingdom is typified by Section 3 of the Coal Industry
Nationalization Act: 'The Minister may, after consultation with the
Board, give to the Board directions of a general character as to the
exercise and performance by the Board of their functions in relation
to matters appearing to the Minister to affect the national interest
and the Board shall give effect to any such directions.' In this language three things are noteworthy: first, the directions are to be of a
general character (i.e. the NCB cannot be asked to work or give up a
particular colliery); secondly, directions are to be given after consulting the Board; and thirdly, the status of the Minister has been
given statutory recognition. In India, the directing authority is invariably the Central Government and not the Minister as such.

Under the TVA Act, the Government of the United States have the
right, in case of war or national emergency declared by Congress,
to take possession of all or any of the property. But if this right is
exercised by the Government, it shall pay reasonable and fair
damages. Further, under Section 4, any member of the TVA Board
(obviously, without assigning any reason) may be removed from
office at any time by a concurrent resolution of the Senate and the
House of Representatives. Section 6 lays down that any member of
the TVA Board who is found by the President of the United States to
be guilty of a violation of this section (which requires all appointments and promotions to be made on the basis of merit and efficiency, no political test or qualification being permitted or given
consideration to) shall be removed from office by the President of
the United States. When the first Chairman of the TVA was removed
by the President on March 23, 1938, the question was whether the
President had such an authority (except when Section 6 was
violated).

It may be mentioned that there are only rare occasions when a
member may have to be removed. At any rate, the problem in India
is not of removing the Board members before the expiry of their
term, but of retaining members sufficiently long so that they can be
properly held accountable for their performance. Government never
find any difficulty in transferring unwanted members to other
Departments and even promoting them if necessary. At least this is
one virtue in having Departmental Secretaries on the Boards of
Government Companies. However, the influence of these Secretaries
has greatly complicated the problem of public accountability. The
LIC-Mundhra Deal of 1957 is an evidence of the existing confusion

and the absence of any clear demarcation of responsibility. There was a four-cornered tussle between the Minister, the Principal Finance Secretary, the Chairman and the Managing Director. For several months, the second and the third offices were held by one person. When he made trunk calls from New Delhi to Bombay, his subordinates found difficulty in finding out whether the voice on the telephone was that of the Departmental Secretary (representing the Minister and the Government) or that of the Chairman (whose proper place was in Bombay and not in New Delhi)! The Mundhra Deal revealed certain other interesting points. If the Finance Minister tells the Departmental Secretary that 'You may look into them', does it amount to a directive? The Departmental Secretary may treat it as an order (if he is in the habit of receiving orders that way), but for a Public Corporation it does *not* amount to a directive. The Chairman and the Managing Director were actually overawed by the personality of the Departmental Secretary when they saw, in the latter's conversation, mandatory directives. Section 21 of the LIC Act clearly states that the directives of the Central Government shall be on 'matters of policy involving public interest' and shall be given 'in writing' so that responsibility for particular decisions can be properly allocated.[24]

(3) *Comptroller and Auditor-General's Control*

Provisions governing the audit of Government Companies in India have already been outlined in Chapter IV.[25] In addition to the usual audit under the Companies Act,[26] through one or more auditors qualified to act as such, the Comptroller and Auditor-General (or any authority and members of the staff deputed by him) may conduct a second audit. Usually, the audited accounts are forwarded to the Director of Commercial Audit who, on behalf of the Comptroller and Auditor-General, may make such comments thereon as he likes.

---

[24] The Chagla Commission, who reported in February 1958 on LIC Investments in Mundhra concerns, formulated seven sterling rules for the working of State Corporations in India: (1) Government directives should be in writing; (2) Chairmen should have business and financial experience; (3) civil servants should be loyal to the Corporation; (4) investment funds should not be used for extraneous purposes; (5) Parliament must be taken into confidence at the earliest stage; (6) Minister must take responsibility for the acts of his subordinates; and (7) Section 27-A of the Life Insurance Act of 1938 should be immediately applied.

[25] See also 'Commercial Audit' in Chapter I.

[26] Although the Articles of Association of many Government Companies provide for the appointment of such auditor(s) by the Company in General Meeting, the Companies Act, 1956, lays down that such auditor(s) would be appointed by the Government on the advice of the Comptroller and Auditor-General. The auditors, so appointed, are to work under his general direction and in accordance with any instructions he might choose to issue.

Very often he does not make any comments. Mr Asoka Chanda, India's Comptroller and Auditor-General, has suggested: 'The provision for an independent audit by the Comptroller and Auditor-General would, obviously, be invoked only where the normal audit reveals gross mismanagement.'[27] However, Mr Chanda has supported the provisions of the Companies Act, 1956, on the following grounds:

An audit conducted merely for the certification of the balance sheets and profit and loss accounts might not, in these circumstances, safeguard the interests of the tax-payers. It would only afford a permanent measure of immunity to officials for mismanagement and inefficiency. Further, when such units are operated side by side with private units within an industry an assessment of comparative efficiency is of the utmost importance. The determination of the unit-cost of production for this purpose therefore becomes necessary. In the case of monopolistic state concerns, it is equally necessary to find and apply a suitable yardstick to assess the degree of efficiency and economy with which these are being operated. An examination of these and other important aspects of management, where necessary, can be covered by the issue of directives. An extension of the scope of audit is also necessary to make the reports more informative to meet the requirements of public accountability.[28]

However, the type of efficiency audit which Mr Chanda has in mind has not developed so far and is not likely to develop unless the mental attitude of auditing staff is revolutionized. Auditors are often concerned more with the observance of formalities than with rationality and economy in the incurring of expenditure. For example, if tenders or quotations are not invited for a particular job it would at once create an audit objection even though, in many cases, the amount involved may be petty and the job may have been executed most economically. On the other hand, a contract might have been awarded at an excessive rate, but the fact may remain unnoticed because it might have been the lowest tender. Under these circumstances, the perpetration of frauds only requires elaboration in paper work. So to say, many auditors follow a 'penny wise, pound foolish' policy. Moreover, many auditors forget the celebrated motto pronounced in the Kingston Cotton Mill case that 'an auditor is a watch-dog, not a blood-hound'. Some auditors start their work with a suspicious mind and would make the working of a commercial enterprise impossible.

[27] Asoka Chanda, *Indian Administration*, George Allen & Unwin, London, 1958, p. 202.
[28] *Ibid.*, pp. 201-2. By the terms public and private companies, Mr Chanda means public and private enterprise. In terms of the Companies Act, he has used misleading terminology.

Mr Paul H. Appleby points out in his 1956 Report: '. . . one of the embezzlements now reported had been conducted over a nine-year span, in spite of auditing. The particular case, interestingly enough, occurred in the Audit Department itself. It makes one ask, "Who audits Audit?" More importantly, who examines the Audit Department with a scrutiny more significant than mere auditing?'[29] This is, however, not quite relevant to the issue. Mr Appleby's analysis is correct that the increased importance attached to the Comptroller and Auditor-General is because of the numerous financial abuses and waste of funds which occurred in the 'first flush of independence'. But Mr Appleby is misinformed when he says that 'This situation has been fully corrected.' However, he has launched scathing criticism against the existing pattern of financial control. He says: 'Auditors don't know and cannot be expected to know very much about good administration. Auditing is *a necessary but highly pedestrian function with a narrow perspective and very limited usefulness*. Any deputy secretary knows vastly more about significant problems in his ministry than the entire staff of the Comptroller and Auditor-General can discover by auditing. The function of auditing is a strictly negative one.' However, even this negative function is of considerable importance, specially in underdeveloped countries, where public officials have not only to act honestly, but they have to demonstrate openly that they have so acted.

(4) *Expert Reviews*

Although auditing itself can be considered as a variety of expert reviews by financial wizards it is, as Mr Appleby suggests, a 'function with a narrow perspective'. Moreover, since it is carried on every year it tends to become mechanical and something of a routine. It may be all right for ordinary Departments of the Government where commercial considerations are less important. But the State Corporations may have much to gain from expert investigations conducted once in several years by highly experienced accountants, engineers and administrators. A special Board of such competent persons may be formed on an all-India basis. If this Board can review the activities of some fifteen to twenty Corporations in a year, it will be possible to have one such expert review in three or four years. Even if it is possible to have a quinquennial review, it will not be bad.

Some difference of opinion may arise with regard to the composition of such a Board. There are many who would advocate a representative Board consisting of Members of Parliament, trade union

---

[29] *Re-examination of India's Administrative System with special reference to Administration of Government's Industrial and Commercial Enterprises*, by Paul H. Appleby, 1956, p. 27.

leaders and other spokesmen of public opinion. Although such a Board may have a wide appeal, there is a danger that it may become more of a political organization and less of an expert body. Another alternative may be to have a Board exclusively consisting of the managers of nationalized industry. Such a Board may be in the nature of a Super-Corporation. No doubt, it will serve a double purpose. On the one hand it will provide for expert reviews by people who have a vast store of practical experience in that very line. On the other hand, it will give an opportunity to the Directors of various Corporations to exchange notes. That is, the investigations will be conducted in an atmosphere of friendly assistance, rather than with any idea of bossing over or blackmailing certain people. The benefits will be mutual. In other words, those who come as investigators will also take back some good ideas to their enterprises. However, there is one danger to be guarded against in such a composition of the Board of investigation. It is possible that fraternal relationship may compel X to speak in favour of Y and Y for X (though such a coincidence may be rare). To overcome this possibility of give and take, the Board may be constituted of ex-managers of State Corporations. However, such a Board could be criticized on the ground that retired persons can always condemn the present incumbents merely to magnify their own level of efficiency. On balance, we would stick to our original suggestion that the Board should consist of highly experienced accountants, engineers and administrators (who may be Directors or ex-Directors of State Corporations).

The nature of investigations which such a Board may be expected to conduct would be based on common sense rather than on procedural details. The task of the Board would be to find out whether the overall performance has been satisfactory, i.e. whether the enterprise is in a sound state of health. It would also draw attention to the directions in which there is greatest scope for improvement. The Board may examine the trends in the various items of cost and revenues. It may analyse the effects of particular price and output policies, incentive bonus schemes, personnel practices and the like. Since public organizations may easily fall a prey to a top-heavy administrative structure, the Board will have to pay special attention to that problem. Finally, the engineers and technical experts on the Board will ensure that an effective machinery of quality control is in operation and that the most economical appliances, considering the size and nature of activity, are being employed.

(5) Users' Committees and Other Advisory Organizations

Consumers' representatives have been appointed to the Governing Boards of State Corporations in France under the tripartite composition. However, this direct participation in management does not eliminate the need for special arrangements to be made within the organization to secure the co-operation of the public in day-to-day business.[30] This co-operation assumes special importance in case of those Corporations which have been granted monopoly status.

The only major experiment in establishing Consumers' Councils in India has been that of the Railways. With a view to establishing contact between the Railway Board and the public, securing broader representation and affording closer contact with railway users, Consultative Committees have been set up in three layers as under:

(a) National Railway Users' Consultative Council at the Centre;

(b) Zonal Railway Users' Consultative Committees at Headquarters level; and

(c) Divisional Railway Users' Consultative Committees at Divisional level.

The Chairman of the National Railway Users' Consultative Council is the Minister for Railways, and the Deputy Minister for Railways is an *ex-officio* member. Besides these two, there were fifty-four members on April 1, 1960, as follows:

(a) Departmental Secretaries (Food and Agriculture, Commerce and Industry, Department of Transport, and Ministry of Steel, Mines and Fuel)	4
(b) Railway Board (all the members)	5
(c) Parliament of India	21
(d) Special Interests (Advocate, Chemist, Labour Leader, Educationist and Industrialist)	5
(e) Agricultural Interests	1
(f) Associated Chambers	1
(g) Federated Chambers	1
(h) All-India Manufacturers' Organization	1
(i) Industries (Coal, Jute, Iron and Steel, Cotton, Cement and Sugar)	6
(j) Different Railways (Central, Eastern, Northern, North-eastern, Southern, Western, N.F., and South-eastern) ...	8
(k) Secretary—Joint Director, Traffic (General) Railway Board	1
	54

Thus one-third strength consisted of official members. Adding the two Ministers, there were 20 spokesmen of the Government. Besides 21 Members of Parliament, there were only 15 representatives of users as such. Further, out of 15, as many as 9 were representatives of big industry. Thus hardly 6 persons were left to speak for the common consumer (in effect only two—the Advocate and the Educationist). Thus even the Users' Committees do not provide enough scope for the free ventilation of the grievances of ordinary

[30] *Some Problems in the Organization and Administration of Public Enterprises in the Industrial Field*, United Nations, 1954, p. 59.

users.[31] Initially, such Committees created some popular enthusiasm. But in course of time they fell into the bureaucratic rut. The layman is not aware of such Committees; and, even if he comes to know of their existence, he tends to look upon them with indifference. The channels of communication are not as smooth, speedy and popular as they should be.

The Articles of Association of Government Companies in India impose no obligations regarding the constitution of Users' Committees. Not many of these Companies are catering to the requirements of the people in general. Most of them are working in particular areas and depending on an assured market to a considerable extent.

In case of some of the Public Corporations, however, there is statutory provision for the appointment of Advisory Committees. Thus the DVC Act authorized the appointment of one or more Advisory Committees for the purpose of securing the efficient discharge of the functions of the Corporation, and in particular for the purpose of securing that those functions are exercised with due regard to the circumstances and requirements of particular local areas. The Air Corporations Act required the constitution of an Air Transport Council consisting of a Chairman and not exceeding eleven members appointed by the Central Government. The Council is competent to investigate any matter relating to the fares, freight rates or other charges in respect of any service or facility provided by either of the Corporations and of the adequacy or efficiency of such service. But investigation is to be made only at the request of the Government. Thus, consumers as such have no say in the matter (although the Government may issue directives on the basis of the recommendations of the Air Transport Council). Further, the Central Government, in consultation with the Corporation concerned, may appoint an Advisory Committee for advising the Corporation in respect of such matters as may be referred to it by the Corporation or as may be prescribed.[32] Again, the consumers have no say with regard to this Committee. The IFC Act provides for the constitution of Advisory Committees on the lines of the DVC Act. The Industrial Finance Corporation of India had five Advisory Committees on June 30, 1958—one each for the Textile, Sugar, Engineering, Chemical and Miscellaneous Industries. These Committees held ten meetings in all during 1957-58 in Delhi and Bombay.

[31] It has been claimed that the Council is 'very broadly and scientifically constituted'—see M. C. Khullar, 'Rôle of Advisory Bodies in Government', *Northern Railway Magazine*, September 1959, p. 36.

[32] A third Committee, whose constitution was mandatory under the Air Corporations Act, is the Labour Relations Committee which advises the Corporation on matters which relate to the welfare of the employees or which are likely to promote and secure amity and good relations between the two.

(6) *Inter-relations of Public Undertakings*

The problem of public accountability may get considerably complicated because of the peculiar inter-undertaking relationships. Thus,
in the case of subsidiary corporations (like the State Bank of India)
and daughter companies (like those sponsored by the Pakistan
Industrial Development Corporation) the formal 'strings' could be
pulled only through the holding (guardian or parent) corporation.
Therefore, the nation's rôle as equity shareholder may be com-
promised to a certain extent. Further, where a corporation is controlled by a number of other corporations (or diverse interests, as in
the case of mixed corporations) public accountability may present
quite a confused picture. In such situations the direct nominees of the
Government would have to shoulder a specially heavy responsibility,
though it is not unlikely that they may follow the line of least resist-
ance and take up an attitude of indifference. While examining the
price policy of public enterprises, we have already made a pointed
reference to the Tata Engineering and Locomotive Co Ltd where
the State had agreed to be a minority shareholder (28 per cent).

Where a number of corporations are working in the same industry
(e.g. the Air Corporations in India) there may be considerable scope
for mutual consultation, joint programmes of development and welfare, etc. Certain common services can be established even by those
corporations which are not in the same industry. In such cases, there
would arise the problem of accurate costing and allocation of expenditure (and benefits). Further, to the extent that competition still
exists between the several corporations within the same industry, or
between the various industries, the pattern of public accountability
would deviate from the conventional requirements prescribed for
public monopolies.[33]

The seller/buyer relationship between several State Corporations
would have its own impact on the question of public accountability.
We have seen that the Hindustan Aircraft Ltd has been subjected
to four different kinds of audit because the Ministry of Defence and
the Railways (as also Road Transport Corporations) have been the
principal customers. As such, a number of public undertakings (like
the Hindustan Insecticides) have got an assured market within the
public sector. In such cases, consumers' organizations have little
importance.[34]

[33] The recent amalgamation of the publicly-owned fertilizer units in India
(through the creation of the Fertilizer Corporation of India) indicates the
advantages of placing consolidated responsibility in the hands of a single
organization.

[34] However, two State Corporations may have grievances against each other.
See the interesting comment made by the Chairman of the Eastern Shipping
Corporation (a Government Company) on the working of the Hindustan
Shipyard (another Government Company).

CHAPTER X

CONCLUSIONS

There has been much talk about socialism on party platforms in India since 1947. But the number of persons employed in the public sector at the end of March 1959 was about 64 lakhs, which works out to only 4 per cent of the total working population in India. The corresponding figure was 24.3 per cent in Great Britain and 12 per cent in the USA in 1950. As of October 1959, public enterprises in the Republic of Korea (in seven selected industries) provided 78 per cent of the employment. The public sector has presented a paradox in India. On the one hand, she is living in an economic framework which is essentially capitalistic. Many of the basic industries like coal mining, electricity supply, petroleum refining, commercial banking, and even iron and steel (until the State-owned steel plants are in full production) are largely in the hands of private enterprise. On the other hand, it is interesting to observe that public enterprise has entered certain consumer goods industries like sugar and paper and has also diverted its energies and resources to undertakings like the Ashoka Hotel.

Marketing Boards have been established even in those countries (like the USA) where public enterprise and socialism are very much at a discount. India is perhaps the only major agricultural country which has failed in this direction. The stabilization of agricultural prices is very necessary because they have been found to be much more sensitive than industrial prices. Moreover, defective marketing adversely affects the pattern of income distribution. State Trading Corporations are functional cousins of the Marketing Boards, and are helpful in negotiating barter agreements and other package deals with socialist countries or even with capitalist countries where there are foreign exchange difficulties. Further, the rôle of State Trading Corporations in promoting standardization and quality control cannot be over-emphasized.

Development Corporations can be helpful not only in filling the gaps in respect of capital, technical guidance and entrepreneurial ability in underdeveloped countries, but as well in giving practical shape to the priorities laid down by the Planning Commission. Development Corporations also perform the finance function although there are a large number of Finance Corporations in India. The financial group of Corporations includes important institutions like the Reserve Bank of India, the State Bank of India, the Life Insurance Corporation of India, the Industrial Finance Corporation of India, and the Central Warehousing Corporation.

River Valley Authorities like the TVA and the DVC cater to the problem of regional development specially in those countries which are rich in water resources. They combine non-commercial functions like flood control and health measures with commercial activities like power supply and irrigation. Multi-purpose projects are best entrusted to Statutory Corporations possessing substantial powers and a high degree of autonomy. However, the Damodar Valley Corporation is the solitary example of a Statutory Corporation managing river valley projects in India. Because of some initial misconceptions about the notion of autonomy experienced in the case of DVC, the other projects managed by Control Boards (Embryonic Corporations) were never entrusted to Public Corporations.

In the field of transport and communications we have Public Corporations like the Indian Airlines Corporation and the Air India International, Government Companies like the Eastern Shipping Corporation and the Western Shipping Corporation, Quasi-Corporations like the Railway Board (and the Posts and Telegraphs Board), and departmental organizations in the matter of road transport. Road Transport Corporations (like the Delhi Road Transport Authority and the Bombay Road Transport Corporation) exist in certain States, but there is scope for many more Corporations, especially in the development of transport facilities in rural areas.

Broadcasting has been entrusted to Public Corporations in a number of countries. Thus we have the British Broadcasting Corporation (and the Independent Television Authority), the Canadian Broadcasting Commission and the Australian Broadcasting Commission. Now that television has been introduced in India, it is opportune that a Radio and Television Corporation be established with a high degree of autonomy. Broadcasting is such a powerful device of propaganda that any misuse of the same by the party in power (and any denial of its use to opposition parties) may cause incalculable harm to the country. Further, it has been experienced that programmes of a high standard may not be originated adequately under departmental organization.

In India, while five Public Corporations were established in 1948, their progress thereafter was very slow. Compelling factors toward the adoption of this form of organization in the case of DVC may be analysed as follows:

(1) The TVA experiment attracted world-wide attention only after 1943 when it had completed the first decade of its working.

(2) A good deal of enthusiasm had been created by the post-1945 nationalization measures, specially those introduced by the British

215

Labour Party.

(3) Because three Governments were involved (Central, Bihar and Bengal) it appeared necessary to establish a Statutory Corporation with adequate powers.

(4) In view of the havoc caused by the flood and famine of 1943 in Bengal, it was desired to plan and execute work with such a speed that another catastrophe might be avoided.

While the DVC has succeeded in controlling floods and supplying sufficiently cheap power, there were inordinate delays in the execution of its projects. There was vacillation and indecision in appointing the Chief Engineer. When a highly qualified American engineer was prepared to come on a certain salary, he was not taken in. Later, the Chairman himself went to the USA and was prepared to offer the desired salary but no suitable person was available. Thus for the first two and a half years the Corporation had no Chief Engineer resulting in inexpert advice, frequent changes in design, increase in costs, and waste of public funds. Although there were a number of highly paid officers, there was no cohesion and co-ordination between them. Many of these difficulties could have been minimized if the Government had not depended so much on civil service personnel.

Whereas in the nationalization of the Reserve Bank, the airlines and the Imperial Bank, Government had followed the policy of announcing their intention sufficiently in advance, shock technique was employed in the case of life insurance so that vested interests may be taken by surprise. In our opinion, the factors which hastened Government decision in the matter may be analysed as follows :

(1) The competitive reduction in the premium rates of life insurance companies gained momentum in 1955 following better mortality experience. It was good strategy on the part of the State to enter the field of insurance at such a juncture and to take credit for making insurance cheaper.

(2) There was an alleged misapplication of some Rs 2 crores in the case of Bharat Insurance Company. Further, twenty-five life insurance companies had gone into liquidation during the last decade and another twenty-five had to be transferred to other companies at a loss.

(3) There was high expense ratio in privately-managed companies because of vast duplication in agents and offices necessitated by competitive conditions.

(4) There was an alarming lapse ratio because of inter-company rivalries, competitive attractions and even statistical juggleries played upon innocent policyholders.

(5) The desire to widen and deepen the channels of public savings.

(6) The problem of answering 'What next?' after the nationaliza-

tion of the Imperial Bank, but before the General Election of 1957.

Out of these six considerations, the sixth one was obviously answered. The first one was initially achieved because LIC premiums were lower than those charged by the top companies. But, on the whole, the (with profit) policyholders have been losers because LIC bonus rates declared in 1959 were substantially lower than those paid by the top companies prior to nationalization. This position stood even when 95 per cent of the surplus is required to be allocated to policyholders. The second consideration, i.e. security for policyholders, has given much satisfaction to the erstwhile policyholders of unsound companies. The fourth consideration, too, has been achieved because the lapse ratio was less than 5 per cent in 1958 as against 35 per cent in 1953. However, there has been little success with regard to the third consideration. The expense ratio in 1958 was 29.2 per cent as against 27.3 per cent in 1953. Finally, much remains to be done for achieving the fifth consideration. Although the new business in 1959 exceeded the annual target under the LIC's Five-Year Plan (1959-63), the investment policy leaves much to be desired. An investment of Rs 10 lakhs per day can not only add substantially to the income potential, it can as well be used for controlling the privately-owned companies and for achieving the planned priorities in the matter of industrial development. However, the LIC has followed quite a negative policy of depending upon brokers' offers. It should have itself taken initiative in studying the Balance Sheets and other relevant data with regard to the various concerns where investments may be most fruitful. The newly-established Investment Research Section has a heavy responsibility in this regard. Further, since the LIC is a long-term investor, a fall in share values caused by Stock Exchange speculation is by no means a danger signal. This point was conveniently ignored by the official witnesses who tendered their evidence before the Chagla Commission. On the average, the performance of the LIC has been better than that of the various concerns prior to nationalization, but the record of top companies remains unbeaten.

Among the Public Corporations in India, the performance of the State Bank of India is perhaps the most creditable. It has completed the uphill task of establishing 400 new branches, mostly in rural and semi-urban areas, a month in advance of the schedule. It was not necessary at all to use the provision regarding extension of time. Further, the working of the State Bank of India had dispelled certain other fears as well. For example, the position of the State Bank as the leading commercial bank of the country has not been affected by recent changes. It has punctiliously observed the code of ethics based on commercial conventions (e.g. secrecy about the financial position of its constituents). The Reserve Bank of India, too, has done well.

But its control over indigenous banking and its contribution to the development of rural credit need further strengthening.

The performance of the Air Corporations can be considered satisfactory, though the nation can legitimately expect something better. Before nationalization, the combined losses of the eight concerns inherited by the Indian Airlines Corporation stood at Rs 110 lakhs in 1949 and at Rs 75 lakhs in 1952. The Corporation had to meet a loss of Rs 84 lakhs in the wage bill and a higher provision of Rs 27 lakhs for depreciation on account of the introduction of costlier aircraft. With a loss of Rs 79 lakhs in 1953-54, the Corporation had thus brought about some improvement. The losses continued to rise until 1956. Thereafter they continued to fall up to 1959. The average annual loss of Indian Airlines during the first six years was about a crore of rupees as against the average annual profit of Rs 25 lakhs in case of Air India International.

The Rehabilitation Finance Administration, the Employees' State Insurance Corporation and the Central Warehousing Corporation have not acquitted themselves sufficiently well. The first has suffered from a top-heavy organization, always suffering losses during the first ten years of its existence. The last two have been rather slow in implementing their schemes. The Industrial Finance Corporation of India, too, did not do well up to 1952. Thereafter, there was a considerable improvement in its working.

In India and certain other countries like France, Italy, Sweden, South Africa and Canada the joint stock company has come to be accepted as a vital instrumentality of the public sector. After the exit of the British Labour Party from office in 1951, the case for Public Corporations seems to have been considerably weakened. After their third successive defeat in October 1959, the prospect must be considered worse. Even before that election, the Labour Party were dissatisfied with the old (1945-51) technique of nationalization. They wanted to make experiments with mixed ownership through State shareholdings. In India there were only four Government Companies in 1949. They achieved great popularity after the registration of the Sindri Fertilizers and Chemicals Ltd on December 18, 1951. Out of forty-six Government Companies registered up to June 30, 1959, thirty-four are exclusively owned by the Central Government, four are joint enterprises of the Centre and the State Government concerned, five are joint ventures of the Central Government and private interests, and three are jointly owned by the Central Government, the State Government concerned and private interests. The total paid-up capital of Government Companies (including State Government Companies) rose from Rs 66 crores on March 31, 1956, to Rs 498 crores on March 31, 1961. The share of Government Companies in the paid-up capital of all Joint Stock

Companies rose from 6.4 per cent in 1956 to 28.9 per cent in 1961. The average paid-up capital for a Government Company rose from Rs 108 lakhs to Rs 363 lakhs, whereas the overall average was only Rs 7 lakhs on March 31, 1961. This means that Government Companies have a much bigger size than ordinary companies. It may, however, he noted that the Hindustan Steel Ltd alone accounted for a substantial part of the capital.

Most of the Government Companies have been registered as Private Companies (not to be confused with private enterprise) where only two signatures (as against seven in case of Public Companies) are required to be made on the Memorandum and Articles of Association. The usual methodology of promotion is that the President of India (through some Departmental Secretary) and the Secretary of the Department concerned become the first shareholders of the new enterprise. In fact, the same civil servant may put two signatures. In the beginning, this method was described as a fraud on the constitution. But in view of the famous decision in Salomon *versus* Salomon & Co (House of Lords, 1897), the legal position was perfectly sound. The Government Companies are now the dominant form of public enterprise in India. But we still think that Public Corporations are more competent for the job because they can be granted special powers by Parliament and their affairs are more open to public scrutiny. Thus, irregularities in the working of the DVC and the LIC attracted much greater attention than (the much greater) wastage of public funds in the case of Hindustan Steel. However, the formal distinction between Public Corporations and Government Companies has narrowed down in recent years.

Government Companies of an industrial character have often experienced difficulty in security foreign technical aid on satisfactory terms. The initial career of many such Companies was tarnished by the delays in the process of execution. In the case of Hindustan Shipyard there was a delay of twenty-nine months in the delivery of the first ship to the Eastern Shipping Corporation (also a Government Company). Another ship, MV *Andamans,* suffered from a deficiency in stability. Under the technical agreement with ACL of France large sums of money were paid by the Hindustan Shipyard, but the target of four ships in a year remained a 'theoretical one'. In July 1958 this agreement was terminated and another agreement was arrived at with LFW of West Germany. In the case of Hindustan Machine Tools, although the agreement with Messrs Oerlikon of Switzerland had been signed on March 28, 1949, the production of component parts was started as late as October 1954. Up to December 1955 only twelve lathes could be assembled. Twenty months had been spent in obtaining the approval of the Standing Finance Committee and another eight months in correspondence and visits. The technical experts took some ten months to arrive at a decision with regard to the design of lathe. Later, the design had to be altered because it was 'discovered' that the earlier design was not quite suitable. In the case of Hindustan Insecticides, while a good deal of assistance was provided by international organizations, much time was spent in negotiating an agreement with DCM Chemical Works (Delhi). The Joint Plan of Operations was drawn up on July 7, 1952, and the Ministry of Production had claimed that the factory would go into production by the end of 1953. This target was shifted to September 1954 and the factory actually commenced production on March 25, 1955. In the case of Hindustan Antibiotics this delay was less marked. Whereas the target of full production was to be achieved by December 31, 1954, that level was actually reached in February 1956. In the case of Hindustan Cables, the work of technical consultants (Messrs Standard Telephones and Cables Ltd of England) was found to be satisfactory. But in the case of Hindustan Steel there were enormous delays and much loss was caused by changing the site of the Rourkela Plant. The time lag between the signing of the Memorandum and the completion of the project (revised schedules) was eighty-four months in the case of Rourkela, seventy-one months in the case of Durgapur and fifty-eight months in the case of Bhilai. Thus the Russian technical assistance fructified in the shortest period.

Commercial Companies, with the exception of Ashoka Hotels Ltd, have put up quite a satisfactory performance. The Eastern Shipping Corporation was managed by the Scindias (as Managing Agents) up to August 15, 1956. Even after that date, the Corporation has done well. Except for the year 1954-55, the entire period up to March 1959 was a profitable one. Of course, the Corporation has a small fleet and it is necessary to strengthen its position. The State Trading Corporation has made useful contribution to the tiding over of the foreign exchange crisis by negotiating Special Payments Agreements (mostly with Socialist countries). However, the activities of the Corporation need to be rationalized and broadbased. Its dependence on cement agency business, which was the object of much criticism, is already on the decline. The Export Risks Insurance Corporation has done fairly well during the short period of its existence. With effect from October 1, 1959, it was able to reduce the premium rates on an average by 10 per cent.

The performance of Development Companies has been quite disappointing. The National Industrial Development Corporation has reduced itself into a Finance Corporation concerned with the grant of loans to jute and cotton textile industries. This task could have been performed by the IFC. The NIDC should have concentrated its attention on promoting the entrepreneurial spirit, procuring technical assistance, sponsoring training programmes and the like. But the NIDC has preferred to roost in comfortable nests and not many enterprises have been promoted by it. As against this, the Pakistan Industrial Development Corporation has achieved tremendous success. Again, the National Small Industries Corporation in India has not been able to justify its existence. The main idea behind the establishment of this Corporation was to operate the scheme of Government purchases as a trading scheme. But, out of Rs 161.35 crores worth of contracts placed by the Director-General of Supplies and Disposals during 1958-59, the value of contracts placed with the assistance of the Corporation was just Rs 2.56 crores. The Hire Purchase Scheme has been running at a loss from the very beginning. Marketing operations through mobile vans resulted in miserably low sales; and revenue losses during the four years (1955-59) aggregated Rs 8.67 lakhs, besides the capital loss of Rs 2 lakhs arising from the disposal of nine vans. Thus there was a total loss of Rs 10.67 lakhs on sales aggregating Rs 6.13 lakhs. The operation of wholesale depôts also resulted in heavy losses. The export activity revealed some profit but the same has substantially declined because of the uneconomic existence of seven export cells. The Estimates Committee found on an on-the-spot study that 54,000 pairs of shoes costing Rs 8.09 lakhs were lying unsold. The Russian order was not for these particular type of shoes but for other types.

It is suggested that the members of Governing Boards should be appointed for five, six or seven years so that they may take interest in their work and try to achieve real improvements in their organization. Many of the Public Corporations in India have not appreciated this point. The Life Insurance Corporation had seen three Chairmen in less than two years' time. The DVC Chairman, between April and October 1959, enjoyed two 'three-month' tenures. In case of Government Companies the position is worse. During the first two years of the working of National Small Industries Corporation, the average stay of the representative of the Ministry of Finance on the Board of Directors was only three and a half months. During the first four years (February 1955 to February 1959), the Corporation had seen five Chairmen. In the case of Sindri Fertilizers and Chemicals, three Managing Directors came into picture during the year 1953-54.

We feel that a Board to be really effective should meet once a month. The decennial average of meetings in the case of TVA (1949-58) works out to 14.4. In case of IFC this average was only six. It may be added that a small Board of three to seven members is likely to feel an adequate sense of responsibility. However, the average size of the Boards of Public Corporations in 1957 was 14.8, with 8.2 Officials and 6.6 Non-officials. In March 1959, with regard to fourteen Government Companies falling within the jurisdiction of the Ministry of Commerce and Industry, the average size of the Board was 9.9, with 6.8 Officials and 3.1 Non-officials. Departmental Secretaries are often appointed as Board members and hold concurrent positions. Thus the Principal Finance Secretary was appointed as the first Chairman of a giant organization like the LIC. Sometimes the mutual jealousies of various Ministers are carried down to the Departmental Secretaries, thus causing delays and obstructions. Full-time Boards are therefore preferable. While technological considerations go in favour of the functional Board, sociological considerations suggest the superiority of the policy Board. In the ultimate analysis, sociological considerations may triumph. However, in case of industrial corporations, due place must be given to functional experts, though they may not be formally put in charge of particular departments.

Whereas the appointment of trade union leaders on the Board as representatives of the labourers in that undertaking may compromise the position of labour leaders, State Corporations must not lag behind in setting up a suitable machinery for workers' participation. It is all the more necessary because State Corporations are often running essential services, any breakdown in which may paralyse the entire life of the nation. However, even when Joint Management Councils are established, the workers would not like to disturb the sanctity of trade unions as a forum where they can speak out their heart and mind fearlessly. More keen than the workers are outside leaders to maintain the status of trade unions. In fine, workers' participation, to be really meaningful, must start at the lowest level.

A study of the price and sales policy followed by the State Corporations in India reveals a bias in favour of Government Departments (and other public organizations including International Agencies), a bias in favour of bulk customers (even though they may be private organizations), a bias in favour of long-term contracts, and a bias in favour of the region or locality where the production operations are carried on (including bias in favour of their employees). A very interesting example is provided by the DVC, which entered into an agreement for bulk sale of power with the Calcutta Electric Supply Corporation Ltd on April 15, 1954. During the year 1957-58, the DVC provided 32 per cent of the total sale of power to that party, but received only 22 per cent of the gross revenues therefrom. The sixteen-year agreement (1945-61) between TELCO and the Government of India created much difficulty. In 1955-56, Chittaranjan locomotives were much cheaper than TELCO engines.

The principle of import parity prices was applied for some time to TELCO, but more fully in the case of Hindustan Shipyard. The latter has all along been receiving subsidies from the Government of India. Some of the State Corporations like the Hindustan Insecticides and the Hindustan Antibiotics are required to operate on no-profit basis. Some Corporations are *expected* to incur losses because of developmental, humanitarian, social or political considerations. A notable example is that of the State Bank of India, which is expected to support the (newly established) unprofitable branches. The Rehabilitation Finance Administration in India and the Pakistan Refugees Rehabilitation Corporation are instances of political necessity. Both the Corporations always suffered losses during the first ten years.

We do not agree with Meade when he says that the principle is to socialize just those industries where marginal cost is below average cost and loss is incurred by equating price with marginal cost. We feel that industrial development cannot be promoted merely by supplying cheap power. Finance is the main hurdle. The profits of State Corporations will act as propellers of Socialist industrialization. In 1958-59, aggregate profits of twenty-seven profitable Corporations amounted to Rs 53.57 crores, whereas the aggregate losses in respect of six unprofitable Corporations amounted to Rs 1.43 crores only. After allowing for Government subsidies amounting to Rs 0.90 crores, the net positive figure amounted to Rs 51.24 crores. However, as much as Rs 40 crores came from the Reserve Bank of India. The State Trading Corporation, the Employees' State Insurance Corporation, the State Bank of India, the Sindri Fertilizers and Chemicals and the Hindustan Antibiotics together contributed another Rs 10 crores. According to the Draft Outline of the Third Five-Year Plan, State enterprises (other than Railways) are expected to contribute Rs 440 crores. This means that the State Corporations should yield Rs 88 crores annually. In the initial year this figure may not be reached but the profits may grow progressively as the Plan advances.

The term 'public accountability' stands for the organizational techniques and procedural devices employed by the nation, as equity shareholder, to pull the strings of State Corporations. The central feature of public accountability is often described as parliamentary control. This is based on the assumptions that Parliament is the true representative of public opinion, that it is sovereign and has the final say in all matters. In actual practice, these assumptions may prove to be too theoretical.

Up to the end of 1953 it was strongly urged in India that while the ordinary Departments were fully accountable to Parliament, and the Public Corporations were accountable within the limits of the incorporating legislation, Government Companies (for the most part) fell outside the periphery of public accountability. The last part of this contention was finally exploded in 1956 when the Companies Act made special provisions for Government Companies.

It has been suggested by Professor Galbraith, who submitted a comprehensive paper to the Krishna Menon Committee, that Parliamentarians, when they question individual decisions of Companies, force the Ministers to protect themselves by asking for advance information and approval of all decisions. Our analysis, however, is just the other way. Since Ministers withhold important information and do not take Parliament into confidence, Members of Parliament are forced to seek information by pressing questions. But for Parliamentary questioning, the entire LIC-Mundhra Deal would have remained undiscovered.

The idea of establishing a Special Committee of Parliament on Nationalized Industries deserves full support. The Estimates Committee and the Public Accounts Committee have created rich traditions of non-political and non-partisan scrutiny in India. We hope that the Third Committee will imbibe those very traditions. The two Committees are already overworked. As time passes, and more Corporations come into existence, the volume of work will increase. Parliament itself is overburdened with work. It has no time to go into the working of so many Corporations. But if Parliament loosens the strings, it will open the flood-gates of corruption and inefficiency. Moreover, many of the difficulties and shortcomings of State Corporations can be better appreciated in a Committee of manageable size rather than in a big assembly. A Committee of outside experts will have its own value, but it will not inspire as much confidence among Members of Parliament as a Committee constituted from within Parliament. We may expect that a well-informed Parliament will interfere less in the working of State Corporations because damaging questions, on many occasions, are the product of ignorance and hearsay.

DAMODAR VALLEY CORPORATION

This may be described as the Indian counterpart of the American Tennessee Valley Authority. The long gap of fifteen years between the birth of these two institutions is accounted for by the fact that the TVA experiment attracted worldwide attention only when it had completed its first decade. The publication of three important books—TVA, *A Study in Public Administration,* by C. H. Pritchett (1943); TVA, *Democracy on the March,* by David Lilienthal (1944); and TVA, *Lessons for International Application,* by Herman Finer (1944)—is an important pointer in this direction. As luck would have it, the year 1943 had seen possibly the most killing famine in civilized history—according to official estimates, 35 lakhs of people lost their lives in Bengal. Further, 'during a comparatively minor flood, all traffic had to be suspended between the stations above and below Burdwan from the 18th of July, 1943, to the 8th of October, 1943. . . . Calcutta would have been flooded and Burdwan destroyed if a breach in the left bank had occurred at a time when the peak flow was equal to that of the 1913 flood'.[1] So it was a question of sheer survival. The ten-man Damodar Flood Enquiry Committee of 1943 favoured the solution of the problem on the TVA model. The Government of India commissioned the Central Technical Power Board to study the proposal. This Board secured the services of Mr W. L. Voorduin, a senior engineer on the staff of the TVA. The Board in its *Preliminary Memorandum* favoured the creation of a Damodar Valley Authority as an example in the multi-purpose development of a watershed for India and also as an agency for national defence. Mr Mathews, Chairman of the Central Technical Power Board, also favoured a 'single unified administration'. He felt that for efficient administration, and regardless of its originating sponsors, the Authority must be invested with a high degree of autonomy for conducting the undertaking.[2]

The Damodar Valley Project was placed in charge of an ICS administrator in May 1946. The Damodar Valley Corporation Bill was introduced on December 1, 1947, and placed on the Statute Book on March 27, 1948. Mr N. V. Gadgil, then Minister for Works, Mines and Power, while moving the Bill, had expressed the hope that the DVC will

---

[1] Central Technical Power Board, *Preliminary Memorandum on the Unified Development of the Damodar River,* reprinted 1948, p. 8. (Serious floods occurred in 1823, 1848, 1856, 1859, 1863, 1882, 1890, 1901, 1905, 1907, 1913, 1916, 1923, 1935 and 1943.)

[2] *Report of the Damodar Valley Corporation Enquiry Committee,* June 3, 1953, p. 11.

provide 'water for irrigation, power for industries and employment all round', and that 'a valley of death and destruction' would turn into 'a valley of prosperity and happiness'. Thus was born the DVC on July 7, 1948.

The functions of the Corporations are outlined as follows in Section 12 of the DVC Act:

(a) the promotion and operation of schemes for irrigation, water supply and drainage;

(b) the promotion and operation of schemes for the generation, transmission and distribution of electrical energy both hydro-electric and thermal (in this respect the DVC enjoys certain monopoly rights);

(c) the promotion and operation of schemes for flood control in the Damodar River and its tributaries and the channels, if any, excavated by the Corporation in connection with the scheme and flow conditions in the Hoogly River;

(d) the promotion and control of navigation in the Damodar River and its tributaries and channels, if any;

(e) the promotion of afforestation and control of soil erosion in the Damodar Valley; and

(f) the promotion of public health and the agricultural, industrial, economic and general well-being in the Damodar Valley and its area of operation.

One unfortunate feature of the DVC legislation is that no attempt has been made therein to lay down broad priorities amongst the various objectives. Thus, in the operation of dams, flood control may run into conflict with power generation and the latter with irrigation.[3] Further, while the TVA Act directs the Board to maintain its principal office within the Tennessee Valley, the DVC Act is silent on the point. This has resulted in much emotional controversy. There have been moves and counter-moves with regard to the shifting of DVC headquarters from Calcutta to some place in the Damodar Valley. Similarly, the absence of clear instructions in the DVC Act with regard to purchase policy has caused much avoidable criticism.

Certain political considerations created a lot of difficulty. Thus the agreement of the Bihar Government depended on issues like (a) irrigation in Bihar, (b) her right to appoint her representative on the board, (c) resettlement of displaced families, and (d) the procedure for land acquisition to be followed by DVC. Similarly, Bengal raised questions about (a) allocation of costs, (b) central contribution to flood control, and (c) construction priorities. All these bickerings went to undermine the autonomy of the Corporation.[4]

One of the major objectives in fostering the institution of Public

[3] Sudhir Sen, 'The Future of Public Corporations', *Capital Annual Review*, Calcutta, December 1953. Dr Sudhir Sen, first secretary of the DVC, would allot priority No. 1 to flood control, though in the list of functions it occupies the third place.

[4] This has also worked to limit the scope of development activities. Thus it was suggested at the Conference of Participating Governments held in July 1954 that the Corporation may henceforth undertake developmental activities ancillary to the projects only, and that the expenditure on such

Corporation was to move away from the rut of bureaucracy. But practical experience in this regard has been rather disturbing.[5] For example, in December 1954 the Damodar Valley Corporation appointed another officer as a General Construction Superintendent, Electrical and Mechanical, in the scale of Rs 1,800-100-2,000 for direct control and supervision of the Hydro-electric Power Station at Maithon. In May 1955, the Corporation observed that in spite of a large number of highly-paid officers there was no cohesion and no co-ordination between them and on July 12, 1955, appointed a Deputy Project Manager in the scale of Rs 1,300-60-1,600 in order to *'co-ordinate the different activities of the various sections and to help the Project Manager in the discharge of his onerous duties'*. On September 27, 1955, the Corporation appointed a Chief Construction Engineer for eighteen months on a salary of $18,000 per annum subject to the Indian Income Tax limited to the USA tax on his income. He actually joined in the first week of October 1955 and his services were terminated on March 13, 1956, i.e. after a little over five months, with three months' pay *in lieu* of notice.[6] Notwithstanding the above appointments, the scheduled date of completion of the Maithon Dam proper by June 1956 could not be adhered to.

It may be noted that as early as September 20, 1952, the Government of India in the Ministry of Irrigation and Power—in accordance with the recommendations made in the Fifth Report (1951-52) of the Estimates Committee of Parliament—had set up the Damodar Valley Corporation Enquiry Committee under the Chairmanship of Mr P. S. Rau, ICS. The question of appointment of a Chief Engineer for the DVC was considered so important that it was added as a separate term of reference on January 20, 1953. The verdict of the P. S. Rau Committee on this issue is worth recounting: '. . . it may sound incredible, but it is true that for the first two and a half years of its existence the Corporation had no Chief Engineer in charge of its multifarious and highly technical operations. . . . For this vacillation and indecision

activities may be charged to the respective project accounts. See the Audit Report on the Accounts of the Damodar Valley Corporation for the year 1953-54, dated October 8, 1955, p. 2.

[5] The DVC Service (Conduct) Regulations, 1955, notified on July 28, 1956, are very much on the lines of Central Civil Services (Conduct) Rules, 1955. For example, no employee of the DVC may make any statement 'which has the effect of an adverse criticism of any current or recent policy or action of the Central or a State Government or the Corporation'. Further, no employee can participate in a radio broadcast or contribute any article or write any letter to any newspaper or periodical without the previous sanction of the Corporation. However, when the Ministry of Home Affairs clarified, in their Memorandum dated January 15, 1957, that Government servants 'are now not required to obtain any sanction to broadcast on All-India Radio, if such broadcasts are of a purely literary, artistic or scientific character', the same principle was adopted by the DVC.

[6] *Audit Report on the Accounts of the Damodar Valley Corporation,* for the year 1955-56, dated November 17, 1956, pp. 7-8. The Corporation explained that the officer did not prove a success and was also unlikely to improve.

in appointing the Chief Engineer the Corporation is as a whole technically responsible, but we regret to have to say that the personal responsibility of the Chairman in the matter is by no means negligible.'[7]

Section 4 of the DVC Act provides that 'The Corporation shall consist of a Chairman and two other Members appointed by the Central Government after consultation with the Provincial Governments'. Section 5(1) originally provided that every member shall be a whole-time servant of the Corporation. This clause was deleted by DVC (Amendment) Act, 1957. This amendment gives discretion to the Central Government to appoint whole-time or part-time Members, as may be necessary according to the state of work of the Corporation. Members of the Central or any Provincial Legislature, and those having any interest in a subsisting contract with the Corporation, are disqualified from the membership of the Corporation. According to DVC rules,[8] the Chairman, Members, Secretary and Financial Adviser of the Corporation shall be appointed for such term not exceeding five years as the Central Government may think fit and shall be eligible for reappointment. Under the DVC (Conduct of Business) dated October 27, 1951, as amended on May 20, 1959, no matter relating to revenue and expenditure shall be included in the agenda of any meeting or be circulated for decision unless previous advice has been taken thereon from the Financial Adviser. The Agenda note shall contain the views of the Financial Adviser on all such matters. The independent status of the Financial Adviser is revealed from the chart opposite.[9]

The business of the Corporation shall be transacted either at meetings of the Corporation or by circulation of files amongst the members and the Financial Adviser.[10] Notice of a meeting shall ordinarily be given to every Member and the Financial Adviser at least three days before the meeting. Any two Members shall form a quorum at a meeting of the Corporation.

It would not be wrong to say that the DVC organization has been in a state of flux during recent years.[11] The changes in administration have

[7] *Report of the Damodar Valley Corporation Enquiry Committee* (1952-53), June 3, 1953, p. 70.

[8] Originally issued vide Ministry of Works, Mines & Power Notification of April 23, 1948. New rules inserted vide Ministry of Irrigation and Power Notification dated April 8, 1958.

[9] By courtesy of the Damodar Valley Corporation.

[10] Regulation 3 formerly provided that 'Normally meetings shall be held at least once a week'. Later, it was amended to read 'Ordinarily meetings shall be held once a week'. The present position is that a meeting of the Corporation is 'to be held ordinarily once a month'. (DVC Compilation of Regulations, etc., March 1960, p. 71.)

[11] The term of the first Board, appointed in 1948, expired in July 1953. Thereafter, an interim Chairman worked up to April 1954, when Mr P. S. Rau, ICS, took over as Chairman. Mr Rau went away as Adviser to the Raj Pramukh of Travancore-Cochin in March 1956 and returned in December 1956. Mr J. P. L. Shenoy, ICS (Retired), assumed charge of the office on April 12, 1958. On April 12, 1959, Mr T. Sivasankar took over as Part-time Chairman, for three months. His term was extended by another three months. On October 12, 1959, Mr S. Lall was appointed as Part-time Chirman.

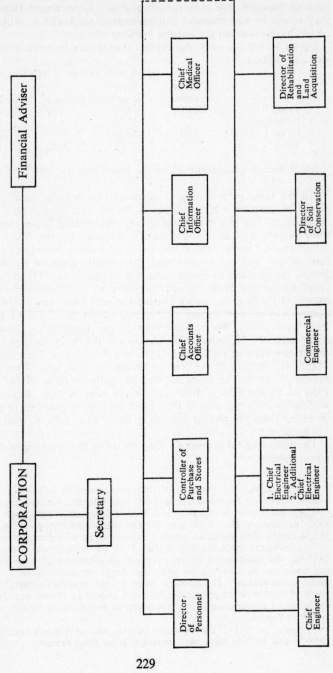

DVC ORGANIZATION CHART
(March 31, 1957)

Financial Adviser

CORPORATION

Secretary

Director of Personnel

Controller of Purchase and Stores

Chief Accounts Officer

Chief Information Officer

Chief Medical Officer

Chief Engineer

1. Chief Electrical Engineer
2. Additional Chief Electrical Engineer

Commercial Engineer

Director of Soil Conservation

Director of Rehabilitation and Land Acquisition

been so frequent that even for an ordinary Government Department they would be bad enough.[12] Administrative exigencies in other walks of life have disturbed the normal working of DVC.

Up to March 31, 1958, the capital expenditure incurred by the DVC stood as follows:[13]

	Central Government	West Bengal	Bihar	Total
PROVIDED BY				(Rs Crores)
1. Power	20.59	20.59	20.59	61.76
2. Irrigation ...	—	32.30	0.35	32.65
3. Flood Control ...	7.00	14.80	—	21.80
4. Total	27.59	67.68	20.93	116.20

(N.B. *Because of approximations, the figures may not always 'add up'*)

All the three participating Governments contributed equally to the power programme which represents 53 per cent of the total capital expenditure. The irrigation programme, representing 28 per cent of the total outlay, was almost exclusively financed by the West Bengal Government. Capital expenditure on flood control, representing 19 per cent of the total outlay, has been increasingly financed by the West Bengal Government in recent years. Up to March 31, 1954, the Central Government and West Bengal had spent an equal amount on flood control (Rs 4.09 crores each). During the next four years (1954-58) the Central Government's share of expenditure on flood control was less than Rs 3 crores, whereas the West Bengal Government contributed more than Rs 10 crores. Considering all the three programmes together, the share of the Central Government fell from 32 per cent as on March 31, 1950, to 28 per cent on March 31, 1954, and 24 per cent on March 31, 1958. The share of West Bengal rose from 39 per cent in 1950 to 50 per cent in 1954 and 58 per cent in 1958. Bihar's share declined from 29 per cent in 1950 to 22 per cent in 1954 and 18 per cent in 1958. Thus the DVC is becoming more and more a West Bengal Corporation.[14]

The following table gives an idea regarding the working of the DVC power system:[15]

[12] Om Prakash, 'The Problem of Entrepreneurship in Socialist Economy', *Indian Journal of Economics,* July 1958, Vol. XXXIX, No. 152, pp. 65-6.

[13] *Annual Report of the Damodar Valley Corporation and Audit Report,* 1957-58, Calcutta, March 1959, p. 50. The capital actually provided was Rs 117.54 crores, there being an unspent balance of Rs 1.34 crores.

[14] According to the Audit Report (July 1959) on the Accounts of the DVC for 1957-58, 'the question of inter-Governmental allocation of expenditure on soil conservation, afforestation and other developmental advities . . . is still under consideration'. The opinion given by the Attorney-General in February 1956, that developmental expenditure should be shared equally by the participating Governments, was not accepted by the Governments of Bihar and West Bengal.

[15] Figures up to 1957-58 are based on the Annual Reports and those for 1958-59 and 1959-60 have been obtained from Press release.

APPENDIX A

	Gross Revenue (Rs lakhs)	Quantity Sold (million KWh)
1953-54	55	108
1954-55	84	163
1955-56	136	283
1956-57	200	420
1957-58	349	807
1958-59	477	1,081
1959-60	605	1,313

The gross revenue per KWh sold fell from 5.3 *Naye Paise* in 1953-54 to 4.8 nP in 1955-56 and 4.3 nP in 1957-58. Thereafter, it improved to 4.6 nP in 1959-60. The gross receipts realized from the sale of electrical energy for the four years 1953-54 to 1956-57 were Rs 477 lakhs against the working expenses of Rs 271 lakhs as exhibited in the provisional Annual Pro Forma Revenue Accounts of the DVC Power System. But taking into account Rs 401 lakhs for interest and depreciation charges, the total expenses for that period aggregated Rs 672 lakhs, thus resulting in a deficit of Rs 195 lakhs for the four-year period.

LIFE INSURANCE CORPORATION OF INDIA

The President of India issued the Life Insurance (Emergency Provisions) Ordinance on January 19, 1956, to provide for the taking over, in public interest, of the management of life insurance business *pending nationalization thereof*. The idea was that adequate steps should be taken to protect the interests of policyholders. This Ordinance was repealed on March 21, 1956, on which date the President gave his assent to the Life Insurance (Emergency Provisions) Act, No. 9 of 1956.[1] Formal nationalization was effected under the Life Insurance Corporation Act, No. 31 of 1956, which received the assent of the President on June 18, 1956. The Life Insurance Corporation of India came into existence on September 1, 1956. The Corporation shall consist of such number of persons not exceeding fifteen as the Central Government may think fit to appoint thereto, and one of them shall be appointed by the Central Government to be the Chairman thereof.[2]

The original capital of the Corporation was to be Rs 5 crores provided by the Central Government after due appropriation made by Parliament. The general duty of the Corporation is to carry on life insurance business, whether in or outside India, and 'the Corporation shall so exercise its powers under the Act as to secure that life insurance business is developed to the best advantage of the community'.

The Central Office of the Corporation shall be 'at such place as the Central Government may by notification in the Official Gazette specify' (Bombay). The Corporation 'shall establish a zonal office at each of the following places, namely Bombay, Calcutta, Delhi, Kanpur and Madras, and, subject to the previous approval of the Central Government, may establish such other zonal offices as it thinks fit'. There may be established as many Divisional Offices and Branches in each Zone as the Zonal Manager thinks fit.[3]

---

[1] *The Gazette of India,* Extraordinary, Part II, Section I, No. 19, New Delhi, Thursday, March 22, 1956.

[2] No qualifications and disqualifications were laid down for the members except that they will have no such financial or other interest as is likely to affect prejudicially the performance of their duties. Thus Members of Parliament can become members of the Corporation.

[3] As on December 31, 1957, the Northern Zone consisted of four Divisions and the Central Zone five Divisions. The Eastern, Southern and Western Zones comprised of eight Divisions each. There appeared to be a case for the amalgamation of the Northern and Central Zones whose total business (between September 1, 1956, and December 31, 1957) aggregated Rs 42 and Rs 45 crores respectively as against Eastern Zone's Rs 77 crores, Southern Zone's Rs 87 crores and Western Zone's Rs 77 crores.

Under section 19(1), the Corporation may entrust the general superintendence and direction of its affairs and business to an Executive Committee consisting of not more than five of *its members,* and the Executive Committee may exercise all powers and do all such acts and things as may be delegated to it by the Corporation. Section 19(2) provides that the Corporation may also constitute an Investment Committee to advise it in matters relating to the investment of its funds. The Investment Committee shall consist of not more than seven members, of whom not less than three shall be members of the Corporation, and the remaining members shall be persons (whether members of the Corporation or not) who have special knowledge and experience in financial matters, particularly matters relating to the investment of funds. In the discharge of its functions under the Act, the LIC shall be guided 'by such directions in matters of policy involving public interest as the Central Government may give to it in writing'.[4]

That the primary motive of nationalization was to protect the interests of the policyholders is revealed in several sections: section 26 lays down that the Corporation shall have an actuarial valuation at least once in every two years; section 28 provides that 'not less than 95 per cent of such surplus shall be allocated to or reserved for the policyholders of the Corporation and the remainder may be utilized for such purposes and in such manner as the Central Government may determine'; and section 37 prescribes that all policies issued by the Corporation (including bonus) and all policies issued by any insurer the liabilities of which have vested in the Corporation (including bonus declared, whether before or after the appointed day) shall be guaranteed as to payment in cash by the Central Government.[5] Further, section 38 puts a bar to the liquidation of the Corporation 'save by order of the Central Government and in such manner as that Government may direct'.

The investment policy of the LIC has been under heavy fire. A major criticism has been with regard to the importance attached to investments in the private sector. Thus the investments in Ordinary Shares of Companies which formed 6.9 per cent of the investments on August 31, 1956, rose to 8.0 per cent on June 30, 1957. Investments in debentures remained constant at 6.0 per cent, whereas those in Preference Shares increased from 3.9 per cent to 4.1 per cent. Thus the percentage share of Shares and Debentures rose from 16.8 per cent to 18.1 per cent.[6] The share of Government and approved securities, as a whole, declined

---

[4] The words 'in writing' are very important because in the Mundhra deal of 1957, inquired into by the Chagla Commission (1958), and later by the Vivian Bose Board (1958) and the Union Public Service Commission (1959), no such directions had been issued by the Government. It could therefore be argued that if the Chairman and the Managing Director behaved like lambs, and were led away by the talk of the Principal Finance Secretary (or even of the Minister), Government of India, they did so at their own risk.

[5] This is subject to the limitation contained in Section 14 which permits a reduction in the Corporation's liability in certain cases (with regard to policies issued by erstwhile insurers).

[6] These figures are based on the *Interim Report on the Activities of Life Insurance Corporation of India,* August 1957, pp. 18 ff.

from 73.1 per cent to 72.1 per cent. The position as at December 31, 1957, is not quite comparable with the breakdown as it stood on August 31, 1956, and June 30, 1957, since the Corporation have resorted to a different pattern of classification. The share of Indian and State Government and other approved securities stood at 65.7 per cent on December 31, 1957. On the same date the share of Debentures and Shares of joint stock companies in India stood at 17.8 per cent. Taking into account four items—(1) Central Government Securities, (2) State Government Loans, (3) Approved Securities, and (4) Debentures, Preference and Ordinary Shares in Joint Stock Companies—it would appear that 77.37 per cent of the holdings were in the public sector, and 22.63 per cent in the private sector (the private sector including a part of the Approved Securities also). However, the share of the public sector rose to 78.1 per cent as on December 31, 1958, and to 78.6 per cent by July 1959, whereas investments in the private sector declined to 21.9 per cent in December 1958 and to 21.4 per cent in July 1959. Of course, it is true that the investment policy of the LIC between September 1, 1956, and June 30, 1957, was inclined in favour of the private sector.[7] However, investments in the private sector, if safe and sound, may not be open to objection. Such investments would, in fact, make for State control of private enterprises through the back door.

Unfortunately, even the basic principles governing sound investment —security of capital and adequacy and regularity of yield—have been ignored in certain transactions. There is a clear finding of the Chagla Commission: 'From a review of the evidence it seems clear to me that whatever might be said about Jessop, Angelo Bros., and Smith Stainstreet, the purchase by the Corporation of Richardson and Cruddas, B.I.C. and Osler shares did not constitute a sound and prudent investment. It would, therefore, be seen that this particular transaction was not entered into in accordance with business principles and was also opposed to propriety on several grounds.' The Vivian Bose Board came to the conclusion that the 'transaction was improper and contrary to business principles and practices and resulted in investments which the Corporation should not have made'. The Attorney-General, Mr M. C. Setalvad, rightly stressed that these public funds are of a special character; they are public trust funds. In his brilliant arguments before the Chagla Commission, on January 29, 1958, Mr Setalvad referred to the 'complete neglect of ordinary methods'.[8]

Further, although the Corporation had an Investment Committee

[7] During this period, the Corporation purchased Ordinary Shares of Rs 5.67 crores (sales amounting to Rs 0.06 crores only, there was a net increase of Rs 5.61 crores). The net increase in Debentures was Rs 1.40 crores (Rs 1.52 crores *minus* Rs 0.12 crores). The net increase in Preference Shares was Rs 1.61 crores (Rs 1.62 crores *minus* Rs 0.01 crores). As against this, the purchase of Government of India Securities stood at Rs 4.16 crores (and with sales as high as Rs 3.89 crores, the net increase was only Rs 0.27 crores—excluding Rs 9.19 crores net increase in State Government Securities).

[8] Mr Sachin Choudhury, Counsel for LIC, conceded that the Corporation had purchased 'a number of ordinary shares irrespective of whether the companies paid dividends or not'. Mr H. M. Patel gave a strange reply on

consisting of experienced persons, the Committee was either not consulted in advance, or it failed to undertake due scrutiny, perhaps relying a little too much on the Chairman and high dignitaries in the Government. The Investment Committee was consulted with regard to the transactions of March 9, 1957, and April 5, 1957. But it was not consulted with regard to the transaction of April 25, 1957 (50,000 shares of Jessop & Co), and, according to the Chagla Commission, 'the evidence is that Mr Patel put through a trunk call from Delhi to Mr Vaidyanathan and asked him to make this investment'. With regard to the four transactions subsequent to June 24, 1957, except with regard to the transaction of September 14, 1957, the Investment Committee was not consulted.

Mr A. Subbiah, who resigned from the membership of the Investment Committee in 1959 after a brief honorary service of eight months, is reported to have found 'too much uncontrolled concentration of power without responsibility in the hands of top executives'. The Investment Committee as well as the LIC Board were presided over by the same person, who played the dual rôle of Chairman and Chief Executive of the Corporation. The Investment Committee used to meet once in a few weeks for a couple of hours to consider some 150 to 200 offers from brokers. The Executive in charge of the Corporation's investments simply presented the offers without adequate scrutiny, background information or suitable recommendations. Moreover, the members were not given any advance information

It would appear that the administrative machinery had been both inefficient and ineffective to handle the complicated task of investing in the shares and debentures of hundreds of companies operating in different spheres of industrial activity. The policies and procedures actually adopted by the Corporation for investing its funds were contrary to recognized business principles, against all canons of sound investment and weighted heavily in favour of outside interests to the detriment of the interests of policyholders. Interested parties, who wanted to get rid of their investments at high prices, could mislead the Corporation by raising false alarms regarding the collapse of the stock market. And the most pitiable thing was that the Corporation, which had to invest some Rs 10 lakhs every day, did little on its own initiative. It should have investigated the Balance Sheets and secured other relevant data about the various corporate enterprises in the private sector with a view to ascertaining the best avenues of investment. The Corporation should not have left itself to the mercy of stockbrokers and other outside influences. The newly-established Investment Research Section has a heavy responsibility in this regard.

The following extract from the LIC Report is enough indication of the legal flaws in some of the investments:[9] 'It is apprehended that the

January 23, 1958, that if they purchased good scrips, it would only result in their prices going up. Does it mean that the LIC should buy the most worthless shares because they need the greatest support?

[9] LIC, *Report and Accounts* for the period September 1, 1956, to December 31, 1957, pp. 8-9.

Corporation's title to some of these shares may be open to challenge. Moreover, in respect of the shares of Richardson Crudas Ltd, purchased by the Corporation, it is possible that a portion of the shares which have already been registered in the Corporation's name may turn out to be spurious.'[10] The total amount involved in such spurious scrips may be insignificant in the context of the vast investments held by the LIC. But the very fact that spurious shares were purchased by an organization which specializes in the art of investment indicates that even elementary vigilance was not practised on certain occasions.

Finally, the Corporation bartered away its autonomy and deviated from its statutory obligation to safeguard the interests of policyholders. It is difficult to improve upon the judicious verdict pronounced by the Chagla Commission: 'In the investments it may make and in the investment policy it may pursue, it must be guided by its own officers and by the statutory commitment set up under the Act. The only control that Government can exercise is under section 21 and that control is restricted to matters involving public interest, and what is equally important is that the control can only be exercised by directions given in writing . . . Government could not tell the corporation that it should or should not invest in any particular shares, it could not tell the corporation that it should help a particular industry, much less a particular individual; but it could tell the corporation that it should invest its funds in certain industries which were essential for the successful working of the second Five-Year Plan or to give effect to a particular economic or financial policy laid down by Government . . . there was a tendency on the part of the Finance Ministry to look upon the corporation as a wing or branch of that Ministry and to issue orders to it in the belief that the corporation was bound to carry out those orders. If one thing is more important than any other, it is that the Chairman of the Corporation should be an independent official who is conscious both of his position and the stature of the corporation under the Act.' Further, nowhere was it stated in the LIC Act that the Corporation should help to stabilize the stock market. Those who have waxed eloquent on this point must seek a fresh mandate from Parliament. Moreover, a very important point, *which has been missed throughout the deliberations,* is the fact that *a falling market was by no means a danger signal to the Corporation.* The LIC is not a professional speculator, and there was no danger of a 'Bull Squeeze'. *The Corporation is, by and large, a purchaser of investments; normally, it is not a seller.* The working results and dividends of the companies were of real importance—and to these little

[10] Mrs Tarakeshwari Sinha, Deputy Finance Minister, disclosed in the *Lok Sabha* towards the close of 1959 that the following shares were found to be duplicate: (1) Richardson and Crudas Ltd—100 ordinary shares of Rs 10 each costing Rs 1,529, and 1,000 preference shares of Rs 100 each costing Rs 80,539; (2) Osler Electric Manufacturing Company Ltd (in liquidation)— 13,000 ordinary shares of Rs 5 each costing Rs 5,244. Further, in respect of 57,000 ordinary shares of Richardson and Crudas Ltd of Rs 10 each it was found that shares bearing similar distinctive numbers were held by others. It could not be ascertained as to which of these shares were spurious, those held by the Corporation or those by others.

attention has been paid—rather than temporary ups and downs on the stock exchange in their share values. The Chagla Commission held that there was no crisis on the stock exchange; but even if there were bearish conditions, any wise investor would have preferred to wait and to take advantage of falling share values.

The resignation of Mr T. T. Krishnamachari, who was Finance Minister when these unhappy transactions were negotiated, was formally accepted by the President on February 13, 1958. The new Finance Minister, Mr Morarji Desai, announced a new investment policy in the *Lok Sabha* on August 25, 1958. Under the new policy, the maximum holdings of the LIC in the ordinary shares of companies was raised from 10 per cent to 30 per cent of the subscribed ordinary capital (with a further provision for exceeding this limit with the prior approval of the Central Government). This provision was intended to ensure effective control of the Corporation over the companies in which it makes investments. Thus the Corporation will behave not merely as an investment trust, but as an active holding corporation. Further, under the new policy, the Corporation can make investments in the shares of Private Limited Companies with the prior approval of the Central Government. Barring these two provisions, the Corporation was placed on the same footing as were the life insurance companies prior to nationalization. With the application of section 27-A of the Insurance Act to the Corporation, the investments were to be conformed to the following pattern: at least 50 per cent of the life funds in *Government and Approved Securities*; not more than 15 per cent in *Other Investments*; and the balance of 35 per cent in *Approved Investments*. Approved investments have been redefined as shares of any company on which dividends of not less than 4 per cent (including bonus) have been paid for five years immediately preceding (the purchase) or at least five out of seven years immediately preceding (the purchase). The Corporation, under the new policy, must also submit, like former life insurance companies, returns and statements of accounts to the Controller of Insurance to enable the latter to ensure that the interests of the policyholders were safe. This will enable the Controller to point out to the Government any mistakes committed by the Corporation.

The following table gives an idea of the new business procured immediately before and after the nationalization of life insurance:

| Year | IN INDIA | | OUTSIDE INDIA | |
	No. of Policies	Sum assured (Rs crores)	No. of Policies	Sum assured (Rs crores)
1955	7,96,030	240.51	35,461	20.33
1956	5,49,401	187.69	17,956	12.59
1957	8,10,738	277.67	5,055	5.40
1958	9,54,771	339.06	5,399	5.62
1959	11,14,122*	417.46*	7,912	9.47

(*Excluding *Janta* Policies which amounted to Rs 2.01 crores in 1959)

During the first year of nationalization, the business suffered a severe fall. However, the LIC was in existence for only four months in 1956. For the greater part of the year, life insurance was under emergency administration of the Government. Thereafter, since 1957, the business has shown continuous improvement. 1959 was the first year of the LIC's own Five-Year Plan (1959-63) which has fixed a target of Rs 1,000 crores to be achieved by 1963. New business secured in 1959 exceeded the annual target of Rs 415 crores by about 14 crores (taking into account *Janta* policies and foreign business). The average sum assured per policy in India (excluding *Janta* policies) was higher at Rs 3,805 in 1959 as against Rs 3,015 in 1955 and Rs 3,666 in 1958. The average sum assured in respect of foreign business was Rs 11,966 in 1959 as against Rs 5,733 in 1955 and Rs 10,409 in 1958. However, foreign business as a whole was at a very low level during 1957 and 1958. In 1959 there was substantial improvement, but it was still less than half of the level attained in 1955. In case of *Janta* policies, the maximum insurable limit was Rs 999. These policies were intended to popularize life insurance in rural areas where medical examination and such other formalities were a source of hindrance. The total amount of business under this simplified plan of insurance stood at Rs 1.61 crores in 1958 and Rs 2.01 crores in 1959.[11] Although it represented an advance of 25 per cent, the experiment, as a whole, has not been very encouraging.

The total business in force on December 31, 1958, was Rs 1,682 crores under 62.3 lakh policies, out of which Rs 1,584 crores (59.7 lakh policies) was in India and Rs 98 crores (2.6 lakh policies) was outside India. The life insurance fund as at December 31, 1958, stood at Rs 447.81 crores as against Rs 361 crores on January 1, 1956. Thus the net aceretion in three years was Rs 86.81 crores giving an annual rate of about Rs 29 crores, which is not quite encouraging. The premium income in 1958 amounted to Rs 73.08 crores as against Rs 58.55 crores in 1955. This gives an annual increase of about Rs 5 crores, which is again rather low.[12]

Certain comparable figures from the United States will indicate the extent of backwardness and the possibility of future progress in India. At the end of 1958, there were 124 million individual policyholders in the United States, i.e. more than twenty times the Indian figure. The amount of business in force stood at $515 billion (i.e. roughly Rs 2,50,000 crores), i.e. more than 150 times the Indian figure. In 1958 alone, new life insurance sold in the United States aggregated $66,831 million (i.e. roughly Rs 32,000 crores), more than ninety times the Indian figure. The number of new policies issued in the United States during 1958 stood at 24,492,000, more than twenty-five times the Indian figure.

[11] In 1958 the number of *Janta* policies issued was 24,325, the average sum assured per policy working out to Rs 662.

[12] The first valuation report (as on December 31, 1957)—see *Commerce* (Bombay), July 18, 1959—revealed a net surplus of Rs 29.01 crores (95 per cent of it, i.e. Rs 27.56 crores, allocated to policyholders). The 'special group' bonus (policies of Oriental, Norwich Union, etc.) was Rs 21 per thousand on whole life policies and Rs 16.80 on endowment policies. The Oriental, before nationalization, had declared Rs 22½ and Rs 18 respectively. The bonus on the policies of LIC (and Bombay Mutual, New India, etc.) has now been Rs 17½ and Rs 14 respectively.

HINDUSTAN STEEL LIMITED

In January 1954, the Hindustan Steel Ltd was originally promoted with an authorized capital of Rs 100 crores, and a paid-up capital of Rs 5 lakhs, of which Rs 4 lakhs were contributed by the Government of India and Rs 1 lakh by the German combine. The latter was to have proportionate representation on the Board of Directors. In May 1954 the German combine submitted a Preliminary Project Report for a plant of half a million ton ingot capacity. After it was approved, the Technical Consultants submitted the Final Project Report in January 1955. Meanwhile, it was decided to increase the capacity of the plant from half to one million ton steel ingots per annum, with the result that a Supplementary Agreement was signed between the Hindustan Steel Ltd and Messrs Krupp-Demag on July 21, 1955. Under the agreement entered into with Messrs Krupp-Demag, the latter were to invest in the Rourkela Steel Project an amount in Deutsche Marks not exceeding the equivalent of Rs 9.5 crores, so as to associate them in the management—particularly during construction and initial operation—with a stake in the Company. Besides, it was hoped that such an association would attract further financial assistance from abroad. The German investment was to be regulated from time to time in relation to the volume of orders for purchase of machinery and equipment in Germany. However, the linking of the investment by the Combine with the orders for plant and machinery to be placed on them, to some extent, limited the area from which purchases of equipment could be made. Moreover, at a later stage it turned out that German investment under the agreement would amount to borrowing at nearly 12 per cent interest. Consequently, their financial collaboration with the Company was dispensed with.[1]

The share of Messrs Krupps-Demag was taken over by the Government of India in December 1956. The two other Steel Projects, Bhilai and Durgapur, were under the direct control of the Ministry of Iron and Steel (now Ministry of Steel, Mines and Fuel) created by a Presidential Order dated May 28, 1955. This position continued till March 1957, when the preparatory work on the two projects was over. Plant and machinery had been ordered and arrangements made for civil engineering work practically in all major sections of the plants. At this stage, Government considered that it would be advantageous if all the three projects were brought under a unified Company management.

---

[1] *Estimates Committee*, 1958-59, Thirty-Third Report, Second Lok Sabha, Ministry of Steel, Mines and Fuel, Lok Sabha Secretariat, New Delhi, February 1959, p. 18.

Accordingly, Hindustan Steel (Private) Limited was re-registered on April 1, 1957, in the State of West Bengal with an authorized capital of Rs 300 crores 'to construct, manage and administer the three steel plants of Rourkela, Bhilai and Durgapur'.[2] The authorized capital of Hindustan Steel is divided into 30,00,000 Equity Shares of Rs 1,000 each. In addition to purchasing all the shares, Government had advanced a loan of Rs 190 crores by the end of February 1960.[3]

Under the Articles of Association of Hindustan Steel Ltd, the President is to determine the number of Members of the Board of Directors, and also to make their appointment. The General Managers, the Financial Adviser and the Chief Accounts Officers of the projects are also to be appointed by the Government. Proposals or decisions of the Board of Directors in respect of capital expenditure exceeding Rs 40 lakhs and other important matters are subject to the approval of the Government.[4] Further, the Board of Directors of Hindustan Steel[5] have set up a Committee for the disposal of business in between the meetings of the Board of Directors. This Committee consists of the Chairman, the Deputy Chairman, the Director of Finance *and such other Directors as may be available*. The decisions taken by it are final, and do not require ratification or confirmation by the Board. The Committee is entitled to meet thrice a week. Between September 1957 and August 1958, it actually met eighty-nine times (roughly, twice in a week), whereas the Board met only seven times. The quorum for the Committee's meeting is two, and the number of Directors attending the meetings has varied from two to four. During this period, no non-official Director ever attended any meeting of the Committee.

The working of Steel Projects has presented the following unsatisfactory features:

(1) *Increase in the Estimates.* The following table presents the original estimates for the three one-million ton ingot steel plants, on the basis of which provision was made in the Second Five-Year Plan, as also the revised estimates given to the *Lok Sabha* on August 13, 1957:

[2] *Administrative Problems of State Enterprises,* Report of a Seminar, December 1957, p. 76.

[3] The amount actually expended on the erection of the Steel Plants, according to the Estimates Committee (February 1959), was Rs 197 crores —Rs 87 crores on Rourkela Plant, Rs 70 crores on Bhilai Plant and Rs 40 crores on Durgapur Plant.

[4] In a note received on February 17, 1959, it was pointed out that 83 cases had been referred by the Company to the Government under the Articles of Association, 68 cases being of capital expenditure exceeding Rs 40 lakhs. In addition, 607 cases of imports, etc., were referred to the Government for sanction of foreign exchange. One directive was issued by the Government regarding housing standard in the steel townships.

[5] The Head Office of the Hindustan Steel Ltd remained in New Delhi till December 24, 1959, but was shifted to Ranchi on December 26, 1959. This was to meet quite a strong criticism regarding the administrative distance from the scene of action.

APPENDIX C

Plant	Total Estimate (Rs in crores)		Component of Foreign Exchange (Rs in crores)	
	Original	Revised	Original	Revised
Rourkela ...	128	170	89	122
Bhilai ...	110	131	67.5	78
Durgapur ...	115	138	72	92
Total	353	439	228.5	292

It came to light on January 7, 1959, that the figure of Rs 292 crores did not include the foreign exchange component of the cost of ancillaries. A rough estimate of these items is given below (in crores of rupees):

Item	Rourkela	Bhilai	Durgapur
Township	14	14	14
Ore Mines	10	10	(a)
Fees to Consultants .	2.85	2.50	1.87
Soviet Staff	—	4.50	—
Water Supply	2	1.50	1
Other Expenditure ...	15	15	12
Total	43.85	47.50	28.87

N.B. (a) means 'Not Available'. The investment on Bolani Ores is included, in case of Durgapur Plant, in 'Other Expenditure'.

Thus these items (excluding the Fertilizer Plant) would cost more than Rs 120 crores, thus pushing up the entire cost to Rs 560 crores. Individually, Rourkela would cost about Rs 214 crores (and if we include the Fertilizer Plant it would come to Rs 230 crores), Bhilai Rs 178 crores, and Durgapur Rs 167 crores. Rourkela would still be the costliest plant, but as between Bhilai and Durgapur, the position would be reversed if these rough estimates prove correct.

(2) *Delay in Execution.* The following statement of the time consumed in the completion of various projects (on the basis of revised schedules) is revealing:[6]

	A		B		C	
	Years	Months	Years	Months	Years	Months
Rourkela ...	7	0	4	10	3	11
Bhilai ...	4	10	4	0	3	8
Durgapur .	5	11	5	6	4	10

Note: 'A', 'B' and 'C' stand for three categories of time-lags (up to the final completion) from (A) the date on which the Memorandum was signed; (B) the date of the Final Project Report; and (C) the date on which orders for plant and machinery were placed.

It is a matter of satisfaction to find that production at Rourkela started on February 3, 1959, at Bhilai on February 4, 1959, and at

[6] Thus the Bhilai Steel Plant gets the best out of these projects. This conclusion is also supported by the evidence which the present writer gathered while visiting the several steel plants (under construction) in September 1957.

Durgapur in December 1959.[7] The Bhilai Plant is expected to produce for sale 300,000 tons of pig iron, 200,000 tons of rails and sleeper bars, 160,000 tons of heavy structurals, 260,000 tons of medium structurals and 150,000 tons of billets. The Rourkela Plant is to turn out 200,000 tons of plates 3/16-inch and above, 300,000 tons of sheets and strips (hot rolled), 170,000 tons of sheets and strips (cold rolled) and 50,000 tons of tin plates. In case of Durgapur Plant, when the first stage is completed, the production for sale will consist of 350,000 tons of pig iron, 240,000 tons of merchant sections, 200,000 tons of light sections, 60,000 tons *each* of sleeper bars and forging billets, 30,000 tons of forging blooms, 10,000 tons of *heavy* forging blooms, 34,750 tons of wheels, 14,500 tons of axles, besides 150,000 tons of billets.[8]

During the Third Five-Year Plan (1961-66), the production of steel would be raised to about 10 million tons. There is a proposal to double the capacity of Rourkela, Bhilai, Durgapur and the two private sector units. Further, the foundation for the fourth plant in the public sector is being laid at Bokaro.

(3) *Defective Agreements with Technical Consultants.* Agreements for the three plants were entered into with:

(1) INDIEN GEMEINSCHAFT KRUPP-DEMAG G.m.b.H of the Federal Republic of Germany, in case of Rourkela Plant.

(2) The Government of the U.S.S.R., in case of the Bhilai Plant.

(3) The International Construction Company of the United Kingdom, in case of Durgapur Plant.

The Consultants' Fees fixed in these cases were Rs 2.85 crores, Rs 2.5 crores and Rs 1.87 crores respectively. The first agreement has been subjected to greatest criticism. Messrs Krupp-Demag had furnished general plans both for the plant and the township 'but it was not their responsibility to give detailed plan for the various units'. Accordingly, separate consultants had to be appointed for the civil engineering work in respect of the Rolling Mills and the Steel Melting Shop on a fee of Rs 65 lakhs.[9] The Russian agreement did not provide for any ceiling on the salaries, etc., of the Soviet Chief Engineer and other Soviet

[7] The question of expanding the steel industry was under the consideration of the Government of India since 1945. It was proposed to set up two steel plants of one-half million tons each. But the matter was shelved in 1949 on grounds of financial stringency (dictated by a false sense of economy). The foreign exchange drain caused by the delay has been of the order of total outlay on the three plants. If these plants had been established five years earlier, they would have cost 40 to 50 per cent less.

[8] The actual production at Rourkela up to February 29, 1960, was 234,154 tons of pig iron and 50,329 tons of steel ingots. The Bhilai Plant during the first eleven months of the year 1959-60 produced 391,150 tons of pig iron, 70,000 tons of steel ingots, 44,250 tons of blooms and 31,050 tons of billets. Durgapur had produced 47,000 tons of pig iron by February 1960.

[9] A consortium of four German firms with Messrs Hochtief A.G., Essen, as group leader was entrusted with this work. Messrs Hochtief, however, resigned from the consortium on taking up the contract.

experts engaged in the supervision of construction work.[10] Apart from the agreement, the Bhilai Plant was employing 1,001 Soviet experts directly.[11] The cost of the Soviet staff *directly* employed was estimated at Rs 4.5 crores.

The agreement with the International Construction Company, technical consultants for the Durgapur Steel Works, provided that the fees payable to the consultants would be reduced by £200,000 (Rs 26 lakhs) in case the Government decided to place the contract for the whole or a large proportion of the work with one contractor. Under this provision the Consultants' Fees were reduced from £1,600,000 (Rs 2.13 crores) to £1,400,000 (Rs 1.87 crores). The contract entered into with the Indian Steel-works Construction Co. Ltd (ISCON), a British consortium, involved a package deal. Under that deal most of the designing and engineering work which is normally done by consultants was passed on to plant suppliers. For the various technical services to be rendered by ISCON, the latter are to be paid nearly Rs 15 crores. Thus, although the Consultants' Fees in case of Durgapur are the lowest, the overall cost of technical advice is the highest. Further, under another agreement signed in December 1955, the International Construction Company were appointed as consulting engineers to the Government for a period of six years. Thus, as super-consultants, they were to supervise their own work.

(4) *Irregularities in awarding Contracts.* In case of Rourkela plant, earth-moving machinery, etc., of the value of Rs 60 lakhs was proposed to be hired at a charge amounting to Rs 75 lakhs. Under another contract, a large number of German carpenters were brought from Germany at a total cost of Rs 20 lakhs 'to reinforce the Indian contractors who had fallen behind the schedule'. It appeared that in several cases the antecedents of the contractors had not been verified before the contracts were awarded. Thus the huge contract for civil engineering work for the Rourkela Blast Furnaces was awarded to an indigenous firm against whom the Public Accounts Committee of the Punjab *Vidhan Sabha* had passed strictures (in connection with the Chandigarh Capital Project) while dealing with the Appropriation Accounts of the Punjab Government for the year 1952-53 and the Audit Report for 1954.[12]

(5) *Lack of Adequate Planning in Other Matters.* We have already

[10] It was revealed in the *Lok Sabha* on November 8, 1958, that an expenditure of Rs 93.4 lakhs had already been incurred on the Soviet Engineer and Soviet experts (as against a ceiling of Rs 70 lakhs in the German agreement).

[11] The monthly salaries of these experts were: 1 Chief Engineer, Rs 4,500; 35 Leading Specialists, Rs 2,850 each; 123 Specialists, Rs 2,400 each; 214 Technicians and Leading Foremen, Rs 2,200 each; 35 Interpreters, Rs 1,950 each; 107 Foremen and Adjusters, Rs 1,800 each; and 468 Other Technicians, Rs 1,500 each.

[12] The Committee had strongly recommended their black-listing in view 'of an utter lack of good business principles'.

referred to the delay in execution, which is a clear indication of inadequate planning. It has been estimated that this delay would involve an expenditure of about Rs 10 lakhs *per day at each of the plants*. Further, the site of the Steel Plant at Rourkela had to be shifted at an additional cost of Rs 3 crores, the original site having been found to be rocky. The enormous increase in the cost of earthwork caused thereby is evident from the following figures:

Earthwork	Original Value of Contract (Rs in lakhs)	Revised Estimated Value (Rs in lakhs)
Zone A	57.53	146.00
Zone B	58.92	158.64
Zone C (I)	104.55	426.75
Zone C (II)	3.08	426.75
Zone D	132.50	153.75

Not only this, there has not been proper co-ordination even in the planning of the three steel plants. Most of the negotiations and deliberations were proceeding simultaneously; yet there is so much of undesirable divergence between the various schemes. Again, from the standpoint of decentralization in industry, the position is not very satisfactory. Technically, the three plants are located in three different States—Rourkela in Orissa, Bhilai in Madhya-Pradesh and Durgapur in West Bengal. But, geographically, they are not as spread out as might be suggested by the size of the country. These locations have satisfied three competing States; but they have failed to satisfy strategic considerations.

STATE TRADING CORPORATION OF INDIA LIMITED

The necessity of augmenting foreign exchange resources for the Second Five-Year Plan dictated the urgency of establishing a State trading organization. The State Trading Corporation of India (Private) Limited was registered on May 18, 1956, with an authorized capital of Rs 1 crore divided into 1,00,000 equity shares of Rs 100 each. The paid-up capital was initially Rs 5 lakhs; but it was raised to Rs 10 lakhs in October 1956, and to Rs 1 crore in March 1957. The share capital was wholly subscribed by the Government of India. During the year 1958-59 the authorized capital of the Corporation was increased to Rs 5 crores and the paid-up capital to Rs 2 crores.

The objectives of the Corporation as set forth in the Memorandum of Association are to 'organize and effect exports and imports into India of such goods and commodities as the Company from time to time determine . . .', and 'to do all such other things as are incidental or conducive to the attainment of the above object'. In practice, the management of the Corporation has, 'having regard to the business already being transacted by other companies or organizations, endeavoured to seek out opportunities to make its contribution to the building up of the country's commerce with new markets and new sources of supply; to providing facilities to augment exports; to securing, wherever possible, improvements in terms of trade and economies in imports; and to arranging to the extent practicable for import and distribution of certain essential raw materials at stable prices'.[1] The Corporation has followed diverse techniques of operation:

(1) *Direct Trading.* This method was restricted to some of the transactions only. Thus the Corporation procured, stocked and shipped the ores sold to foreign buyers. With effect from July 1, 1957, export of iron ore was required by the Government of India to be canalized through the Corporation.

(2) *Joint Sales Programmes.* This approach was adopted in case of the manganese ore. Joint sales programmes were worked out with the principal producers. The total quantity of manganese ore covered by the Corporation's contracts up to June 30, 1957, was of the order of 4,00,000 tons. In view of the slackness of international demand the scheme did not work well during 1957-58 and 1958-59.

[1] The State Trading Corporation of India (Private) Limited, First Annual Report, dated November 16, 1957, §3 (pages not numbered).

(3) *Link Arrangements.* Imports of essential items were linked with exports of Indian manufactures. Thus the import of textile machinery was negotiated with Dia Machinen Exports, Berlin; and gunnies were sold to the Sundries Import Corporation of Viet Nam in exchange for rice. A general arrangement for the purchase and sale of goods on link basis was entered into with the Hungarian Chamber of Commerce. A Special Account was operated by the Corporation to link the purchase of Egyptian cotton with the sale of Indian goods to Egypt. Under the Wheat-Manganese Barter Deal with the Commodity Credit Corporation of the United States, India was expected to supply, by March 31, 1961, 1,12,000 tons of Indian-made ferro and over 1,50,000 tons of manganese ore.

(4) *Business Associates.* In a number of cases while contracts for purchase or sale were concluded by the Corporation, deliveries of consignments on board the ship for export, and the handling and distribution of goods on import, have been looked after by the Corporation's business associates.

(5) *Servicing Agent.* As a servicing agent the Corporation has tried to bring together buyers and sellers, assisting them in implementing business contracts and using its good offices to settle disputes amicably. Further, producers of shoes, handicrafts and woollen fabrics were enabled to organize production for export.

(6) *Government Agency.* The Government of India entrusted to the Corporation the task of acquiring cement from manufacturers, importing it from abroad, and distributing both indigenous and imported cement at an equalized price f.o.r. destination railhead. For these services, the Corporation was given a service fee at $1\frac{1}{4}$ per cent of the gross turnover. It was scaled down to $\frac{3}{4}$ per cent in 1957-58 and to $\frac{1}{2}$ per cent in 1958-59. The cement agency account revealed a surplus of Rs 5.01 crores during 1956-57, Rs 4.10 crores during 1957-58 (remitted to the Government of India) and Rs 2.39 crores during 1958-59.

(7) *Procurement Business.* The import and distribution of soda ash, caustic soda and raw silk were entrusted to the Corporation with effect from July 1, 1956. The Corporation endeavoured to procure these commodities at the cheapest possible price and with the smallest possible outlay of foreign exchange, significant quantities being imported from new sources against payment in rupees. Government departments and industrial enterprises were assisted in procuring essential plant and machinery on economical terms. Thus gypsum was supplied to the Sindri Fertilizers and Chemicals (Private) Limited. Further, the Corporation concluded a contract for the purchase of a diesel cargo vessel of 10,000 DWT from Yugoslavia for the use of the Western Shipping Corporation, and two patrol launches were ordered on behalf of the Central Board of Revenue. The Corporation also procured essential requirements in some vital sections of the country's economy, e.g.

machine tools for both small-scale and large-scale industries, newsprint for newspapers, tractors for cultivation, raw films for cinema industry and X-ray films for hospitals. During the year ended June 30, 1959, the Corporation procured 1.8 lakh tons of low-grade ore for Hindustan Steel Ltd.

Minerals constitute the core of the Corporation's business in the field of exports. The Corporation entered into a long-term agreement with the Japanese steel mills providing for the sale of 7.2 million tons of iron ore, spread over a period of five years, against which 1.3 million tons were contracted to be supplied during 1957-58 'at a price fair both to the buyer and the seller'. An agreement for the supply of a further two million tons of iron ore from the Rourkela area (for a period of ten years in the first instance, commencing from 1964) was concluded between the two countries in March 1958.[2]

The Corporation was 'engaged in exploring overseas markets, and studying business techniques, but it has not so far been possible to take many active steps to promote the export of difficult-to-sell items'.[3] A Special Trade Development Fund was created during 1957-58 with an initial allocation of Rs 15 lakhs. On June 30, 1959, it stood at Rs 51 lakhs. The Corporation has organized trade teams composed of exporters participating in the Fairs at Poznan, Leipzig, Zogreb and Budapest.

During the year 1958-59 there were twenty-five items of export, e.g. iron ore, manganese ore, chrome ore, mica, tobacco, gunny bags, raw jute, handicrafts, shoes, woollen fabrics, cotton waste, hides and skins, crude drugs and condinements, and eighteen items of import, e.g. caustic soda, soda ash, raw silk, ammonium sulphate and other chemicals, skimmed milk, newsprint and copper.[4] The turnover in commodities directly traded by the Corporation was of the order of Rs 35.95 crores during 1958-59 (with a gross profit of Rs 3.33 crores) as against previous year's turnover of Rs 28.58 crores (with a gross profit of Rs 2.13 crores) and a turnover of Rs 10 crores (with a gross profit of Rs 35.42 lakhs) during the year 1956-57. The Corporation suffered a loss on soda ash amounting to Rs 3.82 lakhs in 1956-57 and Rs 6.96 lakhs in 1957-58. It has been explained that the losses were incurred 'with a view to maintaining the price of the commodity at a steady level, despite fluctuations in procurement prices' (in the larger public interest). Further,

[2] In respect of manganese ore, 'the comparatively high level of internal prices did not make it easy for the management to convert limited trading opportunities into firm sales'—Second Annual Report, dated April 29, 1959, p. 3.

[3] The State Trading Corporation of India Limited, Second Annual Report, dated April 29, 1959, p. 4.

[4] The Government of India authorized the State Trading Corporation to export 2 lakh tons of Indian cement during the period January 1958 to June 1959. By March 1959 the Corporation had contracted to sell 1,55,550 tons. The customers were Ceylon, Saigon (South Viet Nam), Cambodia, Persian Gulf Ports, East Pakistan, East Africa, Madagascar, Afghanistan and Aden. With effect from June 1959 the Government of India canalized the exports of salt through the Corporation.

during the year 1957-58 there was a loss of Rs 1.39 lakhs on tobacco. In order to provide against seasonal fluctuations in prices, a Price Fluctuation Fund was raised during the year 1957-58. The Fund stood at Rs 40 lakhs on June 30, 1959.[5]

The Corporation has followed a conservative dividend policy, declaring 6 per cent on the first year's working and 7 per cent for the second and the third year respectively. The dividends consumed only Rs 6 lakhs in 1956-57 (out of a net profit of Rs 32.63 lakhs), Rs 7 lakhs in 1957-58 (out of a net profit of about Rs 105 lakhs), and Rs 14 lakhs in 1958-59 (out of a net profit of Rs 134 lakhs).

On the positive side of the Corporation's achievements must be placed the Special Payments Arrangements promoted by the Corporation to tide over the foreign exchange crisis. During the year 1957-58 such Arrangements aggregated Rs 930 lakhs with seven countries—Egypt (552 lakhs), German Democratic Republic (188 lakhs), Hungary (64 lakhs), Poland (48 lakhs), Yugoslavia (34 lakhs), Rumania (23 lakhs) and Czechoslovakia (21 lakhs).

But several criticisms might be levelled against the working of the Corporation. First, its activities have been confined (excepting Japan) mostly to Communist countries. It is true that these countries offer special facilities for State Trading. But, unless it is proposed to establish other Corporations of a similar nature, the said Corporation must succeed in tackling more difficult situations. Secondly, there has been no proper allocation between the spheres of action of this Corporation and private businessmen. This means overlapping and duplication of effort. The Corporation will have little justification for its existence if it merely snatches away some business from the erstwhile channels of foreign trade. It must show overall improvement from the standpoints of quantum of trade, efficiency and standards of business morality. Thirdly, it would appear that the Corporation has failed to take advantage of the experience of private traders. While in most of the Government Companies it has been customary to keep a few industrialists on the Board of Directors, the State Trading Corporation started with an all-official structure.[6]

---

[5] The State Trading Corporation, Third Annual Report, dated April 4, 1960.

[6] According to the First Annual Report, all the eight Directors were Government officials—four Joint Secretaries of the Ministry of Commerce and Industry (including the Chairman), a Joint Secretary of the Ministry of Finance, the Director General of Supplies and Disposals, the Director General of Shipping, and Director of Railway Board. One of the nominees of the Ministry of Finance was in office for less than a month; and the average tenure of the first three nominees of that Ministry (consecutively) was about three and a half months.

NATIONAL INDUSTRIAL DEVELOPMENT
CORPORATION LIMITED

The establishment of industrial development corporations in the post-war world has brought a new institutional pattern to the fore in the economies of under-developed countries. With the avowed objective of accelerating the rate of industrial growth and of overcoming the initial hesitancy of private enterprise, particularly in the launching of large-sized basic and key industries, these corporations have come to be regarded as an important step in bringing about a 'balanced economy'. The accent of such Corporations is on 'enterprise' whether private or public. As such, they are looked upon as a vital agency whose mission it is to reconcile the conflicting claims of the public sector and the private sector.[1]

In this respect, Pakistan showed the way to India. The Pakistan Industrial Development Corporation (PIDC) was created under Act No. XLV of 1950 and it started functioning on January 12, 1952. The birth of industrial development corporations in India is a later event. The Committee on Finance for the Private Sector appointed by the Reserve Bank of India under the Chairmanship of Mr A. D. Shroff, a well-known industrial magnate, submitted its report in May 1954. The Committee recommended that three development Corporations should be established: (a) an Industrial Development Corporation, owned and managed by the Government of India; (b) a privately-owned and managed Industrial Development and Finance Corporation; and (c) a Special Development Corporation for small industries.

All the three Corporations were registered under the Companies Act. The first one (State-owned Corporation), the National Industrial Development Corporation (NIDC), was established on October 24, 1954, as a Private Limited Company. The second one (privately-owned), Industrial Credit and Investment Corporation of India, was registered on January 5, 1955, in Bombay as a Public Limited Company. This Corporation 'is solely concerned with the promotion, expansion and modernization of industries in the private sector'.[2] The third development corporation, the National Small Industries Corporation, was registered as a Private Limited Company on February 4, 1955. Here we proceed to discuss the NIDC.

[1] Cf. Om Prakash: Industrial Development Corporations in India and Pakistan, *The Economic Journal* (Royal Economic Society, England), March 1957, p. 40.

[2] *Chairman's Speech* at the Statutory Meeting of the ICIC by Sir A. Ramaswami Mudaliar on July 28, 1955 (Cyclo-styled), p. 2. After the nationalization of life insurance in 1956 the ICIC shares held by privately-owned insurance companies passed into the hands of the public sector. Even then, this Corporation is not a Government company.

The authorized capital of the NIDC was fixed at Rs 1 crore divided into 1 lakh shares of Rs 100 each. This is equivalent to the authorized capital of the Pakistan Industrial Development Corporation, divided into 100 shares of Rs 1 lakh each. However, in spite of ambitious objectives and high expectations, the NIDC could achieve very little as compared to the PIDC. The Directors' First Report, dated March 23, 1956, states: Although the Corporation was set up in October 1954, it was not until a year later that it received the approval of Government to the following projects being promoted by it:

    (i) Establishment of steel foundries, forges and steel structural shops;
    (ii) Manufacture of intermediates for dyestuffs;
    (iii) Manufacture of wood pulp;
    (iv) Manufacture of carbon black;
    (v) Manufacture of sulphur from pyrites;
    (vi) Manufacture of printing machinery;
    (vii) Manufacture of air compressors and fractional horse power motors; and
    (viii) Manufacture of refractories.

Further, it may be recalled that in September 1954 the *Lok Sabha* (Parliament) had passed a resolution favouring the rationalization of jute and cotton textile industries. The Government saw in the NIDC, established in October 1954, a convenient vehicle for the implementation of that resolution. This was all very nice. But later events suggested that the NIDC were being reduced to the status of a Finance Corporation. Appendix I of the Directors' Report dated March 23, 1956, had laid down: 'The Corporation will undertake financing only in so far as it is incidental to the development of an industry.' But what was contemplated as an ancillary business soon threatened to be the main activity of the NIDC. More than half of 'A Review of Progress' for the year ended June 30, 1958, is devoted to the granting of loans. It would appear that the NIDC has preferred to roost in comfortable nests.

The First Directors' Report had referred to eight projects. 'A Review of Progress' for the year ended June 30, 1957, stated: 'Having regard to the allocation of funds in the Second Plan for the NIDC projects and to the priorities indicated in the Plan, it is proposed with the approval of Government to concentrate on projects relating to: (a) the manufacture of industrial machinery in the field of heavy engineering; (b) the production of the primary intermediates required by the organic chemical industries like drugs, dyestuffs and plastics; and (c) some crucial raw materials like aluminium and synthetic rubber.'[3] 'A Review of Progress' for the year ended June 30, 1958, repeated the sentence 'Having regard . . . relating to', retained the (a) category as it was, but amalgamated (b) and (c) categories by stating: '(b) some crucial industrial raw materials like raw film, aluminium and synthetic rubber and primary intermediates for the drug, dyestuff and plastic industries.'[4]

Some preliminary steps had been taken by the NIDC regarding the

[3] *The National Industrial Development Corporation Private Limited,* June 1957, p. 2.
[4] *Ibid.,* June 1958, p. 2.

Heavy Machine Building Plant, the Heavy Foundry/Forge and the Coal Mining Machinery Plants. But these were entrusted to the Heavy Engineering Corporation registered on December 31, 1958.

In 1957 a team of Russian experts submitted a preliminary report for the manufacture of Optical and Ophthalmic Glass. Later, a contract was entered into with M/s Technoexport of Moscow for the preparation of a detailed project report. The factory was planned to manufacture 200 tons of Ophthalmic Glass and 10 tons of Optical Glass per annum. Foreign exchange component of the cost was to be met out of the Russian credit of 500 million roubles. The project is to be located at Durgapur, where the Coal Mining Machinery Project is also being set up. Pending a final decision regarding the agency which would ultimately handle the Optical Project, it was decided to entrust it to the Heavy Engineering Corporation.

The designs and specifications for a phosphorus plant were to be prepared by a team of Indian engineers after they had completed their training at Wilson Dam in the USA. The Tennessee Valley Authority had agreed to assist the NIDC and to train up the engineers.

For the development of drugs and pharmaceutical industries, a second team of experts from the USSR visited India between August 3 and October 15, 1958. On May 29, 1959, an agreement was signed with the USSR Government for co-operation in establishing in India enterprises for the manufacture of antibiotics, synthetic drugs and special intermediates, drugs from medicinal plants, surgical instruments, and endocrines and glandular products. The Russian credit of 80 million roubles is to be repaid by equal annual instalments within a seven-year period (beginning one year after the completion of delivery of complete equipment for all enterprises). A contract was signed with Messrs Technoexport of Moscow on September 5, 1959, for technical assistance in selecting construction sites and in collecting initial data necessary for designing these projects.

Regarding the scheme for the production of Carbon Black, besides the interest shown by a private party in establishing it on the basis of work earlier done by the NIDC, the Rumanian Government provided the services of two experts to undertake a fresh project survey. These experts visited India between June 7 and July 14, 1958.

Up to June 30, 1958, the NIDC had received loan applications from 34 Jute Mills for Rs 8.41 crores. Applications of 17 mills for Rs 3.38 crores were granted. But the actual amount drawn stood at Rs 1.36 crores only. In case of Cotton Mills, applications had been received from 69 mills for Rs 27.43 crores. Applications of 14 mills for a sum of Rs 3.05 crores were sanctioned. But the actual amount drawn stood at Rs 75 lakhs only. Up to November 1, 1959, the Government had advanced a sum of Rs 4.18 crores to the NIDC for granting loans to various units. Besides these two industries, 'Government have recently decided to utilize the Corporation as an agency for advancing loans to the units manufacturing machine tools.'[5]

[5] NIDC: *A Review of Progress*, June 1958, p. 7.

THE NATIONAL COAL BOARD

The decision to nationalize the coal mining industry was announced in the King's Speech of August 15, 1947, only a month after the Labour Party had come into power. After the vesting date (January 1, 1947), the National Coal Board (NCB) was charged with the duties of: (a) working and getting the coal in Great Britain to the exclusion (save as in this Act provided) of any other person; (b) securing the efficient development of the coal-mining industry; and (c) making supplies of coal available, of such qualities and sizes, in such quantities and at such prices, as may seem to them best calculated to further the public interest in all respects, including the avoidance of any undue or unreasonable preference or advantage.

The policy of the NCB shall be directed to secure consistently with the proper discharge of their duties: (a) the safety, health and welfare of persons in their employment; (b) the benefit of the practical knowledge and experience of such persons in the organization and conduct of the operations in which they are employed; and (c) that the revenues of the Board shall not be less than sufficient for meeting all their outgoings properly chargeable to revenue account on an average of good and bad years.

The Board shall be a body corporate by the name of the National Coal Board, with perpetual succession and a common seal and power to hold land without licence in mortmain. It shall consist of a Chairman and eight to eleven other members,[1] to be appointed by the Minister of Fuel and Power from amongst persons appearing to him to be qualified as having had experience of, and having shown capacity in, industrial, commercial or financial matters, applied science, administration, or the organization of workers. A person shall be disqualified for being appointed or being a member of the Board so long as he is a member of the House of Commons.

The Coal Industry Nationalization Act received Royal Assent on July 12, 1946, and the first members of the National Coal Board were appointed by the Minister of Fuel and Power on July 15, 1946 (although the Members had been meeting since April as an Organizing Committee, and had discussed many urgent problems). There were nine members, including the Chairman, all of them serving full-time. Except for the

---

[1] Originally the Board was to consist of only nine members including the Chairman. But it was provided in the Coal Industry Act, 1949, that there would be a Chairman and not less than eight nor more than eleven other members (one of these to be Deputy Chairman). The Minister could appoint a second Deputy Chairman from among the members. Apart from the Chairman, not more than eight of the members could render whole-time service.

Chairman (Lord Hyndley) and the Deputy Chairman (the late Sir Arthur Street), *the Members of the Board were to take charge of executive Departments, as well as to share in forming the Board's policy.* Each Member had special knowledge of a particular field of the industry's past activities or of an activity which was to be developed by the Board. The portfolios allocated to the Board Members were Production (two members), Marketing, Finance, Manpower and Welfare, Labour Relations, and Scientific Department.

The Fleck Report (February 1955) suggested the following pattern for the National Coal Board:

(1) Chairman
(2) Deputy Chairman
- (a) Free of routine duties.
- (b) Presiding over Board and Executive.
- (c) Watch over work of Headquarters.
- (d) Senior appointments.
- (e) Contacts with the Government.
- (f) Board items of policy.

(3) Full-time Member—Production, Carbonization, Opencast and Small Ancillaries.
(4) Full-time Member—Marketing and Purchasing.
(5) Full-time Member—Industrial Relations.
(6) Full-time Member—Staff.
(7) Full-time Member—Finance.
(8) Full-time Member—Scientific and Medical.

(9) Part-time Member
(10) Part-time Member
(11) Part-time Member
(12) Part-time Member
- (a) To give advice on special problems.
- (b) To serve on one of the Board's Committees according to bent and experience.
- (c) To advise the Minister on the appointment of Full-time Members and other important matters.

Although the Fleck Committee laid great emphasis on the rôle of full-time Members, they were not prepared to do away with part-time Members. Their idea was that the part-time Members of the Board would be men known as having proved themselves outstanding in some phases of industrial leadership, and holding leading positions in the industry of the country; they would be representative of the best industrial thinking, and would be men in whose judgment the community could have confidence. Their experience and balanced judgment, the Committee felt, would be a source of strength to the full-time members.[2]

It is significant to observe that in spite of the 1955 reorganization,[3]

[2] National Coal Board, *Report of the Advisory Committee on Organization* (Fleck Report), February 1955, pp. 56-7. Dr A. Fleck disagreed with the recommendations of the Committee in certain respects. He recommended two Deputy Chairmen (instead of one) and six Part-time Members (instead of four).

[3] Out of 61 recommendations of the Fleck Committee, 4 were not meant for the Board as such. Of the remaining 57, 44 were accepted forthwith. In the case of 10 other recommendations, the NCB expressed their agreement. The remaining 3 recommendations were subjected to further consideration. The rules of guidance for the reconstitution of the Board, *inter alia,* were:

the output of coal and the productivity per man year has not shown any significant improvement. On the other hand, the position has actually deteriorated in certain spheres. It can be argued that the first Board (1946-51) did very well, but after 1952 there has been a sort of stagnation in the British coal industry. The following is indicative of this tendency:

Year	Coal Output (Million Tons)			Productivity (Tons per man year)
	Deep-mined	Opencast	Total	
1947	186.5	10.2	196.8	262
1948	196.7	11.7	208.5	272
1949	202.7	12.4	215.1	282
1950	204.1	12.2	216.3	293
1951	211.3	11.0	222.3	302
1952	212.7	12.1	224.8	297
1953	211.8	11.7	223.5	297
1954	213.6	10.1	223.6	302
1955	210.2	11.4	221.6	299
1956	209.9	12.1	222.0	298
1957	210.1	13.6	223.6	296
1958	201.5	14.3	215.8	288

Notes:
  (i) Because of approximation, figures may not always 'add up'.
  (ii) Figures for the earlier years may not tally with those contained in the respective Annual Reports because certain revisions have been incorporated in recent Reports.
  (iii) Up to 1955, Reports of the National Coal Board were made strictly according to the calendar year (year ending December 31). The Report for 1956 covered the period up to December 29 (364 days or 52 weeks). The Report for 1957 covered 52 weeks up to December 28; but the Report for 1958 was for 53 weeks ending January 3, 1959 (ordered by the House of Commons to be printed on May 14, 1959). However, figures for 1958 (except costs, profits and losses) were calculated on the basis of a 52-week year.

It is evident from the above table that the total coal output in 1958 was at a level which stood more than eight years back between 1949/1950. The level of productivity in 1958 was also at the 1949/1950 level. After 1954 productivity, measured by tons per man year, had presented a consistent fall. However, measured by tons per manshift, the productivity in 1958 stood at 1.265 as against 1.231 in 1957. But even here there was a stagnation during the years 1954-1957. From 1.231 in 1954, the figure fell to 1.225 in 1955, rose to 1.232 in 1956, and again fell to 1.231 in 1957. The period 1947-1951 had presented a much better record when productivity rose from 1.074 in 1947 to 1.108 in 1948, 1.160 in 1949,

(1) The Members should be able to work together as a team; (2) Normally, the full-time Members must come from within the industry (with sound age distribution to ensure continuity); (3) The Minister, before appointing part-time Members, should seek the advice of industrial and labour leaders (the part-time Members were to be consulted in the appointment of the Chairman, Deputy Chairman and full-time Members); and (4) Salaries should be substantially raised. The reorganization took effect on February 21, 1955.

1.194 in 1950 and 1.210 in 1951. The figure fell to 1.193 in 1952; thereafter, it improved to 1.224 in 1953 and 1.231 in 1954. The Board can take pride in the fact that the output of Opencast Coal has shown consistent improvement during the five years 1954-1958. But the output as a whole has been far from satisfactory.

Since 1954, absenteeism among the coal miners has been continuously on an increase. The attendance per week fell from 4.71 in 1954 to 4.56 in 1955, 4.65 in 1956, 4.61 in 1957 and 4.38 in 1958. In this respect the record of the first years (1947-1951) is definitely better, though not consistent. The attendance rose from 4.69 in 1947 to 4.71 in 1948; fell to 4.76 in 1949; and from to 4.72 in 1950 and 4.81 in 1951. This was an achievement difficult to excel. The figure fell to 4.79 in 1952 and 4.67 in 1953; it improved to 4.71 in 1954.

The number of workers in 1947 stood at about 711,000. It rose to 724,000 in 1948—a record figure for the period 1947-1958. The number had fallen to 697,0009 by 1950. It rose to 699,000 in 1951 and 716,000 in 1952. Thereafter, there was a consistent fall up to 1956 (703,000). The figures rose to 710,000 in 1957, but again fell to 699,000 in 1958. The level of employment in 1958 was about the same as in 1951, but the level of output was considerably lower.

Workers' earnings per manshift have presented a consistent increase —from 28s 10d in 1947 to 62s 5d in 1958. This increase was relatively greater than the rise in total costs (per ton of saleable coal) from 41s 3d in 1947 to 83s 11d in 1958. Sale proceeds rose from 40s 3d per ton (giving a loss of one shilling) to 82s 0d (giving a profit of sevenpence). The widest margin of profit existed in 1949 when costs stood at 45s 0d (lower than the previous year's figure—45s 7d) and proceeds at 47s 11d (a profit of 2s 11d per ton). The overall financial picture of the NCB is not quite encouraging. The Board suffered deficits in seven out of the twelve years (1947-1958). The years of unprofitable working were 1947 (£23.3 million), 1951 (£1.8 million), 1952 (£8.2 million), 1954 (£3.8 million), 1955 (£19.6 million), 1957 (£5.3 million) and 1958 (£3.5 million). As against a total loss of £65.5 million, profits during five years aggregated only £32.7 million—1948 (£1.7 million), 1949 (£9.5 million), 1950 (£8.3 million),1953 (£0.4 million) and 1956 (£12.8 million).

THE TENNESSEE VALLEY AUTHORITY

The TVA was established under the 'Tennessee Valley Authority Act of 1933' (May 18, 1933). The preamble to the Act reads: 'To improve the navigability and to provide for the flood control of the Tennessee River; to provide for reforestation and the proper use of marginal lands in the Tennessee Valley; to provide for the agricultural and industrial development of the said valley; to provide for the national defence by the creation of a corporation of Government properties at and near Muscle Shoals in the State of Alabama, and for other purposes.' The immediate need was 'to control the destructive flood waters in the Tennessee River and Mississippi River Basins'. The Act laid down: 'The board of directors first appointed shall be deemed the incorporators, and the incorporation shall be held to have been effected from the date of the first meeting of the Board.' Such a provision is not to be found in any of the Indian legislations enacted for such purpose.

Under Section 2 of the TVA Act, the Board of Directors of the Corporation shall be composed of three members, to be appointed by the President, *by and with the advice and consent of the Senate.* The term of office of the members first taking office after the approval of this Act shall expire as designated by the President at the time of nomination, *one at the end of the third year, one at the end of the sixth year, and one at the end of the ninth year,* after the date of approval of this Act. Each of the members of the Board shall be *a citizen of the United States* and shall (besides a dwelling house) receive a salary of $10,000 a year (later raised to $20,500 in the case of the Chairman and $20,000 in the case of the other members of the Board) to be paid by the Corporation as current expenses. All members of the Board shall be *persons who profess a belief in the wisdom of the Act.*

Section 3 of the Act gives full power to the Board to appoint and remove all kinds of employees *'without regard to the provisions of Civil Service laws',* but *'No regular officer or employee of the Corporation shall receive a salary in excess of that received by the members of the Board'.* Further, all contracts to which the Corporation is a party, and which require the employment of labourers and mechanics, shall contain a provision that *'not less than the prevailing rate of wages for work of a similar nature prevailing in the vicinity shall be paid to such labourers and mechanics'.*

Section 6 restricts the powers granted to the Board under Section 3. In the appointment of officials and the selection of employees, and in the promotion of any such employees or officials, no political test or qualification shall be permitted or given consideration, but all such appointments and promotions shall be given and made on the basis of merit and efficiency. *Any member of the Board who is found by the President of the United States to be guilty of a violation of this Section shall be removed from office by the President of the United States,* and any appointee of the Board who is found by the Board to be guilty of a violation of this Section shall be removed from office by the Board.

Under Section 4, the TVA shall have succession in its corporate name and may sue and be sued in that name.[1] It may use a corporate seal which shall be judicially noticed. It may adopt, amend and repeal 'by-laws'. Any member of the TVA Board *may be removed from office at any time by a concurrent resolution of the Senate and the House of Representatives.*[2] The Corporation was granted general freedom to enter into contracts and 'such powers as may be necessary or appropriate for the exercise' of its functions.[3]

The Board was authorized and directed to pay to States concerned, and the counties therein, for each fiscal year beginning July 1, 1940, the following percentages of the gross proceeds derived from the sale of power by the Corporation (fiscal year beginning July 1):

1940	....	10	per centum
1941	....	9	,, ,,
1942	....	8	,, ,,
1943	....	$7\frac{1}{2}$	,, ,,
1944	....	7	,, ,,
1945	....	$6\frac{1}{2}$	,, ,,
1946	....	6	,, ,,
1947	....	$5\frac{1}{2}$	,, ,,
1948 and each fiscal year thereafter		5	,, ,,

The Board shall file with the President and with the Congress, in December of each year, a financial statement and a complete report as to the business of the Corporation covering the preceding governmental

[1] A total of thirty-eight preliminary injunctions were sought against the TVA during its first five years, of which twelve were denied and twenty-six granted. Of the latter, twenty-five were later dissolved, and one was made permanent. The temporary injunctions were estimated to have cost $13 million to the TVA and its consumers. The development of power operations was greatly hampered. (C. Herman Pritchett, *The Tennessee Valley Authority*, A Study in Public Administration, Chapel Hill, 1943, the University of North Carolina Press, pp. 264-5.)

[2] Dr Arthur E. Morgan, the first Chairman of the TVA, was, however, removed by the President of the United States under his executive authority on March 23, 1938.

[3] The TVA was 'clothed with the power of Government' in several respects, e.g. the access to the Patents Office (and free supply of the copies of documents) and the authority to exercise the right of eminent domain for acquiring real estate. However, any conveyance by the Corporation (except leases for less than 20 years) of property exceeding $500 requires the approval of the US President. Further, any transfer of real property for erecting thereon docks and buildings requires Congressional approval.

fiscal year.[4] The report shall include an itemized statement of cost of power at each power station, the total number of employees and the names, salaries, and duties of those receiving compension at the rate of more than $1,500 a year.[5] The Board shall file with each annual report, a statement of the total cost of all power generated by it at all power stations during each year, the average cost of such power per kilowatt hour, the rates at which sold, and to whom sold, and copies of *all contracts* for sale of power. Useful data shall be reported by the Board to the Congress from time to time with appropriate analyses and recommendations.

The following is the organization chart of the Tennessee Valley Authority:[6]

BOARD OF DIRECTORS
General Counsel
Office of the General Manager

Division of Personnel	Office of Engineering	Office of Power	Office of Chemical Engineering	Division of Agricultural Relations
Division of Law	Division of Water Control Planning	Division of Power Utilization	Division of Chemical Development	Division of Forestry Relations
Division of Finance	Division of Design	Division of Power Supply	Division of Chemical Operations	Division of Health and Safety
Division of Property and Supply	Division of Construction	Division of Power Operations		Division of Navigation and Local Flood Relations
Division of Materials		Division of Power Engineering and Construction		Division of Reservoir Properties

The Office of Engineering plans, designs and constructs hydro-electric and steam-electric plants and other large plant facilities. It also controls the flow of water 'in the present system of thirty dams on the Tennessee River and its tributaries'. It has provided for *a rotation training pro-*

[4] The Comptroller General of the United States shall audit the transactions of the Corporation and shall submit his report in quadruplicate—one copy for the President of the United States, one for the Chairman of the Board, one for public inspection at the principal office of the Corporation, and one copy to be retained by him for the uses of the Congress.

[5] It is an indirect way of controlling higher appointments. But the limit is rather low, specially in the light of American standards. $1,500 a year comes to Rs 600 per month. As against this, in India it is usual to control only those appointments wherein the maximum salary is Rs 1,500-2,000 per month.

[6] Source: Division of Personnel, Knoxville, Tennessee, June 1959. The total number of persons employed by the TVA stood at 13,174 on June 30, 1949, and at 16,056 on June 30, 1958.

gramme with a view to giving the young engineer an opportunity to learn about varied engineering jobs. Approximately one week's training is imparted to all engineering and architectural graduates in the office of the Chief Engineer. In the Division of Water Control Planning, approximately seventeen weeks' training is given to Civil Engineers, and two weeks' instruction to Electricals, Mechanicals and Architects. In the Division of Design, Civil Engineers have to spend seventeen weeks and others twenty-five weeks. Finally, in the Division of Construction, Civil Engineers are again trained for seventeen weeks; and the Electricals, Mechanicals and Architects are trained for twenty-four weeks. Thus all the four kinds of Engineers have to spend fifty-two weeks, i.e. one full year, in the process of training.

The Office of Power operates and maintains the power system, plans, designs and constructs the power transmission and communication system; markets the power; plans for future power needs, and takes steps to ensure an adequate supply. The generating capacity of the system exceeds 11 million kilowatts, making it by far the largest system in the United States. Another 2 million kilowatts is expected to be in service by 1962. The power requirements of the region are currently growing at the rate of about 800,000 kilowatts a year. There are approximately 6,600 employees in the Office of Power (about 40 per cent of TVA's employment), of whom roughly 10 per cent are engineers. Its training programme is different from the one adopted in the Office of Engineering. The training starts with introductory assignments in Chattanooga for two months (briefly covering the engineering work in the entire Office of Power). Thereafter, the trainees are transferred to *one* of the Divisions. In the Division of Power Engineering and Construction there is about ten months' scheduled work and related study *on a division basis*. In the Division of Power Operations, there is about twenty-two months' scheduled work and related study *in one branch* of the division. The Division of Power Supply provides for about ten months' scheduled work and related study *on a division basis*. In the Division of Power Utilization there is approximately ten months of scheduled work and related study *in one branch of the division*. After the completion of training (which varies from a year to two years), the trainees are placed in a regular engineering position in the division.

The Office of Chemical Engineering is located at Wilson Dam, Alabama. The major unit develops and administers programmes and policies involving research and development of chemical processes, production of fertilizers, and munitions. It gives administrative direction and guidance to research activities based upon chemistry, chemical engineering and metallurgy.

Beginning with the fiscal year 1938 and extending through 1944, the financial statements of the Tennessee Valley Authority were examined annually by independent public accountants *as well as* by the United States General Accounting Office. Under the provisions of the Government Corporation Control Act, 1945, Government Corporations, unless otherwise expressly provided by law, are not permitted to use their funds to pay the cost of private audits of their accounts. The TVA, however, has an internal Auditing Branch. Government audit, through the Auditing Branch of the Division of Finance, is responsible for detailed pre-audits of all disbursements as well as continuous field audits, on a test-check basis, of financial transactions and monthly financial statements. In connection with its field audits, it reviews the system of internal control and accounting procedures. These continuous audits as well as its audit of the financial statements at June 30 (close of the fiscal year) are made in accordance with generally accepted auditing practices applicable in the circumstances and include all procedures considered necessary.[7]

Between 1948 and 1958, TVA's operating revenues from power operations increased by roughly 400 per cent. The following table gives the position for the fiscal years ending on June 30:[8]

	1948 $	1958 $
I—Sales of Electrical Energy:		
(a) Municipalities and Co-operatives	23,519,611	80,686,929
(b) Commercial and Industrial	10,979,328	35,176,890
(c) Federal agencies	6,156,193	113,093,737
(d) Electric utilities	5,786,948	1,289,166
(e) Rural (retail)	161,498	—
Total outside sales	46,603,578	230,246,722
(f) Interdivisional sales	1,831,299	1,970,467
Total sales	48,434,877	232,217,189
II—Rent and other revenues	334,647	1,330,977
TOTAL OPERATING REVENUES	48,769,524	233,548,166

The share of municipalities and co-operatives fell from about 49 per cent in 1948 to 35 per cent in 1958. Commercial and industrial sales have declined from about 23 per cent to 15 per cent. Electric utilities had their share reduced from about 12 per cent to ½ per cent. Interdivisional sales fell from about 4 per cent to ¼ per cent. Rural retail sales which were already insignificant have disappeared from the scene. Federal agencies have had a big jump from about 13 per cent in 1948 to 49 per cent in 1958. The Atomic Energy Commission and other Federal Agencies purchased in the 1958 fiscal year 30 billion kilowatt-hours from TVA. By way of comparison, *all the utilities* in the entire State of New York sold about 40 billion kwh. In only four States outside the Valley were *total* sales as great as what TVA sold to the Federal Government *alone*. Users of TVA power save more than $100 million a year compared with what they would have to pay for the same amount of electricity priced at the average of the rate scheduled throughout the United States. It may be mentioned in this connection that the net

[7] Report by E. Arnold Sunstrom, Comptroller, dated September 2, 1949.

[8] Table constructed on the basis of Financial Statements for the fiscal years ended June 30, 1949, and June 30, 1958.

income from power operations has not been able to rise as fast as the gross revenues. The net income rose from about $17 million for the 1948 fiscal year to about $55 million for the 1958 fiscal year (whereas gross operating revenues had risen from $49 million to $234 million). Operating expenses have risen faster, from $32 million for the 1948 fiscal year to $179 million for the 1958 fiscal year. Production expenses rose from $14 million to $111 million, depreciation from $9 million to $44 million, administration expenses from $3 million to $9 million, and transmission expenses from $4 million to $9 million.

The total fixed assets of the TVA rose from $876 million on June 30, 1948, to $2,098 million on June 30, 1958. On the latter date, power assets stood at $1,755 million, navigation assets at $159 million and flood control assets at $184 million. The Tennessee River System is the most completely regulated river system in the world. Between 1933-1958, the freight traffic on the Tennessee rose from 33 million ton-miles to about 2 billion ton-miles. Flood control operations have dated from 1936, when Norris Dam, TVA's first multi-purpose project, was placed in operation. However, this system has been in essentially full operation only since 1945 when Kentucky Dam was completed. Since 1936, the system has regulated more than twenty floods that would have caused damage at Chattanooga. These include the flood of February 1957 which, without regulation, would have been the second highest ever recorded at that point. It would have come within four feet of the highest flood ever recorded, that of 1867. The reservoir system reduced this flood by twenty-two feet, averting about $66 million of damage. The total of flood damage averted at Chattanooga and on the lower Ohio and Mississippi Rivers now exceeds $140 million. This is equal to about 75 per cent of the total investment of $184 million in flood control facilities.[9]

In respect of 'Tax and In-Lieu Payments' the TVA had paid during the twenty-six fiscal years (actually a few days more than twenty-five years) ended June 30, 1958, $51.4 million. After adding payments made by distributors ($72 million), the total payments amounted to $123.4 million. Out of this sum the States received $28 million, the Counties $42.6 million, and the Municipalities $52.8 million. Throughout twenty-five years of operation (1933-1958) the return on power investments has averaged about 4 per cent. But there appears to be a declining trend. In the 1958 fiscal year the return was only about 3 per cent ($55 million on an investment of $1,755 million). The net income had fallen from $58 million in 1957 to $55 million in 1958.

[9] TVA 1958, *25th Anniversary Year*, United States Government Printing Office, Washington, 1959, p. 25.

INDEX

262